Artificial Intelligence:
The Very Idea

D0169219

⌐b

Bradford Books

Mind Design, John Haugeland, 1981

The Modularity of Mind, Jerry A. Fodor, 1983

The Science of the Mind, Owen J. Flanagan, Jr., 1984

Matter and Consciousness, Paul M. Churchland, 1984

Computation and Cognition, Zenon Pylyshyn, 1984

Artificial Intelligence:
The Very Idea

John Haugeland

A Bradford Book
The MIT Press
Cambridge, Massachusetts
London, England

Second printing, 1986
© 1985 by The Massachusetts Institute of
Technology

This book was set in Palatino and Univers by The
MIT Press Computergraphics Department and printed
and bound by Halliday Lithograph in the United States
of America.

Library of Congress Cataloging in Publication Data

Haugeland, John, 1945–
  Artificial intelligence.

  "A Bradford book."
  Bibliography: p.
  Includes index.
  1. Artificial intelligence. I. Title.
Q335.H38 1985   001.53'5   85–5916
ISBN 0–262–08153–9

*Dedicated to my mother
and the memory of my father
Carol and John Haugeland*

Contents

Acknowledgments

For offering numerous comments and suggestions on the entire manuscript, I am especially indebted to Dan Dennett, Bert Dreyfus, Drew McDermott, and Al Newell. For further help of many kinds, I am also grateful to Pedro Amaral, Joe Baim, Bob Brandom, Rob Cummins, Pat Hayes, Peter King, Wendy Lehnert, Bob Moore, Zenon Pylyshyn, and Betty and Harry Stanton. Anyone who knows all these people, or even very many of them, knows that I could not have accepted every recommendation they made; still, the book is much better than it would have been without their combined assistance. Finally, for devoting countless hours and late nights (more, indeed, than anyone but me), I would thank my tireless, ever faithful, never complaining, handmade computer—but I sold it.

There are a number of topics I would like to have treated but didn't, notably behaviorism, parallel processing, nonmonotonic reasoning, and the "background" of everyday practice; I am not sorry, however, to have neglected flip-flops, machine code, Godel incompleteness, Eliza, phenomenology, or the fifth generation.

Pittsburgh
March 1985

Artificial Intelligence:
The Very Idea

Clockwise from left: Galileo Galilei, Nicolaus Copernicus, Thomas
Hobbes, René Descartes, David Hume, Charles Babbage, Alan Turing,
John von Neumann, John McCarthy, Allan Newell

Introduction

Minds: Artificial and Natural

What are minds? What is thinking? What sets people apart, in all the known universe? Such questions have tantalized philosophers for millennia, but (by scientific standards anyway) scant progress could be claimed . . . until recently. For the current generation has seen a sudden and brilliant flowering in the philosophy/science of the mind; by now not only psychology but also a host of related disciplines are in the throes of a great intellectual revolution. And the epitome of the entire drama is *Artificial Intelligence,* the exciting new effort to make computers think. The fundamental goal of this research is not merely to mimic intelligence or produce some clever fake. Not at all. "AI" wants only the genuine article: *machines with minds,* in the full and literal sense.[1] This is not science fiction, but real science, based on a theoretical conception as deep as it is daring: namely, we are, at root, *computers ourselves.* That idea—the idea that thinking and computing are radically the same—is the topic of this book.

We've all chuckled nervously over the cartoon computer typing out "I think, therefore I am" or some comparable profundity. But when it comes to taking Artificial Intelligence seriously, people tend to split into "scoffers" and "boosters." Scoffers find the whole idea quite preposterous—not just false, but ridiculous— like imagining that your car (really) hates you or insisting that a murderous bullet should go to jail. Boosters, on the other hand, are equally certain that it's only a matter of time; computers with minds, they say, are as inevitable as interplanetary travel and two-way pocket TV. The remarkable thing is how utterly confident each side is: "It's so obvious," they both say (while thumping the table), "only a *fanatic* could disagree." Well, here we shall not be fanatics in either direction, no matter who disagrees. Artificial Intelligence is neither preposterous nor inevitable. Rather, it is based on a powerful idea, which very well might be right (or right in some respects) and just as well might not.

More specifically, we have three ambitions: first and foremost, to explain, clearly and with an open mind, what AI is really all about; second, to exhibit the philosophical and scientific credentials behind its enormous appeal; and finally, to take a look at what actually has and has not been accomplished. Along the way we shall have to develop an abstract account of what computers are; confront some knotty metaphysical puzzles about "meaning" in a material universe; disentangle various common-sense confusions about language, knowledge, personality, and even common sense itself; and, in general, delve into quite a stack of tricky and controversial issues. Since this is an unusual juxtaposition of problems, some part of what follows will be new, even to professional scientists and philosophers. But the discussion as a whole is designed deliberately for nonspecialists; technical assumptions in any area have been carefully avoided.

Fiction, Technology, and Theory

The concept of Artificial Intelligence did not, of course, spring up from nowhere, nor did it originate with computers. Its proper intellectual heritage is the subject of chapter 1; but in the meantime, we can distinguish two familiar and well-developed themes on intelligent artifacts in science fiction. One is the "creature feature" genre, starring monsters or androids—basically like natural animals except for being man-made (and thus somehow peculiar, superior, or horribly flawed). Included are the mythical creations of Hephaestus and Dr. Frankenstein as well as miscellaneous anthropoid slaves, indistinguishable from ordinary people save for serial numbers, emotional oddities, and the like. The other genre is populated by various mechanical "robots": typically blinking, clanking contraptions, with springs and pulleys in lieu of flesh, wires for nerves, and maybe wheels instead of legs—plus emotional limitations even more serious than the androids'.

While the monster theme often invokes mystery and black magic, robots tend to be extrapolations of industry's latest high-tech marvel. Early designs were based on the intricate gear and ratchet mechanisms that so enchanted Europe when clockworks were new; and, through the years, steam engines, automatic looms, hydraulic controls, and telephone switchboards have all fueled fantastic projections. Contemporary Artificial Intelligence, needless to say, is rooted in fancy programmable electronics; in particular, no current work is based on chemical wizardry or bioengineering (it belongs at IBM, not at du Pont or Genentech). AI, therefore, is direct heir to the contraption line. But there's one crucial difference: whereas few respectable scientists ever tried to build intelligent clockworks or switchboards (let alone androids), research on intelligent computers is big time. Why?

The real issue has nothing to do with advanced technologies (or corporate specialties), but with deep theoretical assumptions. According to a central tradition in Western philosophy, thinking (intellection) essentially *is* rational manipulation of mental symbols (viz., ideas). Clocks and switchboards, however, don't do anything at all like rational symbol manipulation. Computers, on the other hand, can manipulate arbitrary "tokens" in any specifiable manner whatever; so apparently we need only arrange for those tokens to be symbols, and the manipulations to be specified as rational, to get a machine that *thinks*. In other words, AI is new and different because computers actually do something very like what minds are supposed to do. Indeed, if that traditional theory is correct, then our imagined computer ought to have "a mind of its own": a (genuine) *artificial mind*.

To call something a symbol or a manipulation is to characterize it quite abstractly. That doesn't mean the characterization is vague, formless, or even hard to understand, but rather that inessential details are omitted. Consider, for instance, two ways of specifying the motor for an appliance. One engineer might describe it in great detail, giving the precise shape of each little part, what it's made of, how it's attached, and so on. (That would be a "concrete" characterization, the opposite of abstract.) Another engineer, however, might stipulate only the minimum horsepower required, the space into which it has to fit, and how quietly it must run—leaving the details up to the motor designer. The resulting motor could be made of metal or plastic, be round or square, be based on one physical principle or another, and still satisfy the abstract specifications exactly.

According to the symbol manipulation theory, intelligence depends only on a system's organization and functioning as a symbol manipulator—which is even more abstracted from concrete details than are horsepower and noise level. Hence low-level specifics, such as what the symbols are made of or their precise shapes, are irrelevant to whether the system might be intelligent; the symbols need only satisfy some higher-level, abstract specifications. In other words, various "details," like whether the underlying structure is electronic or physiological (or hydraulic or fiber optical or whatever), are entirely beside the point. By the same token, contemporary computer technology is relevant only for economic reasons: electronic circuits just happen to be (at the moment) the cheapest way to build flexible symbol manipulating systems.

But the lesson goes deeper: if Artificial Intelligence really has little to do with computer technology and much more to do with abstract principles of mental organization, then the distinctions among AI, psychology, and even philosophy of mind seem to melt away. One can study those basic principles using tools and techniques from computer science, or with the methods of experimental psychology, or in traditional philosophical terms— but it's the same subject in each case. Thus a grand interdisciplinary marriage seems imminent; indeed, a number of enthusiasts have already taken the vows. For their new "unified" field, they have coined the name *cognitive science*. If you believe the advertisements, Artificial Intelligence and psychology, as well as parts of philosophy, linguistics, and anthropology, are now just "subspecialties" within one coherent study of cognition, intelligence, and mind—that is, of symbol manipulation.

Artificial Intelligence in this sense (as a branch of cognitive science) is the only kind we will discuss. For instance, we will pay no attention to commercial ventures (so-called "expert systems," etc.) that make no pretense of developing or applying psychological principles. We also won't consider whether computers might have some alien or inhuman kind of intellect (like Martians or squids?). My own hunch, in fact, is that anthropomorphic prejudice, "human chauvinism," is built into our very concept of intelligence. This concept, of course, could still apply to all manner of creatures; the point is merely that it's the only concept we have—if we escaped our "prejudice," we wouldn't know what we were talking about.

Be that as it may, the only *theoretical* reason to take contemporary Artificial Intelligence more seriously than clockwork fiction is the powerful suggestion that our own minds work on computational principles. In other words, we're really interested in

AI as part of the theory that *people* are computers—and we're all interested in people.

What Is Intelligence?

How shall we define intelligence? Doesn't everything turn on this? Surprisingly, perhaps, very little seems to turn on it. For practical purposes, a criterion proposed by Alan Turing (1950) satisfies nearly everyone. Turing was annoyed by fruitless disputes over word meanings; he thought you could never find out anything interesting about what machines could do by armchair philosophizing about what we mean by 'think' and 'intelligent'. So he suggested that we ignore the verbal issue and adopt a simple test which he devised; then we could concentrate on building and observing the machines themselves. He predicted that by the year 2000 computer systems would be passing a modest version of his test and that contrary "definitions" would eventually just look silly (and quietly fade away).

Turing's test is based on a game, called the "imitation game," played by three mutual strangers. Two of them are "witnesses," and they are of opposite sex; the third player, the "interrogator," tries to guess which witness is which, purely on the basis of how they answer questions. The trick is that one witness (say the man) is trying to fool the interrogator (by systematically pretending to be the woman), while the other (the woman) is doing all she can to help the interrogator. If the interrogator guesses correctly, the woman wins, otherwise the man does. In order to avoid any extraneous clues, like tone of voice, all questions and answers are transmitted via teletype. So far no computers are involved. Turing's idea, however, was to substitute a computer for the male witness and see whether, against average women opponents, it can fool the average (human) interrogator as often as the average man can. If it can, it "passes" the test.[2]

But why would such a peculiar game be a test for general (human-like) intelligence? Actually, the bit about teletypes, fooling the interrogator, and so on, is just window dressing, to make it all properly "experimental." The crux of the test is *talk*: does the machine talk like a person? Of course this doesn't mean sounding like a person, but rather saying the sorts of things that people

Box 1
Why IQ Is Irrelevant

It might seem that we already have a perfectly reasonable standard of intelligence: namely, performance on an IQ test. There are, however, two things wrong with that supposition. First, IQ tests are intended to measure *degree* of intelligence, on the assumption that the subject has some intelligence to measure. But for computers that assumption is the issue; we must know whether it makes sense to attribute intelligence to them at all before we can ask how much of it they have. Second, IQ tests are designed specifically for people, and thus they may depend on indicators that are actually valid only in this special case.

To take a simplified example, it might be found that some peculiar skill, like solving logic problems or comparing line diagrams, is reliably correlated with how smart a person is; so a test could take advantage of this correlation, for purposes of convenient measurement. But that doesn't mean that such a task actually requires intelligence; it could happen that a manifestly unintelligent device could perform splendidly, by virtue of some coincidence or gimmick. (The fact that many people can't remember how to extract square roots doesn't mean that pocket calculators are more intelligent than they.) What we need is a general test for whether an entity is intelligent at all (in the human sense, of course) and not a special purpose measuring device convenient for use in schools or the army.

say in similar situations. But again, why should that be a sign of general intelligence? What's so special about talking? Turing says: "The question and answer method seems to be suitable for introducing almost any one of the fields of human endeavor that we wish to include." That is, we can talk about pretty much anything.

Further, and more important, to converse beyond the most superficial level, you have to know what you're talking about. That is, understanding the words alone is not enough; you have to understand the topic as well. Turing points out (1950, p. 446) how similar his imitation game is to an oral quiz and gives us a sample:

Interrogator: In the first line of your sonnet which reads "Shall I compare thee to a summer's day," would not "a spring day" do as well or better?
Witness: It wouldn't scan.
Interrogator: How about "a winter's day"? That would scan all right.
Witness: Yes, but nobody wants to be compared to a winter's day.
Interrogator: Would you say Mr. Pickwick reminded you of Christmas?
Witness: In a way.
Interrogator: Yet Christmas is a winter's day, and I do not think Mr. Pickwick would mind the comparison.
Witness: I don't think you're serious. By a winter's day one means a typical winter's day, rather than a special one like Christmas.

This student has displayed not only competence with the English language, but also a passable understanding of poetry, the seasons, people's feelings, and so on—all just by talking. The same could be done for politics, fine wines, electrical engineering, philosophy . . . you name it. What if a machine could pass all those examinations? That's why the Turing test is so powerful and compelling.

It's also quite convenient in practice; typing and reading at a terminal, after all, are the standard means of interacting with a computer. Since there's no physical barrier to having a friendly conversation with a machine, AI research is free to attack the underlying theoretical issues. By accepting the Turing test (in spirit, if not the letter), scientists can concentrate almost entirely on the "cognitive" aspects of the problem: what internal structure and operations would enable a system to say the right thing at the right time? In other words, they can dispense with messy incidentals and get on with computational psychology.

"They can only . . ."

Many people are especially doubtful about "automating" creativity, freedom, and the like. No computer, they suppose, could ever be truly inventive, artistic, or responsible, because "it can only do what it's programmed to do." Everything depends, however, on just what this alleged limitation means. In one technical and boring sense, of course, it's perfectly true that computers always follow their programs, since a program is nothing but a careful specification of all the relevant processes inside the machine. That, however, doesn't prove anything because a similar point might be made about us. Thus, assuming there were a "careful specification" of all the relevant processes in our brains (laws of neuropsychology, or something like that), it would be equally easy to say: "We—or rather our brain parts—always act only as specified."[3] But, obviously, no such fact could show that we are never creative or free—and the corresponding claim about computers is no more telling.

The underlying problem with the argument is that it ignores distinctions of *organizational level.* A stereo, for instance, can be desribed as a device for reproducing recorded music, as a complicated tangle of electronic components, or as a giant cloud of subatomic particles. What you can say about it depends on the level of description you adopt. Thus, none of the components (let alone the particles) could properly be termed "high fidelity"; that characteristic makes sense only at the level of music reproduction. Likewise, none of our individual brain functions, and none of the individual operations in a computer, could properly be termed "creative" or "free"; such descriptions belong at a completely different level—a level at which one speaks of the system or person as a whole.[4]

Unfortunately, confusions remain because the notion "is-programmed-to" is ambiguous. Instead of the above sense, in which programming refers to a detailed specification of internal processes, one can use the term more broadly, to describe a system's overall design or intended capacities. For example, I might say "this computer is programmed to keep the payroll accounts" or "that computer is programmed to find the best flight path in bad weather." These descriptions apply to the system as a whole; yet even at this level it seems that the systems "can only do what they're programmed to do"—as long, anyway, as they don't malfunction. Here the underlying problem is quite different: namely, it's simply not clear that being "programmed" (in this sense) is incompatible with being creative or free. After all, why not just program the system to be creative, free, or whatever? Then it would have those characteristics by design.

You might think that being "programmed for creativity" is a contradiction in terms. But it can't be, as we can see by again considering ourselves. In some sense, surely, we are elaborate integrated systems with an overall design—the result of evolution, perhaps. Thus when we're healthy (not malfunctioning), we "only do what we're designed to do." But then, assuming that creativity and freedom are not (always) unhealthy, we must be "designed for creativity," etc. This is no contradiction because the relevant sense of "design" relates only to overall capacities and characteristics; but that's also the very sense of "programming" in question.

Still, there's one last argument: it's only a metaphor to say that we were "designed" by evolution; evolution is not an actual designer, but only a mindless natural process. Computers, on the other hand, are quite literally *programmed* by actual (human) programmers. So when we're creative, it's all our own; but when a computer printout contains something artistic, that's really the programmer's artistry, not the machine's. But wait: how does that follow? Why should an entity's potential for inventiveness be determined by its ancestry (like some hereditary title) and not by its own manifest competence? What if, for instance, the very same computer system had resulted from an incredible laboratory accident; could *that* make any difference to whether the resulting

Box 2
Why Not Start with Learning?

Sometimes it seems that learning is to psychology what energy is to physics or reproduction to biology: not merely a central research topic, but a virtual definition of the domain. Just as physics is the study of energy transformations and biology is the study of self-reproducing organisms, so psychology is the study of systems that learn. If that were so, then the essential goal of AI should be to build systems that learn. In the meantime, such systems might offer a shortcut to artificial adults: systems with the "raw aptitude" of a child, for instance, could learn for themselves—from experience, books, and so on—and save AI the trouble of codifying mature common sense. But, in fact, AI more or less ignores learning. Why?

Learning is *acquisition* of knowledge, skills, etc. The issue is typically conceived as: given a system capable of knowing, how can we make it capable of acquiring? Or: starting from a static knower, how can we make an adaptable or educable knower? This tacitly assumes that knowing as such is straightforward and that acquiring or adapting it is the hard part; but that turns out to be false. AI has discovered that knowledge itself is extraordinarily complex and difficult to implement—so much so that even the general structure of a system with common sense is not yet clear. Accordingly, it's far from apparent *what* a learning system needs to acquire; hence the project of acquiring some can't get off the ground.[5]

In other words, Artificial Intelligence must start by trying to understand knowledge (and skills and whatever else is acquired) and then, on that basis, tackle learning. It may even happen that, once the fundamental structures are worked out, acquisition and adaptation will be comparatively easy to include. Certainly the ability to learn is essential to full intelligence; AI cannot succeed without it. But it does not appear that learning is the most basic problem, let alone a shortcut or a natural starting point.

system was creative? Or, turning the tables, what if you or I had been concocted out of petroleum by-products at Exxon; would that mean that all our later inventions and artworks automatically belonged to a team of chemists? I certainly hope not.

Of course, if those inventions had actually been dreamt up in advance by the relevant programmers or chemists and merely stored in the machine or us for later "playback," then the credit would be theirs. But that's not at all the way AI works, even today. What gets programmed directly is just a bunch of general information and principles, not unlike what teachers instill in their pupils. What happens after that, what the system does with all this input, is not predictable by the designer (or teacher or anybody else). The most striking current examples are chess machines that outplay their programmers, coming up with brilliant moves that the latter would never have found. Many people are amazed by this fact; but if you reflect that invention is often just a rearrangement (more or less dramatic) of previously available materials, then it shouldn't seem so surprising.

None of this proves that computer systems *can* be truly creative, free, or artistic. All it shows is that our initial intuitions to the contrary are not trustworthy, no matter how compelling they seem at first. If you're sitting there muttering: "Yes, yes, but I *know* they can't; they just couldn't," then you've missed the point. Nobody knows. Like all fundamental questions in cognitive science, this one awaits the outcome of a great deal more hard research. Remember, the real isssue is whether, in the appropriate abstract sense, we are computers ourselves.

Galileo instructing Milton

1 The Saga of the Modern Mind

Copernicus and the End of the Middle Ages

Our commonsense concept of "the mind" is surprisingly recent. It arose during the seventeenth century, along with modern science and modern mathematics—which is no mere coincidence. These historical roots are worth a look, not only because they're fascinating, but also because they give a richer perspective on cognitive science (which is, after all, just the latest theory in the series). Fortunately, the story itself is rather more suspenseful and intriguing than one might expect. One scholarly confession first, however: in bringing out the main contours, I have streamlined historical fact, omitting miscellaneous important people and subtle distinctions. For instance, I mention "the medievals" as if they were all alike, which is a scandal; and many of the ideas I associate with, say, Galileo or Descartes were really current at the time and were being discussed by many writers. Still, the larger drama is about right, and that's what matters.

Though the plot didn't really get rolling till the time of Hobbes and Descartes, it began building steam a century or two earlier, as the Middle Ages gave way to the Renaissance. The medieval world view was largely a Christian adaptation of ancient Greek philosophy and science, especially the works of Plato and Aristotle. The principal modification was putting God at the foundation, as creator and cause of everything (else) that exists. Prior to the creation, however, the Creator did need *ideas* of all that there would be (His plans, you might say); and these ideas played an important role for philosophers. In the first place, obviously, ordinary worldly objects were just more or less corrupt materializations of God's original, perfect ideas. (The corruptions, of course, must also have been planned by God; but medieval rationalizations for that got rather sticky and needn't concern us.)

The human intellect or soul had ideas too, something like God's; but their status and relation to objects was more problematic. One charming story (loosely Platonic in inspiration) had the thought/thing relation as really the base of a triangle, with God's intellect at the apex. Human ideas were *true* insofar as they were more or less accurate copies of God's ideas; mundane objects, in turn, were also true, though in another sense, insofar as their construction more or less conformed to those same divine ideas, now seen as designer's blueprints. Thus our thoughts could be "true of" things only via a detour through the original plans that they each imperfectly matched, in their respective ways.

A more common (and more Aristotelian) approach skipped the detour through the apex and postulated a direct relation between thought and thing at the base. But what relation could that be? By virtue of what could an idea in a mind be of or *about* some particular worldly object(s)? The most appealing and also standard answer was that ideas are like pictures or images: they *resemble* the objects they stand for, and they stand for those objects because they resemble them. Thus a thought could be true of a thing by "conforming" with it directly—that is, by sharing the same *form*. In a sense, the mind was just like the world (i.e., in form), only realized in a different substance (mental instead of material). This account of how thoughts could relate to things had the double advantage of intuitive plausibility and the lack of serious competition. As we shall see, however, the emergence of modern science slowly sabotaged the standard resemblance theory and eventually forced a quite different view of mental contents.

Medieval cosmology—the theory of the universe—was also basically Aristotelian. Our Earth was at the very center, surrounded in various rotating spheres by the visible heavens, which were surrounded ultimately by God's heaven, motionless and invisible.[1] The sensible world was composed of five elements: earth, water, air, fire, and the so-called quintessence (fifth element). Each of these had its "natural place" toward which it naturally tended to travel, if it were ever removed. The heavens were composed entirely of quintessence, and since this is where the quintessence belonged, the heavens never changed (the spheres just rotated ceaselessly in place). The other four elements, however, were all jumbled up in the lowest sphere, below the moon; and hence this sphere was in constant turmoil, with things always subject to change and decay. For example, wood was flammable because the fire and air in it "tended" to go up and the earth "tended" to go down, if they ever got the chance. This same fire and air component also explained why wood floated on water while stones and ashes (which were more concentrated earth) did not float—water's natural place being above earth, but below fire and air.

All told, it was a pretty picture; but by the late middle ages there was trouble brewing. For sundry practical reasons, astronomy was the most advanced empirical science. The calendar had to be right, for determining religious holidays; and navigators, venturing ever farther from known waters, needed more accurate astronomical tables. Unfortunately, as more careful observations accumulated, it became progressively harder and more complicated to square them with the accepted geocentric (Earth-centered) theory. The situation was so serious and exasperating, especially with regard to predicting the positions of the planets, that by the thirteenth century Spain's King Alfonso X could exclaim: "If God had consulted me when creating the universe, He would have received good advice!"[2]

On the Revolution of the Spheres, published by the Polish astronomer Nicolaus Copernicus (1473–1543) in the last year of his life, turned the medieval world literally upside down. Its heliocentric (Sun-centered) theory of the universe was surely the most disorienting scientific innovation of all time—though Copernicus's successors were oddly slow in appreciating all its implications. The basic ideas were that

1. the daily motions of the heavens are just an illusion, brought about by rotation of the Earth on an internal axis; and
2. the annual circuit of the Sun through the Zodiac, as well as some of the stranger wanderings of the planets, are equally illusory, due to the Earth slowly orbiting around the Sun.

The Earth itself was reduced to the status of another planet, situated between Venus and Mars in its distance from the Sun at the center.

Not only was this proposal destined to transform astronomy, but it also (eventually) threw the rest of accepted science into disarray. For now the natural places, which were the basis of the account of all mundane movement and decay, were totally dislocated. Which directions were up and down? Why would the four elements of the universe (besides the quintessence) have their natural "tendencies" tied to some peculiar moving point inside the Earth? Where, indeed, were Heaven and Hell? The questions for the theory of motion were equally serious. Why didn't loose objects whirl off the spinning Earth and then get left behind in space as we sailed on around the Sun? Or why, at least, didn't a falling stone come down slightly "behind" (west of) its original location as the Earth rotated out from under it? These were extremely hard problems, and it was many years before the laws of inertia, force, and gravitation were all worked out to solve them.

The modern *mind* was invented ('invented' is the right word) in this same scientific ferment; and its first impulse came from the Copernican distinction between appearance and reality. It is a commonplace, of course, that things are not always what they seem; and, even in ancient times, Plato had elevated this into a philosophical principle: *never* are things *really* what they seem. The ordinary objects of perception, he maintained, are only pale imitations of true reality, like mere shadows cast on a wall by a dancing fire. (For Plato, true reality was the realm of perfect eternal "forms"—later appropriated as God's intellect, full of divine ideas.)

Copernicus, however, needed a more drastic distinction. The illusion of the Sun rising in the east is no pale shadow or imperfect mental picture of the Earth's rotation—it's totally different. The same can be said for the Sun's motion through the Zodiac, and even more so for the planets' complicated wanderings back and forth among the stars. According to the new theory, astronomical appearances weren't even similar to reality. That opened breathtaking new possibilities for the sorts of things science could conceivably discover; and at the same time, by undermining resemblance, it drove a crucial wedge between the mind and the world—a wedge that ultimately transformed our whole understanding of thinking and ourselves.

Galileo and the New Science

One final stop, before Hobbes draws the fateful computational conclusion, is the great Italian physicist Galileo Galilei (1564–1642), who enters our story in several ways. He is perhaps most famous for introducing the telescope into astronomy and thereby discovering the moons of Jupiter, the mountains on Earth's moon, the changing phases of Venus, and so on. These were all important factors in the ultimate triumph of Copernicanism. (For his trouble, Galileo was tried by the Inquisition and sentenced to house arrest for the last eleven years of his life.) But in the history of the modern mind (and also in the development of modern physics), what is most important is his application of mathematics to the problem of motion.

Galileo was convinced that the only way to understand physical nature is in terms of mathematical relationships among quantitative variables. He himself expresses the idea both colorfully and lucidly:

Philosophy is written in that great book, the universe, which is always open, right before our eyes. But one cannot understand this book without first learning to understand the language and to know the characters in which it is written. It is written in the language of mathematics, and the characters are triangles, circles, and other figures. Without these, one cannot understand a single word of it, and just wanders in a dark labyrinth.[3]

Mathematics, for Galileo, was essentially geometry (and arithmetic). This is evident, for example, if you look at his proof of Theorem 1 (see box 1), where he relies on geometrical concepts and relationships to say things that we would say with algebraic equations.

What matters historically, though, is not just *that* Galileo used geometry, but *how* he used it. Traditionally, geometry was the study of figures and relations in space. But Galileo conceived of it more abstractly. So, for example, lines in his diagrams wouldn't

Box 1
Galileo's Theorem 1

The time it takes a uniformly accelerated body to cover any given distance, starting from rest, equals the time it would take the same body to cover the same distance at a constant rate of speed equal to half the maximum speed finally achieved by the accelerated body.[4]

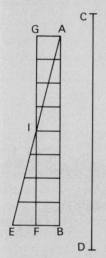

Let line AB represent the time in which some body uniformly accelerated from rest covers the distance represented by line CD. Let line BE (intersecting AB at any angle) represent the maximum speed achieved by that body at the end. Then all the line segments parallel to BE and connecting intervening points on AB to line AE represent the gradually increasing speeds during time interval AB. Let F be the midpoint of BE, and draw lines FG and AG, parallel to BA and BF, respectively, thereby constructing parallelogram AGFB, which is equal in area to triangle AEB (with side GF bisecting AE at I); and suppose the parallels in triangle AEB are extended straight out to line IG. Then we have the aggregate of all the parallels contained in the quadrilateral equal to the aggregate of those comprised in triangle AEB; for the ones in triangle IEF exactly match those in triangle GIA, and trapezoid AIFB is common to both cases.

Now, the instants in time AB correspond one for one to the points in line AB; and, taking the parallels from all those points, the portions enclosed by triangle AEB represent the increasing speeds, while, likewise, the portions contained in the parallelogram represent nonincreasing speeds, of which there are just as many, even though they are all equal. Hence it is apparent that exactly as many momenta of speed are consumed in the accelerated motion (given by the increasing parallels in triangle AEB) as in the constant motion (the parallels in parallelogram GB); for surely the deficit of momenta at the beginning of the accelerated motion (as represented by the parallels in triangle AGI) is made up by the momenta represented by the parallels in triangle IEF. Thus two bodies will clearly travel through the same distance in the same time, when the motion of one is a uniform acceleration from rest, while that of the other is constant, with just half the momentum of the accelerated motion at its maximum speed.
Q. E. D.

always represent lines or even distances in space, but might just as well represent times, speeds, or any other interesting physical variable. Theorem 1 is a case in point: though it is about bodies traveling a given distance, no line in the diagram represents either the paths or the distance. (As if to emphasize this fact, Galileo draws CD off to the side and then never mentions it again.) Instead, the lines actually represent times and speeds. Thus point A is the "starting point," but only in time, not in space; points further down from A on the line AB represent later instants, not subsequent positions. Lines GF and AE don't represent anything; but, in effect, they determine the speeds as functions of time. That is, all the equal line segments drawn over to GF from points on AB represent equal speeds at all those times, while the gradually lengthening segments from AB to AE represent gradually increasing speeds (i.e., uniform acceleration). The distances traveled are then represented by (of all things!) the respective "aggregate" *areas*;[5] hence the proof reduces to the trivial theorem that triangle AEB encloses the same area as parallelogram AGFB.

Obviously Galileo's main contribution is not the proof itself but the abstract representation in which such a proof could be given. Discovering and validating this strange way of representing instantaneous velocity, uniform acceleration, total distance, and so on cost Galileo many years of struggle. It looks so simple or even clumsy now; but it is one of the great achievements of the human intellect. What made it really significant, though, was not any particular result but rather the fact that now all the familiar techniques of geometry could be used to establish all kinds of results. Euclid's whole deductive system could be abstracted away from geometric shapes and applied instead to motions. For example, given the empirical hypothesis that falling bodies accelerate uniformly, Galileo was able to *prove* his classic "times-squared" law;[6] and, assuming the motion of a projectile to be a combination of uniform horizontal motion and vertical free-fall (a stunning insight in itself), he could show that the actual path would be a parabola.

Like Copernicus before him, Galileo didn't "philosophize" much about the mind or soul; hence, though his dramatic new uses of geometry had important consequences for the theory of mental representation, it took Hobbes and Descartes to bring them out. Galileo did, however, draw one famous and influential conclusion about "metaphysics"—that is, about what's really real:

I believe that for external bodies to excite in us tastes, odors, and sounds, nothing is required in those bodies themselves except size, shape, and a lot of slow or fast motions [namely, of countless "tiny particles"]. I think that if ears, tongues, and noses were taken away, then shapes, numbers, and motions would well remain, but not odors, tastes, or sounds. The latter are, I believe, nothing but names, outside of the living animal—just as tickling and titillation are nothing but names, apart from the armpit and the skin around the nose.[7]

In neighboring paragraphs Galileo also included colors and heat in the same category: qualities that aren't really present in external objects as such but arise only in our perceptions. This general idea is as old as the Greek "atomist" Democritus (fifth century B.C.), but Galileo gave it a whole new credibility. For he held that nature herself is "written in mathematical characters" (i.e., shapes, sizes, and motions) and supported that doctrine with totally unprecedented precision and detail, by actually deciphering those characters in his laws and proofs.

Most philosophers since Galileo have accepted some form of this distinction between properties that objects really have in themselves and properties that only appear in them because of the nature of our perceptual apparatus. Perhaps the best known discussion is by the English philosopher John Locke (1632–1704), who called the two groups "primary" and "secondary" qualities, respectively.[8] But the important point, from our perspective, is that the distinction drives in the Copernican wedge between how things seem and how they really are; that is, it further separates thought from the world. As we shall soon see, however, Galileo's methods of mathematical representation were destined to have an even deeper influence on the evolving modern mind.

Hobbes — The Grandfather of AI

"By RATIOCINATION, I mean *computation*," proclaimed the English philosopher Thomas Hobbes (1588–1679), prophetically launching Artificial Intelligence in the 1650s.[9] This slogan, he explained, conveys two basic ideas. First, thinking is "mental discourse"; that is, thinking consists of *symbolic operations*, just like talking out loud or calculating with pen and paper—except, of course, that it is conducted internally. Hence thoughts are not themselves expressed in spoken or written symbols but rather in special brain tokens, which Hobbes called "phantasms" or thought "parcels." Second, thinking is at its clearest and most rational when it follows methodical rules—like accountants following the exact rules for numerical calculation. In other words, explicit ratiocination is a "mechanical" process, like operating a mental abacus: all these little parcels (which, of course, need not stand only for numbers) are being whipped back and forth exactly according to the rules of reason. Or, in cases where the rules are being ignored or bent, the person is simply confused.

Here is how Hobbes himself elaborated the point in his magnum opus, *Leviathan*:

When a man reasoneth, he does nothing else but conceive a sum total, from addition of parcels; or conceive a remainder, from subtraction of one sum from another. . . . These operations are not incident to numbers only, but to all manner of things that can be added together, and taken one out of another. For as arithmeticians teach to add and subtract in numbers; so the geometricians teach the same in lines, figures, . . . angles, proportions, times, degrees of swiftness, force, power, and the like; the logicians teach the same in consequences of words; adding together two names to make an affirmation, and two affirmations to make a syllogism; and many syllogisms to make a demonstration.[10]

Hobbes no doubt overstretched the metaphor of "addition," but we can wink at that after all these years. More interesting is his inclusion of time, swiftness, force, etc. in the domain of geometricians; clearly he is thinking of Galileo.

Hobbes greatly admired Galileo, and in 1634 journeyed all the way to Italy just to meet him. More particularly, the great Italian's discovery that physics could be conducted with all the methodical rigor of geometric proof directly inspired Hobbes's conception of intellectual method in general. Thus his momentous suggestion that thinking *as such* is basically computation was clearly an extrapolation from Galileo's idea that the study of motion is basically geometry. And Hobbes's own main philosophical work was (wild as it seems) an attempt to do for politics what Galileo had done for physics. Needless to say, his definitions and proofs were not quite as precise and convincing as Galileo's (or we might live in a better world today); but his overall approach transformed the field—and, in recognition of that, he is often called "the father of modern political science."

Closer to our present topic, Hobbes also eagerly embraced the idea that reality itself is fundamentally "mathematical": ultimately nothing but tiny moving particles. Hence he readily agreed that so-called sensible qualities (colors, odors, tickles, and the like) are not really in objects at all but only in perceivers. At this point, however, Hobbes went his predecessor one better; for he argued, as Galileo had not, that if *all* reality is just particles in motion, then that must include the mind and its contents as well.

> All which qualities, called *sensible*, are [nothing] in the object, but so many several motions of the matter, by which it presseth our organs diversely. Neither in us that are pressed, are they any thing else, but divers motions; for motion produceth nothing but motion.[11]

Thus when I receive blue or tickling sensations from a colored feather, these sensations are really just complex patterns of tiny motions in my sense organs and brain; they are no more blue or tickling in themselves than the feather is in itself. Or rather to call them blue or tickling sensations is simply to classify them among certain repeatable patterns of movement in my body. This makes it evident, among other things, that when Hobbes speaks of putting thought parcels together and taking them apart again, he means it literally—at least to the extent that he means real physical manipulations of tiny physical symbols.

But there is a fundamental difficulty in Hobbes's whole program: to put it starkly, he cannot tell (that is, his theory cannot account for) the difference between minds and books. This is the tip of an enormous iceberg that deserves close attention, for it is profoundly relevant to the eventual plausibility of Artificial Intelligence. The basic question is: How can thought parcels *mean* anything? The analogy with spoken or written symbols is no help here, since the meanings of these are already *derivative* from the meanings of thoughts. That is, the meaningfulness of words depends on the prior meaningfulness of our thinking: if the sound (or sequence of letters) "horse" happens to mean a certain kind of animal, that's only because we (English speakers) mean that by it. Hobbes even agrees

> that the sound of this word *stone* should be the sign of a stone, cannot be understood in any sense but this, that he that hears it collects that he that pronounces it thinks of stone.[12]

Box 2
Causal Determination of Meaning

Suppose I am looking at an apple and having an experience *of* it. If we ask why that experience is of that apple (rather than of another apple or of Calcutta), the answer seems clear: that particular apple is *causing* my experience. Moreover, if I later remember the apple, that too is of that apple by virtue of a causal connection (via the initial perception). Finally, perhaps even my *concept* 'apple' gets its meaning from causal relations to various apples, such as those used to teach me the concept in the first place.

Here then is an account of meaning that is neither derivative nor based on resemblance. Does it solve the mystery? Not until questions like the following get answered:

1. **WHICH CAUSES?** Overindulgence causes splitting headaches, but splitting headaches don't *mean* (represent, stand for) overindulgence. When I see the apple, my experience is also caused by the photons entering my eye, the act of opening my eyes, and the microtexture of the apple's skin. Why do some causes generate meanings while others don't?

2. **WHICH MEANINGS?** As I regard the apple, I can see (notice, think of) an apple, a fruit, a particular gift from a student, lunch, its redness, its distance from me, and so on. These all differ in meaning (content), yet the causal connection between the apple and me seems just the same.

3. **INFORMED MEANING:** Mechanic and client alike hear the engine ping; but it "means" more to the mechanic, both in the experience (what kind of ping) and in the concept (what pinging actually is). Again there is more to meaning than is determined by the cause.

4. **NONCAUSAL OBJECTS:** I can think of the number eleven, and mean it; yet the number eleven itself has never caused anything. Likewise, I can think of the future or a possibility that didn't happen, though neither has had any

effects. And what about abstractions: has the *species* raccoon caused anything not caused by individual raccoons?

None of this argues that causal factors couldn't form *part* of a more elaborate approach to original meaning; indeed, much current work is along such lines—but incorporates ideas not available to Hobbes.

Now obviously the meaningfulness of thoughts themselves cannot be explained in the same way; for that would be to say that the meanings of our thoughts derive from the meanings of our thoughts, which is circular. Hence some independent account is required.

I call this the *mystery of original meaning*. For the problem is: Where does meaningfulness *originate*? Some meanings can derive from others, but not all of them can; if the meanings of public symbols (e.g., language) derive from the meanings of internal symbols (e.g., thoughts), then the latter cannot be similarly derivative—they must be the "originals." In other words, Hobbes cannot explain thinking by saying it's *just like* talking or writing, except for being internal. There has to be some further difference that accounts for the fact that thoughts can have original meaning, while word meanings are only derivative. This "further difference" is then clearly the crux of the matter.

The standard resemblance theory did offer a kind of answer: if thoughts, unlike words, resembled or pictured their objects, then this special relation could be the ultimate source (origin) of meaningfulness. Hobbes, however, couldn't use that answer. In making discourse and computation his model of ratiocination, he effectively gave thoughts the structure of sentences or formulae, composed of distinct, arbitrary symbols. Images don't have that structure: a picture of a fat man running is not composed of three separate symbols for "fat," "man," and "running." Thus the rules for manipulating such symbols, as in proofs and derivations, don't work for images either. Therefore, in proposing a computational account of thinking, Hobbes essentially forfeited the resemblance account of meaning. Yet he had, I think, nothing else to offer—which is to say he couldn't solve the mystery of original meaning or explain the basic difference between minds and books.

Descartes

Galileo and Copernicus were outstanding physicists and first-class mathematicians, but they weren't all that much as philosophers. Hobbes was a great philosopher but an inconsequential physicist and a truly abysmal mathematician. That towering French intellect René Descartes (1596–1650) was, on the other hand, a world-shaker at everything he touched. Commonly deemed the "father of modern philosophy," he might equally be called the father of modern mathematics; and his contributions to physics, though eventually eclipsed by Newton's, were for a generation the foundation of the discipline. Perhaps his most lasting mark, however, is in the theory of the mind; for, remarkable as it seems, this is the one point at which all his work comes together.

Descartes's career and outlook began with mathematics, in the history of which he is famed for two enormous innovations: first, his development of analytic geometry, and second, his astonishing interpretation of that development. Analytic geometry is that branch of mathematics in which geometric points, lines, and relationships are represented by numbers and algebraic equations, using the system we now call "Cartesian coordinates" (= graph paper; see figure 1). Of course, parts of the idea were old; astronomers, for instance, had long used a sort of coordinate system to keep track of stars. Descartes's contribution was a systematic approach to *solving geometric problems* by *algebraic methods*. And, while he was at it, he greatly improved the algebra of his time, basically introducing the notation we still use today.

Descartes began his famous work, *La Geometrie*, by saying:

Any problem in geometry can easily be reduced to such terms that one need only know the lengths of a few straight lines in order to construct it.[13]

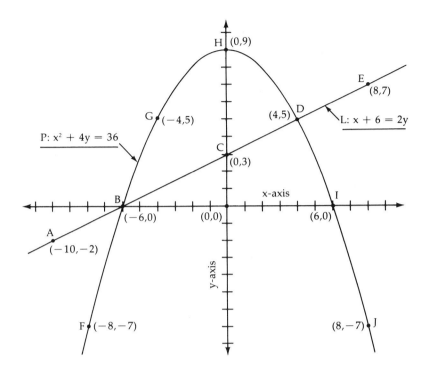

Figure 1   Cartesian Coordinates

A point in the plane corresponds to a pair of numbers, called its "X-coordinate" and "Y-coordinate," respectively. For instance, the point D above corresponds to the pair (4,5) because it is located 4 units out along the X-axis and 5 units up along the Y-axis. The values 4 and 5 (for x and y) also happen to satisfy the equation $x + 6 = 2y$; and, as you can see, the coordinates for points A, B, C, and E satisfy it too. In fact, all and only the points on line L have coordinates which satisfy that equation; hence the equation and the line "define" each other, given the coordinate system. And (first-order) equations like that are now known as "linear" equations.

In a similar way the coordinates of F, B, G, H, D, I, and J all satisfy the (second-order) equation $x^2 + 4y = 36$; and these points (plus all the others determined by the same equation) lie on the curve P, which turns out to be a parabola. (Other equations define circles, ellipses, and so on.) Notice, finally, if the above two equations are taken together and solved for x and y, the only two solutions are $(-6,0)$ and $(4,5)$, which correspond to points B and D, where the two curves intersect.

Most geometers in those days, Galileo and Kepler included, expressed quantitative relationships by means of geometrical proportions, such as:

Line (or area) A (in some diagram) is to B as C is to D

—which quickly got tedious and complicated. Descartes, however,
saw a way to cut through all that. He regarded geometric proportions and numerical operations, like multiplication and division,
as just *different forms* of a single more general relational structure.
So instead of struggling with a lot of complicated proportions,
Descartes calmly talked about multiplying, dividing, and extracting
roots of his line segments (lengths)—and always got other line
segments for answers.

   Geometrically this is a bizarre idea. What could the square root
of a line segment be? Moreover, the product of two lengths ought
not to be another length but an *area*. Descartes's idea was to define
some convenient "unit length" and then treat all those relations
as special cases of proportions. Thus any given length is to its
square root as the latter is to unity; or, unity is to one length as
a second length is to the product of the two. In other words:

If: L is to R as R is to 1,   then: $L = R^2$
If: 1 is to A as B is to C,   then: $A \times B = C$.

All these relations are proportions among lengths; yet, in terms
of them, the "algebraic" operations make perfect sense. The other
side of the coin is that geometric proportions can themselves be
re-expressed as algebraic equations, which in turn means (given
the above quotation) that any geometric problem can be "translated" into algebraic notation and solved by algebraic methods.

   As if unifying algebra and geometry weren't enough, Descartes
also realized that physics was in the same boat. If physical laws
could be represented geometrically and geometrical relationships
could be expressed algebraically, then physics too could be formulated in algebraic terms. Today it seems so obvious that physical
laws can be *equations* that we forget the intellectual leap required

to conceive such a thing. In particular, we forget that science can be quantitative and mathematically rigorous without algebra (not to mention calculus); Galileo (and Kepler, etc.) established that, using geometry.

Inventing analytic geometry was Descartes's first great step; his second step essentially redefined the field of mathematics. He explains the basic idea in a semi-biographical passage in his *Discourse on Method*:

Still, I had no intention of trying to learn all the particular sciences commonly called mathematics. For I saw that, although these sciences treat different objects, they all agree in considering nothing about the objects but the various relations or proportions found in them. Hence I thought it more worthwhile to examine just those proportions in general, free of any specific assumptions about the subject matter—except ones which might make understanding easier. And even then, of course, the assumptions were never binding, for my ultimate aim was a better ability to apply the same proportions to whatever other objects they fit.[14]

Galileo "abstracted" Euclid's methods away from purely spatial problems so he could apply them to physics, and now Descartes drives the principle to its radical conclusion: geometry, algebra, and physics are all equally just "applied math." Mathematics *as such* is not concerned with any specific subject matter (figures, numbers, motions, or what have you), but only with the very abstract relationships that might be found in them, or in any other objects.

Surprisingly, these same discoveries were just as revolutionary in the philosophy of mind as in mathematics. For the essential innovation is a reconception of the relation between symbols and what they symbolize—what we would now call the theory of meaning. Though mathematical notations were the model for Descartes's new ideas, he soon extended them to cover everything meaningful—especially thoughts. In other words, he regarded thoughts themselves as symbolic representations, fundamentally analogous to those used in mathematics; and, as a result, he could apply all his conclusions about representations in general to the special case of the mind. This profound maneuver, and its startling consequences, basically launched modern philosophy.

The new approach to representation has two distinct components: the negative half, rending symbol and symbolized asunder, and the positive half, getting them back together again. The negative half is clearly manifested in the mathematical work: the basic point is that algebraic formulations don't intrinsically represent numbers, and Euclidean formulations don't intrinsically represent geometric figures. Rather, algebra and geometry are two separate notations, each equally adequate for expressing numerical, spatial, kinematic (motional), or any other quantitative relationships. Nothing about either notation connects it, as such, to any particular subject matter.

Extend this negative realization to mental representations (thoughts), and you finally conclude the divorce of thought from thing, mind from world, that began so innocently in the old appearance/reality distinction. Suddenly a thought is one thing and its alleged object quite another—and there is no intrinsic relation between them. My thoughts of numbers are no more connected, as such, to numbers, than algebraic notation is connected, as such, to numbers. Those very same thoughts could equally well represent spatial facts or kinematic facts or even nothing at all (and perhaps I could never tell; see box 3). This disconcerting picture is the essence of the modern mind; we owe it all to Descartes.

The positive half—getting the symbols to symbolize again—turns out to be harder. If we read between the lines in Descartes, we can see him dividing it into two stages (with mathematics again the inspiring example):

1. What makes a notation suitable for symbolizing (representing) some subject matter?
2. What makes a suitable notation actually symbolize (represent) that subject matter?

Descartes barely answers the first question at all; but, via implication and creative anachronism, we can put good words in his

Box 3
Epistemological Skepticism

Being 'skeptical' means doubting, reserving judgment, or remaining unconvinced. 'Epistemological' means having to do with knowledge or the theory of knowledge. Epistemological skepticism is the infamous philosophical stance of doubting whether we can ever really know anything. A classic line goes like this: Given that our senses are often unreliable (we are fooled by illusions, hallucinations, dreams, etc.) and that even our most careful reasonings sometimes go astray, then how can we know for sure, at any particular moment, that we are not being fooled or irrational right then? But if we could never know *that*, we could never know anything.

Descartes used a skepticism like this to introduce one aspect of his new conception of mind (namely the divorce between thought and thing). But, as befits his genius, he first transformed the argument into something far more compelling and sinister. Suppose, he suggested, there were an "evil demon," divinely powerful but malicious, bent on deceiving me about everything. For instance, the demon might create in my mind sense impressions and even theoretical concepts that bear no relation whatever to the outside world; furthermore, he might cleverly arrange them all so that they seem to hang together and make perfect sense. Indeed, my whole life could be a single, diabolically orchestrated hallucination. How would I ever know?

How could Descartes ever dream up such a thing? After all, the illusion of the Sun rising depends directly on the real Earth turning; the ticklings around Galileo's nose are still intimately related to the shapes and motions in the feather. But the evil demon could strip us of all contact with reality whatsoever. Descartes could dream that up because he had a new vision of thoughts as mere symbols in a notational system; and he knew full well that such symbols could equally represent one subject matter or another, or none at all, and the system itself would be no different.

In my own view, epistemological skepticism has been

largely a digression within the history of philosophy and the cause of a lot of wasted effort. In any case the issue is certainly tangential in Artificial Intelligence, and we won't consider it again.

mouth. First, however, we should give a brief nod to his elaborate and sadly influential answer to the second question.

Notice that external notational systems aren't the problem. When external symbols actually represent, it's because they express thoughts, which already represent; they thereby acquire meanings, but only derivative meanings. The real issue, clearly, is those already meaningful thought-symbols; that is, it's a variation on our old friend, the mystery of original meaning. Unlike Hobbes, Descartes at least saw the problem; and he offered an amazing solution. In barest outline, he argued that (1) he could prove, just from what he found within his own mind, that a nice God exists; and (2) it wouldn't be nice to let creatures be radically misguided (especially if they worked conscientiously). Therefore, if we're conscientious, our thoughts will represent reality. Though Descartes's own version was a lot less crude, its main impact was still to send other philosophers after better answers.

Let's return to the first question: What makes a notation "suitable" for symbolizing some subject matter? It isn't just that convenient symbols can be invented for all the relevant items or variables—that, by itself, is trivial. Galileo didn't just say "the area within the triangle represents the distance traveled" and let it go at that. Nor is analytic geometry merely the clever idea of identifying geometric points with numerical coordinates (that wouldn't have cost Descartes much effort). No, what earned these men their reputations was demonstrating how, if you represented things in certain very specific ways, you could *solve problems*.

When a notation can be used to solve problems about a subject matter, then it is suitable for representing that subject matter. Galileo showed how, using his geometrical representations, he could *derive* his famous laws from a few simple assumptions; and thereby he also showed how Euclid's system can be suited to representing kinematics. Descartes did the same for algebra and geometry ("Any problem in geometry can easily be reduced . . .") and then recognized the general point: any number of different notations might be equally suitable for representing any number of different subject matters.

This point about solving problems has two subtle but important corollaries. First, it wouldn't do to get just a few scattered problems right, while giving silly (or no) results on others, for then the occasional successes would seem like mere flukes (or even hoaxes). In other words the notation-cum-problem-solving-method must form an *integrated system* that can be used systematically and reliably in a well-defined area. Second, solving problems obviously involves more than just representing them. There must also be various allowable steps that one can take in getting from (the representation of) the problem to (a representation of) the solution (for example, in derivations, proofs, etc.). Hence the integrated system must include not only notational conventions, but also *rules* specifying which steps are allowed and which are not.

Descartes himself didn't really say all this. Pioneering ideas often bubble beneath the surface in authors who can't quite articulate them. (Later writers will finally get those ideas explicit, while struggling with still newer ones.) Anyway, we can see rules and steps bubbling beneath Descartes's way of distinguishing people from "unreasoning" machines:

> For we can well imagine a machine so made that it utters words and even, in a few cases, words pertaining specifically to some actions that affect it physically. For instance, if you touch one in a certain place, it might ask what you want to say, while if you touch it in another, it might cry out that you're hurting it, and so on. However, no such machine could ever arrange its words in various different ways so as to respond to the sense of whatever is said in its presence—as even the dullest people can do.[15]

Incredible! In 1637 this man could imagine not only the loudspeaker, but also the talking Toyota; perhaps we can forgive him if he couldn't quite imagine mechanical reasoning. For to arrange words appropriately in response to the sense of a previous utterance is just to say something "reasonable," given the context. And what's reasonable (in Descartes's eyes) is determined by the rules of reasoning—that is, the rules for manipulating thought symbols, in the notational system of the mind.[16] So, essentially, Descartes is saying that machines can't think (or talk sensibly—he's anticipated Turing's test too) *because* they can't manipulate symbols rationally.

That, obviously is hitting Artificial Intelligence where it lives. Yet the worry over "mechanical reason" is deep and challenging; it deserves a section of its own.

The Paradox of Mechanical Reason

Descartes was a *dualist*: he believed that minds and the physical universe were two entirely different kinds of substance. Minds, by their nature, can have thoughts in them—beliefs, desires, worries, decisions, and the like—all subject to the order of reason. Meanwhile, the physical universe can, by its nature, have bodies in it—physical objects and mechanisms—all subject to the order of physical law. Note the two radically different notions of 'in'. Thoughts are "in" minds, but not in the sense of being inside a three-dimensional container; minds and their "contents" have no spatial properties at all. The universe, on the other hand, essentially *is* space; all physical objects are within it spatially and always have definite sizes, shapes, and locations. It follows from this contrast that no mind can ever have a physical object in it and likewise that there can never be any thoughts in the physical universe.

Dualism actually has a strong commonsense appeal; and since it would rule out Artificial Intelligence at a stroke, we should pay attention. Suppose Frank remembers Frankfurt, or hankers for a Frankfurter. What could his thought be like *spatially* (the thought itself, not what it's about)? Is it one inch wide (or a millimeter or a mile)? Is it round like a ball (or conical or doughnut shaped)? There is something perverse about such questions; and the problem isn't just that thoughts are fuzzy or hard to measure. I can't even imagine a thought shaped like a fuzzy, one-inch doughnut. Location seems initially easier than size and shape: thoughts are "in our heads," aren't they? But if they have no size or shape, how can they have a place? And anyway, when Frank remembers Frankfurt, exactly how far is it from his recollection to, say, his left earlobe? Of course, science may someday come up with surprising answers; but, on a common-sense level, Cartesian dualism does seem very reasonable.

There is, alas, one fundamental difficulty that no dualist has ever resolved: if thought and matter are so utterly disparate, how can they have anything to do with one another—how can they *interact*? This is the notorious *mind–body problem*, and it has driven dualists to some of philosophy's most desperate gyrations ever (see box 4 for a few samples). Here's how it goes. The laws of physics suffice to explain every movement of every material particle entirely in terms of physical forces; and these forces are all exactly determined by specified physical properties, like mass, distance, electric charge, and various quantum oddments. But if thoughts can have no size, shape, or location, they're even less likely to sport mass, charge, or queer quark quirks; hence, they can never exert any physical forces on matter (or vice versa, presumably). Consequently, all movements of material bodies can be completely explained without reference to anything mental.

So, for a dualist, the price of admitting mind–body interactions would be forfeiture of modern physics, which no mere philosopher could ever afford. On the other hand, foreswearing interactions is also rather awkward. Thus when I decide to raise my hand and then my hand goes up, it sure seems that my (mental) decision *causes* that (physical) movement. Conversely, the (physical) light rays entering my eyes sure seem to cause my (mental) visual experiences of the world. In short, mind–body interaction seems physically impossible; yet without it we could neither perceive nor act. So, despite all its intuitive appeal, dualism is a tough row to hoe.

Most alternatives to dualism turn out to be some sort of *monism*—theories that say there is really only one kind of substance instead of two. In the nineteenth century, the most popular variety of monism was *idealism*, according to which minds and ideas are the only ultimate reality; material objects were regarded either as purely illusory or as special "constructs," somehow built up out of ideas. In our own century, idealism has fallen on hard

Box 4
Dualist Desperados

INTERACTIONISM: Descartes himself actually maintained (to everybody's amazement) that mind and body *do* interact. This, of course, would be an eminently sensible view but for the minor inconvenience of contradicting everything else Descartes believed—and his reasons therefor. He did gingerly restrict the effect to subtle vapors in the pineal organ, a still mysterious body near the bottom of the brain; but somehow that didn't help much with the problem of principle.

PARALLELISM: According to this clever idea, mind and matter are related like two perfect clocks set in motion simultaneously at the creation. Each obeys its own laws and proceeds entirely independently; but, due to God's marvelous planning and workmanship, they "keep time" flawlessly and forever. Thus when the hammer crushes my thumb, and the pain instantaneously clouds my judgment, there is no causal connection, but only another "coincidence," like the noon whistle and the church bells always sounding at 12:00.

OCCASIONALISM: Though mind and body can never affect each other, God can affect anything. So another charming line has watchful Providence intervening helpfully on each "occasion" when mind and matter would interact, if only they could. For instance, that hammer doesn't really affect me (my mind) at all; but God alertly creates for me exactly the excruciation my thumb nerves signal—and then bravely forms on my carnal lips those colorful words I no sooner intend than regret.

EPIPHENOMENALISM: Here's one for agnostics. The universe is a superbly engineered machine, ticking and whirring smoothly, with everything complete and in order. Minds and conscious experiences play no role in the mechanism but are incidental by-products ("epiphenomena"), like the ticking and whirring. This peculiar approach is curiously ambivalent about interaction: matter causes or "gives off" mind, but thought has no effect on matter. So we can watch the world go by, but we can't do anything about it (our impressions to the contrary being but a cruel hoax).

times, and the most popular monism is *materialism*, according to which (naturally) matter is the only ultimate reality. Materialists hold either that thoughts and ideas are purely illusory or else that they are special constructs, somehow built up out of matter. The difficulties that toppled idealism are not particularly relevant to AI; so we mention them only in passing and concentrate on the materialist side.

Materialism, however, has troubles of its own. For one thing, materialists find it hard to say anything terribly comforting about immortal souls; but we set that issue aside. Of more immediate concern is what to say about thoughts, if all reality is ultimately material. The crux of the issue is a deep and traditional conundrum, which I call the *paradox of mechanical reason*. Its resolution is, simultaneously, the philosophical foundation of the Artificial Intelligence boom and also the most attractive current alternative to hopeless dualism and zany idealism (not to mention vulgar behaviorism).

So what's the paradox? Reasoning (on the computational model) is the manipulation of meaningful symbols according to rational rules (in an integrated system). Hence there must be some sort of manipulator to carry out those manipulations. There seem to be two basic possibilities: either the manipulator pays attention to what the symbols and rules *mean* or it doesn't. If it does pay attention to the meanings, then it can't be entirely mechanical—because meanings (whatever exactly they are) don't exert physical forces. On the other hand, if the manipulator does not pay attention to the meanings, then the manipulations can't be instances of reasoning—because what's reasonable or not depends crucially on what the symbols mean.

In a word, if a process or system is mechanical, it can't reason; if it reasons, it can't be mechanical. That's the paradox of mechanical reason. Unfortunately, the issue is just too important to be quietly forgotten. So people have struggled with it courageously, generating a vexed and amusing history that is also somewhat enlightening (at least in retrospect).

Consider again the alternative where the meanings are taken into account. Ironically, the problem is essentially a reenactment, within monist materialism, of the basic dualist difficulty about interactions, only this time the mysterious troublemakers are meanings rather than thoughts. Materialists try to escape the interactionist trap by claiming that thoughts are really just a special kind of material object (viz., symbols), which therefore obviously can "interact" with matter. But the *meanings* of those symbols are not material objects (they are "abstract" or "conceptual" or something). The trouble is, they still have to affect the operation of the mechanism for the manipulations to be reasonable. Hence all the old embarrassments return about exerting forces without having any mass, electric charge, etc.: meanings as such simply cannot affect a physical mechanism.

But suppose this problem could be resolved. (I think many philosophers ignored it, convinced that it had to be resolvable somehow.) Would that finish the matter? Not quite; for the status of the manipulator remains disconcertingly unsettled. We're assuming, for the moment, that it manipulates thought symbols reasonably, by "paying attention" to the meanings of the symbols and the rules of reason. But how, exactly, does that work? Consider Zelda. We imagine a manipulator "reading" the symbols in her mind, figuring out what they mean, looking up various rules of reason, deciding which ones to apply, and then applying them correctly—which generally means "writing" out some new mental symbols (whatever Zelda thinks of next).

This manipulator turns out to be pretty smart. It can read and understand both the symbols it's working on and the rules it's following; it can figure things out, make decisions, apply rules to novel cases, do what it's told, and so on. But so what? Isn't Zelda the manipulator of her own thoughts, and doesn't she understand them as well as anybody? No! That cannot possibly be right. Zelda's thoughts and understandings are the symbols *being manipulated*; if carrying out the manipulations also requires thoughts and understandings, then these latter thoughts and understandings must be distinct from Zelda's. The point of the computational theory is to *explain* Zelda's thinking in terms of rational manipulations of her thought symbols. Her thinking cannot itself be employed in explaining the manipulations, on pain of rendering the account circular.

How humiliating! In order to explain thinking, the theory has to invent an inner "manipulator" who thinks, understands, decides, and acts all on its own. Philosophers have dreamt up various soothing names for this inconvenient little fellow, such as the "faculty of the will" or the lofty "transcendental ego." But the name which sticks is the one used by mocking opponents: he's the *homunculus* (which is just Latin for "little fellow"). Whatever the name, the bottom line is a simple, shattering question: If a thinking homunculus is needed to explain how Zelda can think, then what explains how the homunculus can think? A still smaller homunculus?

We should appreciate that this debacle follows directly from assuming that (rational) thought manipulations require "attention" to what the thought symbols and rules *mean*; for that's what entailed a manipulator who could understand and think on his own. In other words, sticking to the "reason" side of the paradox of mechanical reason leads to the homunculus disaster. What happens if we try the "mechanical" side?

Hume — The Mental Mechanic

Scotland's most celebrated philosopher, David Hume (1711–1776), was the first to spell out consistently the mechanical conception of thinking. The subtitle of his monumental *Treatise of Human Nature* (written in his twenties) announces the central plan of his entire philosophy: "An Attempt to introduce the experimental Method of Reasoning into Moral Subjects."[17] By "moral subjects" Hume meant not only ethics and the theory of justice but all of what he called "the science of man"—beginning with psychology. By the "experimental method of reasoning" he meant the methods of natural science, especially physics.

In other words, Hume proposed to establish a new category of human sciences, explicitly modeled on the wonderfully successful physical sciences. More particularly, he wanted to explain thinking and feeling in terms of how various mental mechanisms work; or, as he put it, to

discover . . . the secret springs and principles by which the human mind is actuated in its operation.

In the same paragraph, Hume effectively compares his own efforts to those of the great English physicist Sir Isaac Newton (1642–1727), whom he describes as having

determined the laws and forces by which the revolutions of the planets are governed and directed.

For he goes on to conclude:

The like has been performed with regard to other parts of nature. And there is no reason to despair of equal success in our inquiries concerning the mental powers and economy, if prosecuted with equal capacity and caution.[18]

So Hume wants to discover the laws and forces by which ideas are governed and directed; he wants to be the Newton of the mind.

The centerpiece of Hume's theory is the famous principle of "association of ideas," which he adopted pretty much intact from the English empiricist John Locke (1632–1704), who, in turn, got a good deal of it from Hobbes. Locke is the philosopher who said the mind starts out as a *tabula rasa* (clean slate), on which experience "writes" the sense impressions basic to all knowledge; then the mind's natural "association" combines and recombines all these fundamental "ideas" into ever more complex and sophisticated science. Locke's main concern was to legitimate Newton's empirical method against the Cartesians (who still wanted physics to be "intuitive," like mathematics). He was using physical knowledge as a kind of acid test for philosophical theories: no theory of the mind could be right, in Locke's view, unless it could show why Newtonian science is good science.

Hume, on the other hand, was inspired by Newton more directly: his theory was designed not merely to accommodate Newton's physics but to imitate it. That is, Hume really put forward a "mental mechanics"; his impressions and ideas were not so much the basic evidence on which all knowledge rested but rather the basic pieces out of which all knowledge was composed—or, better yet, the basic "corpuscles" (particles) to which all the mental forces and operations applied. And the association of ideas is just the general category for all these forces; Hume himself describes it as

a kind of ATTRACTION, which in the mental world will be found to have as extraordinary effects as in the natural, and to shew itself in as many and as various forms.[19]

Obviously he's thinking of universal gravitation (and maybe magnetism).

It is important to appreciate how different Hume is not only from Locke, but also from Hobbes. The latter shared Hume's "mechanical" outlook, even to the point of regarding thoughts as actual movements of matter in the brain. The difference is that Hobbes took thoughts on the model of numerals or words: physical symbols to be manipulated according to the rules of calculation or rational discourse. And that led, as we saw, to the question of how there could be such manipulations, for they seem to require an intelligent manipulator (the homunculus). Hume, however, had no such problem; his science of the mind was to be entirely analogous to physics, plus maybe a bit of engineering.

But, crucially, this analogy occurs at the level of explanation. Unlike Hobbes, Hume didn't claim that ideas actually *are* physical (he didn't, in fact, seem to care much about the materialism/ dualism issue). Rather, he said, ideas are *like* physical particles, in that their interactions are to be explained in terms of natural forces governed by natural laws. Hence the account doesn't beg its own question by assuming some behind-the-scenes intelligence making it all work. There is no more difficulty about "how" ideas obey the laws of association than there is about "how" planets obey the law of gravity; they just do. In other words, Hume, like Newton, can say, "I frame no hypotheses."[20]

Unfortunately, however, in avoiding the homunculus pickle, Hume landed himself in another: What makes his ideas *ideas*, and what makes their interactions count as *thinking*? What, in short, is mental about the mind? Hume has so thoroughly eliminated meaning and rationality from the basis of his account that he might as well be talking about some new and strange kind of physics. In a way, of course, that was the whole point; but he now owes us an explanation of how meaning and reason get back into the picture; otherwise he hasn't produced a "mechanics of the *mind*" after all. Unfortunately, Hume has no such story to tell; indirectly, I think, he even admits it, in his own peculiar brand of "skepticism" (see box 5).

But this just brings us back to the paradox of mechanical reason: either meanings matter to the manipulations, in which case the processes aren't really mechanical (they presuppose an homunculus); or else meanings don't matter, in which case the processes aren't really rational (they're just some meaningless "machine-like" interactions). Hume is simply caught on the second horn of the dilemma. Historically, this is the point at which transcendental idealism thundered to the rescue; that is, Kant, Hegel, and their legions bravely returned to the first horn and gave up on matter. But, as mentioned earlier, this otherwise remarkable and difficult episode is really a digression within the pedigree of Artificial Intelligence. So we will skip over it and plunge back in with confident and all-conquering twentieth-century materialism.

Box 5
Semantic Skepticism

In the section of the *Treatise* entitled "Of scepticism with regard to the senses," Hume describes what he calls the "double existence" theory, according to which our perceptions and the objects they (allegedly) represent are distinct entities. Perceptions are fleeting and dependent on us, whereas objects are supposed to be durable and external; moreover, objects supposedly cause perceptions, which, in turn, resemble them. But Hume (as you might have guessed) thinks all of this is rubbish. Our minds work only with perceptions themselves; that is, we never have any "direct" experience of objects, independent of perceptions. Further, the existence of perceptions could never *logically* imply that anything else exists. Hence these "external objects" can be nothing but figments of our imaginations.

Hume has a subtle and ingenious story about why our imaginations do such a thing to us, why the confusion itself is so irresistible, and why philosophers have no hope of ever clearing it up. But the fact remains that, according to Hume's own theory, mental representation of nonmental objects is inconceivable. Thus, insofar as the meaningfulness of thought essentially involves "representational content," Hume has no place for it. So while Descartes's skeptic asks: "How can I know what I know?" Hume's skeptic grapples with the more basic question: "How can I even mean what I mean?"

Chess is chess, at any scale

Formal Games

Late in our own century it's hard to take the "paradox" of mechanical reason quite so seriously. Obviously (one insists impatiently) there can be reasoning machines—many of us carry them in our pockets. In philosophy, however, nothing is so treacherous as the "obvious." Even if it's true (as it may be) that the paradox is now resolved, we must see exactly *how* the solution works; we must understand just which new ideas and discoveries finally broke through where Hobbes, Descartes, and Hume (not to mention introspective psychologists, psychoanalysts, and behaviorists) had failed. In other words, we must understand, in fundamental terms, what a *computer* really is. The concepts involved are not particularly difficult; but they're not, in fact, all that obvious either.

A computer is an *interpreted automatic formal system*. It will take us two chapters to spell out what that definition says. More specifically, this chapter will explain what an automatic formal system is; then the next can get on to interpreting them, which is where meaning and rationality come in. In the meantime, before we can talk about automation, there's quite a bit to say about old-fashioned, "manual" formal systems.

A *formal system* is like a game in which tokens are manipulated according to rules, in order to see what configurations can be obtained. In fact, many familiar games—among them chess, checkers, Chinese checkers, go, and tic-tac-toe—simply *are* formal systems. But other games—such as marbles, tiddlywinks, billiards, and baseball—aren't formal at all (in the sense we care about).[1] What's the difference? All formal games have three essential features (not shared by other games): they are "token manipulation" games; they are "digital"; and they are "finitely playable." We must see what these mean.

The *tokens* of a formal game are just the "pieces" ("markers," "counters," or whatever) with which the game is played. For instance, chessmen, checkers, and go stones are the tokens with which chess, checkers, and go are played. These tokens happen to be handy little physical objects, which you can pick up and move with your fingers; but formal tokens don't have to be like that. Thus the tokens for tic-tac-toe are usually O's and X's, written down with chalk or pencil; and, for many electronic games, the tokens are actually switch settings and colored light patterns.

Manipulating tokens means one or more of the following:

1. Relocating them (e.g., moving them around on some board or playing field);
2. altering them (or replacing them with different ones);
3. adding new ones to the position; and/or
4. taking some away.

In chess and checkers, for example, the pieces are mostly moved, sometimes removed (captured), and occasionally altered (promoted); but new ones are never added. In go, on the other hand, each play consists of adding a new stone to the board and occasionally also removing some; but once a stone is on the board, it is never moved around or altered. Obviously writing down O's and X's, or flipping switches to turn lights on and off, can also be token manipulations, depending on the game. (Often it is convenient to use the term *move* for any sort of token manipulation, not just relocations.)

In order to define completely any particular token manipulation "game"—any formal system—you have to specify three things:

1. what the tokens are;
2. what the starting position is (or what the alternative starting positions are); and
3. what moves (manipulations) would be allowed in any given position—that is, what the rules are.

A *position*, clearly, is an arrangement or configuration of tokens (at a given moment). Play begins with some starting position and proceeds by modifying the position, one step at a time. Many formal games (chess and checkers, for instance) have a standard starting position that is always the same; but go has several starting positions, depending on the relative strengths of the players; and other systems may allow any number of possible starting positions.[2]

Positions are modified by (and only by) *legal moves*: that is, by token manipulations permitted by the rules. Just which manipulations the rules permit depends, at each point, on the current position and on nothing else. Thus a move that's legal in one position might not be legal in another; but if it is ever legal in a certain position, then it will always be legal whenever that position occurs. The latter point is emphasized by saying that formal systems are *self-contained*; the "outside world" (anything not included in the current position) is strictly irrelevant. For instance, it makes no difference to a chess game, as such, if the chess set is stolen property or if the building is on fire or if the fate of nations hangs on the outcome—the same moves are legal in the same positions, period. The players or spectators might have wider interests, but all that matters in the game itself are the current and possible positions.[3]

A crucial consequence of formal self-containedness is the irrelevance of meaning. By concentrating so far on games, we have neatly postponed any questions about formal tokens having meanings. But it doesn't take a crystal ball to see that those questions are coming (in the next chapter, to be exact). Suffice it to say here that meaning is not a *formal* property—because (roughly) meanings relate to the "outside world." To take a contrived example, imagine a game in which the following string of letters is part of the position: "The cat is on the mat." (And, for clarity, suppose also that no cats or mats are tokens in the game.) Then the point is: nothing about any cat, mat, or cat/mat relations makes any difference to what formal moves are legal in that game. Of course the string of letters might perfectly well mean something (about some cat and mat, say); but that meaning (if any) cannot be relevant to the formal system as such.

Those formal systems we think of as games typically have some special class of positions designated as the goal or "winning" positions. In such games the player or players strive to achieve one of those positions by carefully planning and selecting their moves; when there is more than one player, they are often opponents, competing to see who can reach a winning position first. But it is essential to realize that not all formal systems are competitive or even have goal positions; these characteristics are common in *games* only because they add to the excitement and fun. But many important formal systems are important for reasons quite apart from amusement (computers being a salient case in point).

A simple example of a formal system not involving competition (but still having a goal position) is the familiar solitaire game played with pegs on a board with a cross-shaped array of holes in it. The starting position appears below. The solid dots represent

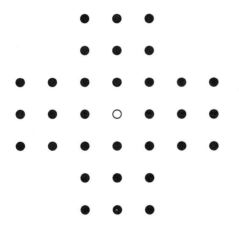

holes with pegs in them, and the circle in the center represents an empty hole (the only one in the starting position). This game has only one kind of legal move: if you have two pegs next to each other in a row or column and an empty hole next to one of them in the same row or column, then you can remove the middle peg, while "jumping" the other peg over to the hole that was empty. (Thus the two holes that had pegs in them end up empty, and the one that was empty gets a peg.) The goal of the game is to remove pegs by a sequence of jumps, until only one remains, and it's in the center.

This solitaire game is a simple but genuine formal system. It is not just an analogy or suggestive comparison; it *is* a formal system. All the essential elements are here; and we will refer back to them periodically to make various points explicit. To be sure, miscellaneous subtle and important complications are lacking from such a primitive example—thereby setting the stage for illustrative contrasts as well.

The first "important complication" is really quite basic and should be introduced right away. In the solitaire game there is only one kind of token: they're all pegs, completely alike and interchangeable. But in most interesting formal systems there are numerous distinct token *types*. In chess, for instance, there are six different types of token (for each side): king, queen, rook, bishop, knight, and pawn. Formal tokens are freely interchangeable if and only if they are the same type. Thus it doesn't make any difference which white pawn goes on which white-pawn-square; but switching a pawn with a rook or a white pawn with a black one could make a lot of difference. Of course it can be a legal move to switch tokens of different types; but that results in a new and different position. Interchanging tokens of the same type isn't a move and doesn't affect the position. By the way, "altering" a token (one of the kinds of manipulation mentioned above) really means changing its type (or replacing it with one of a different type).

Ultimately, the rules are what determine the types of the tokens. The rules specify what moves would be legal in what positions. If interchanging two particular tokens wouldn't make any difference to which moves were legal in any position, then it couldn't make any difference to the game at all; and those tokens would be of the same type. To see the significance of this, consider chess again. In some fancy chess sets, *every* piece is unique; each white pawn, for instance, is a little figurine, slightly different from the others. Why then are they all the same type? Because, in any position whatsoever, if you interchanged any two of them, exactly the same moves would still be legal. That is, each of them contributes to an overall position in exactly the same way, namely, in the way that pawns do. And that's what makes them all pawns.

Formal systems, it was said at the outset, are distinctive in three essential respects: they are token-manipulation games, they are digital, and they are finitely playable. We have seen now something of what "token-manipulation" means, so we may turn to the other two characteristics, beginning with digital systems.

Digital Systems

The word 'digital' generally brings to mind electronic computers or perhaps discrete numeric "readouts" (as in digital clocks, tuners, and thermometers). But digital systems include far more than these—comprising, indeed, a fundamental metaphysical category. Every formal system is digital, but not everything digital is a formal system. The alphabet is digital, as are modern currency (money), playing cards, and the rotary function-switch on your stereo. On the other hand, photographs, gold bullion, pick-up sticks, and stereo volume controls are generally not digital. What's the basic difference?

A *digital system* is a set of positive and reliable techniques (methods, devices) for producing and reidentifying tokens, or configurations of tokens, from some prespecified set of types. Let's distill the main idea out of that: first, we can disregard configurations of tokens ("complex tokens") for the time being and also quietly take reliability and the prespecified types for granted. Second, we can substitute "writing" and "reading" for the more cumbersome "producing" and "reidentifying," but only with two warnings: (1) *writing* isn't just making pen or pencil marks but rather any kind of token manipulation that changes the formal position (thus, putting a peg in the center hole is "writing" a token of the type: peg in center hole); and (2) *reading* implies nothing about understanding (or even recognition) but only differentiation by type and position (an elevator "reads" the button pressings and shows as much by stopping at the proper floors). These simplifications render the definition quite elegant: a digital system is a set of positive write/read techniques.

Clearly everything turns on what 'positive' means. A *positive* technique is one that can succeed absolutely, totally, and without qualification; that is, "positively." The opposite would be methods that can succeed only relatively, partially, or with such qualifications as "almost exactly," "in nearly every respect," or "close enough for government work." Whether a given technique is positive depends heavily on what would count as success. Imagine, for instance, carefully measuring off six feet on a board, drawing a perpendicular line there with a square, and then sawing right along the line. Is that a positive technique? Well, it depends. If the specified goal is to get a board between five feet eleven inches and six feet one inch, then the technique can succeed totally; so it's positive. But if the goal is a board exactly six feet long, then the method is not positive, since it could succeed at best approximately.

A positive technique isn't guaranteed to succeed; success may not even be very likely. The question isn't whether it will succeed (or how often), but rather how well it can succeed: a positive technique has the possibility of succeeding *perfectly*. When we ask instead about the likelihood of success, that's a question of *reliability*. Thus, the above method for cutting a board within an inch of six feet is not only positive but also reliable because it would be successful almost every time. If the goal were to be within a sixteenth of an inch of six feet, then it would still be positive, but it might or might not be reliable, depending on the skill of the sawyer. But if the specification were plus or minus a millionth of an inch, then the technique would be neither positive nor reliable because it is impossible to cut wood that precisely.

Many techniques are positive and reliable. Shooting a basketball at the basket is a positive method (for getting it through), since it can succeed absolutely and without qualification; moreover, for talented players, it is pretty reliable. Counting is a positive technique for determining the number of pencils in a box, and most people can do it reliably. Closing a switch is a positive method for turning on a furnace, and thermostats can do it reliably. On the other hand, there is no positive method for keeping the temperature at exactly 68 degrees: even the best thermostat could only approximate the goal. No technique can positively determine the exact weight of the pencils in a box or get a ball exactly through the center of a basket, and so on.

Digital techniques are write/read techniques. "Writing" a token means producing one of a given specified type (possibly complex); "reading" a token means determining what type it is. A "write/ read cycle" is writing a token and then (at some later time) reading it; a write/read cycle is *successful* if the type determined by the read technique is the same as the type specified to the write technique. A digital system is a set of write/read techniques that are positive and reliable, relative to this standard for write/read success (and some prespecified set of relevant types).

There is considerable latitude in what one counts as producing and then identifying tokens. Thus one could say that getting a ball through a basket and not getting it through are two types of "basket-shooting tokens": shooting the ball is writing a token, and seeing whether it went through or not is reading the token. Then, given a shooter who can reliably hit or miss on command and a judge who can reliably tell hits from misses, you have a simple digital system. But it's kind of silly. Not quite so silly is a multiposition electrical switch. The types are the different possible positions; writing a token is setting the switch to some position; and reading the setting is sending electricity to the switch and having (only) the relevant circuit conduct. This is positive and reliable because the different settings are clearly separated (e.g., by "click stops") and because it is totally unambiguous and determinate which circuit conducts (for each setting).

But the real importance of digital systems emerges when we turn to more complicated cases. Consider, for a moment, the respective fates of Rembrandt's portraits and Shakespeare's sonnets. Even given the finest care, the paintings are slowly deteriorating; by no means are they the same now as when they were new. The poems, by contrast, may well have been preserved perfectly. Of course a few may have been lost and others miscopied, but we probably have most of them *exactly* the way Shakespeare wrote them—absolutely without flaw. The difference, obviously, is that the alphabet is digital (with the standard write/read cycle), whereas paint colors and textures are not.

In the real world there is always a little variation and error. A ball never goes through a basket the same way twice; the angle of a switch is microscopically different each time it's set; no two inscriptions of the letter *A* are quite alike. "Nothing is perfect," we often say. But digital systems (sometimes) achieve perfection, despite the world. How? Essentially, they allow a certain "margin for error" within which all performances are equivalent and success is total. Thus the exact token doesn't matter, as long as it stays "within tolerances."[4] In basketball, a basket is a basket is a basket; and a miss isn't. There are many slightly different ways to inscribe a character which is totally and unqualifiedly an *A*. Hence two copies of a poem can be equally perfect, even though they're in different handwriting (or fonts), as long as each character remains clearly recognizable (and correct).

One reason this is important is that it permits a kind of complexity that is otherwise difficult or impossible. To see how, consider two contrasting conventions for keeping track of money in a poker game. Each uses different colors for different denominations: blue, red, and white for a hundred, ten, and one, respectively. But in one system the unit of each denomination is a colored plastic disk (i.e., a poker chip), whereas in the other system it is a tablespoon of fine colored sand. What are the relative merits of these two arrangements? Well, the sand system allows fractional bets, by using less than a full tablespoon of white sand. You can't do that with chips. But the chip system is digital: there is a positive technique for determining the amount of any wager (namely, counting the chips of each color), and, therefore, every bet is *exact*.

The advantage of the digital arrangement becomes apparent in the case of large, precise wagers. Since a volume of sand can never be measured exactly, there would always be some small error in any sand-system wager—say $\pm$ 2 percent, for purposes of discussion. Now imagine trying to be + 914 units. With chips it's easy: you count out nine blue, one red, and four white ones, and you have it exactly. But with the sand, things aren't so nice. Two percent of 900 units is 18 units; so the expected error on the blue sand (the grains that stick to the spoon and so on) is worth more than all the red and white sand combined. In effect, the imprecision in large denominations swamps the entire significance of small denominations and renders them superfluous. But modest "imperfections" don't affect the value of blue chips. Even when they're scratched and worn, they're still worth exactly 100 white chips; therefore additional white chips are never superfluous.

Of course two percent is not a very accurate measurement, and 914 units is kind of an odd wager anyway. But the difference is a matter of principle: at some point the elaboration and versatility afforded by denominational distinctions is only feasible in a system with positive write/read techniques. The same holds for any complicated system where tiny deviations in one part can make all the difference in the world to other parts; there has to be some way to prevent the influential components from accidentally overwhelming the sensitive ones. Digital designs are one of the most powerful means known for dealing with this problem, which is one of the main reasons they are so important.

By definition every formal system is a digital system. Formal systems can thus get extraordinarily intricate and complicated without getting out of control—a fact important to Artificial Intelligence in several different ways. But first we should consider the more straightforward cases, beginning with our old solitaire example. Why is that digital? "Writing" a token means producing a new position by making a move (that is, by jumping one peg over another and removing the latter), and "reading" that token means recognizing what the new position is (and thereby determining what moves would be legal next). This cycle is positive and reliable because one can (easily) get the pegs unambiguously and totally in and out of the various holes in the board and then tell exactly and flawlessly just which holes they're in. It doesn't matter if a peg is leaning slightly or is not quite centered in the hole: it's still absolutely and perfectly in that hole and no other, as any child can see.

The same is true for chess, though with the added complication of the different piece types. But positively discriminating the pieces (of any decent set) is as trivial as identifying what squares they're on. Again, the wide margin for error, the fact that the pieces are quite distinct and don't have to be exactly centered on the squares, is what makes the positive techniques possible. Billiards, on the other hand, is not digital: the precise positions of the balls can be quite important. Consider the difference between accidentally messing up a chess game and a billiards game. Chess players with good memories could reconstruct the position perfectly (basically because displacing the pieces by fractions of an inch wouldn't matter). A billiards position, by contrast, can never be reconstructed perfectly, even with photographic records and the finest instruments; a friendly game might be restored well enough, but jostling a tournament table could be a disaster.

The digitalness of formal systems is profoundly relevant to Artificial Intelligence. Not only does it make enormous complexity practical and reliable, but it also underlies another fundamental property of formal systems: their independence of any particular material medium. Intelligence, too, must have this property, if there are ever to be smart robots.

Medium Independence and Formal Equivalence

Formal systems are independent of the medium in which they are "embodied." In other words, essentially the same formal system can be materialized in any number of different media, with no formally significant difference whatsoever. This is an important feature of formal systems in general; I call it *medium independence.*

To begin with a familiar example, it obviously doesn't matter to pegboard solitaire whether the pegs are made of wood or plastic, are red or green, or are a quarter or a half an inch high. You could change any or all of these and still play the very same game: the same positions, the same moves, the same strategies, the same skills—everything. And, of course, the changes could be bigger: the pegs could be eliminated altogether and replaced with marbles resting in little craters, X's chalked in squares, or even onion rings hanging on nails. On the other hand, changing the starting position or the rules for jumps would matter: that would make it a different game.

Likewise, chess pieces come in many styles and sizes—though their color usually does matter, to distinguish the opposing sides. Or rather, what really matters is that each piece be positively identifiable, both as to type and side (as well as which square it's on). Consistent with that restriction, however, the sky's the limit. Texas millionaires, for instance, could play chess from their opposing penthouses, using thirty-two radio-controlled helicopters and sixty-four local rooftops. Or, if they owned an eight-story hotel with eight rooms per floor, they might use brightly marked window shades (which the hotel staff redistributes on command).

Such outlandish examples are worth stressing just because medium independence is itself so remarkable; most nonformal games are not independent of their media at all. Doubling (or halving) the dimensions of a football, for instance, would make the game significantly different, especially in the passing and kicking strategies. If the ball were magnified by twenty (not to mention replaced by a helicopter), nothing even resembling ordinary football could be played. Billiards is similarly sensitive to the size (and weight and shape and texture . . .) of billiard balls. Small variations might make only a minor difference; but switching, say, to little wooden pegs or onion rings would be out of the question.

Electronic toys illustrate the point in another way. Each December stores are awash with new and cleverer versions of "pocket hockey," "finger football," and the like, as well as electronic chess and checkers. But there is a dramatic difference between the cases. Pocket hockey has about as much to do with hockey as stick figures do with people: you can see a coarse analogy in a few structural respects, but beyond that they're not even similar. Electronic chess, on the other hand, *is* chess—not grandmaster quality, maybe, but the real thing. Replacing regulation balls and pucks with electronic blips is actually far worse than merely changing their size: a real, live quarterback can't even pick a blip up, let alone pass it or kick it. But luminous displays work just fine as (genuine, full-fledged) chess pieces; Russian champions can attack them (and probably capture them) as well as any other.

The difference isn't simply that some games are intellectual while others are physical. In the first place, professional sports demand a great deal of planning and strategy; and, of course, chess pieces, checkers, and go stones are just as much physical objects as any balls, bats, or cue sticks. Rather it is medium independence itself that explains why, despite these facts, chess still seems so much less "physical" than football or even billiards. The essential point is that nothing in a formal game depends on any *specific* features of its physical medium, as long as the same sequences of legal moves and positions are maintained; hence the game itself seems less directly tied to material embodiment.

Digitalness makes medium independence feasible. Return to the case of Shakespeare versus Rembrandt: since the alphabet is digital, poems are medium independent. They can be chiseled in stone, embossed in Braille, recorded in computer code, or traced romantically in the sand; and, if the order of letters and punctuation remains constant, the poem as such is unaffected. One might think that the same is true for paintings: as long as the "order" of colors, textures, reflectivities, etc. is exactly maintained, a portrait can be indifferently reproduced in oils, acrylics, watercolors, or any medium you like. The trouble is that the relevant properties of paintings cannot, in fact, be exactly duplicated even in one medium, let alone several. It is the digitalness of alphabets that makes exact reproduction—and hence medium independence—of character sequences feasible.

Note that medium independence does not imply that suitable media are entirely arbitrary. You couldn't really play chess (or record poems) with puffs of smoke, since they can't be maneuvered very well and they dissipate too fast. At the opposite extreme, it would be just as hard to use a solid steel chess set, with all its pieces welded permanently to the board. Clearly the medium (the tokens) of a formal system must be manipulable enough that legal moves can actually be made (written) and also durable enough that positions can still be positively recognized (read) when it comes time for the next move. Though many diverse material systems and procedures can meet these requirements, many others cannot: not everything can be digital.

So far our discussion has been confined to a fairly intuitive and direct notion of "sameness": same game, same move, same poem, etc. But in fact this notion is not simple, and some interesting variations arise when it's pushed. Consider the (unfamiliar) formal game defined as follows:

1. The tokens are thirty-three plastic chips, each with two letters written on it: one from early in the alphabet (A–G), and one from late in the alphabet (T–Z).
2. In the starting position, all of the chips are together in a white basket, except for the one marked *DW*, which is all by itself in a black basket.
3. A move consists of exchanging two chips in the white basket for one in the black; but there's a restriction on which chips can be exchanged for which:
   a. *either* all three chips must have the same early letter and sequential late letters, *or else* they must all have the same late letter and sequential early letters;
   b. *and* the middle letter in the sequence can't be on the one chip going from the black basket to the white.

For example:

AX,BX $<=>$ CX and AX,AW $<=>$ AV are legal moves;

but ET,EV $<=>$ EZ isn't legal (no sequential letters);

AW,BX $<=>$ CY isn't legal (no same letter); and

AX,CX $<=>$ BX isn't legal (middle letter in black basket).

The game is played by one person, whose goal is to finish with all the chips exchanged (i.e., all but *DW* in the black basket).

Obviously this game is digital and formal, and therefore medium independent. The chips could be wooden instead of plastic, marked with digits instead of letters, and/or exchanged between boxes instead of baskets; and, of course, it could all be done with labeled helicopters across the English channel. But could there be more dramatic differences than that? A surprising answer may emerge when we finish defining the game; in particular, we still have to specify *which* letter pairs are marked on those thirty-three chips. The specification is merely a list, but the list can be arranged so as to display the starting position in a revealing pattern.

		A V	A W	A X			
		B V	B W	B X			
CT	CU	C V	C W	C X	CY	CZ	
DT	DU	D V		D X	DY	DZ	DW
ET	EU	E V	E W	E X	EY	EZ	
		F V	F W	F X			
		G V	G W	G X			

White basket   *Black basket*

Needless to say, each chip corresponds to one hole in the board for our old solitaire example. Transferring a chip from the white basket to the black is like removing a peg from the board, while transferring a chip back is like putting a peg back in an empty hole. And, given that analogy, the rather complicated rule for chip exchanges corresponds exactly to the rule for peg jumps.

So in some sense the two games are the "same." But it's not simply a case of different media, as discussed earlier. The tokens, the pegs and chips, do *not* correspond; there are thiry-two pegs, all alike, as compared to thirty-three chips, all different. On the other hand, there are thirty-three distinct places where a peg can be, as against only two relevant chip locations. In effect, token distinctions are traded off for place distinctions, leading to the same number of possibilities overall. The correspondence between the two systems is thus complete and exact, but only at a higher or more abstract level than the direct token-for-token, square-for-square correspondence of, say, helicopter chess.

This more abstract correspondence relates complete positions instead of individual tokens and token locations. Moves, then, are conceived as changes in the overall position; so conceived, they also correspond, even though there may be no direct correspondence in the relocations (etc.) of individual tokens. We can express these new intuitions about "higher-level sameness" in an explicit definition. Two formal systems are *formally equivalent* just in case

1. for each distinct position in one system there is exactly one corresponding position in the other system;
2. whenever a move would be legal in one system, the corresponding move (i.e., from the corresponding position to the corresponding position) would be legal in the other system; and
3. (all) the starting positions correspond.

Hence there is also an exact correspondence in the positions legally accessible from the starting positions in the two systems: if you can get there from here in one, you can get there from here in the other.[5] (If the systems are understood as games with goal positions, then these ought to correspond as well.)

Our earlier illustrations of medium independence are, of course, just special cases of formal equivalence: namely, when the positions and moves correspond because the individual tokens and token arrangements correspond. Clearly helicopter chess is formally equivalent to chess played in the more ordinary way. But these are also both formally equivalent to chess played by mail, where the moves are made by writing formulae (like: P–K4) on postcards rather than by relocating physical pieces. If you let your imagination roam a little, you can see that many otherwise quite disparate formal systems might nevertheless have the same structure of position-accessibility as chess and thus be formally equivalent to it.[6]

The notions of medium independence and formal equivalence are crucially important to Artificial Intelligence and to computational psychology in general. Though some of the significance can only emerge as our discussion proceeds, the basic point can be stated crudely: brain cells and electronic circuits are manifestly different "media"; but, maybe, at some appropriate level of abstraction, they can be media for equivalent formal systems. In that case, a computer mind might be as much a real (genuine) mind as helicopter (or computer) chess is genuine chess, only in a different medium. Of course, we have some work to do before we can turn that into anything more than a tantalizing hint.

Finite Playability and Algorithms

So far we have been fairly casual (not to say "informal") about the definitions of formal systems, avoiding mathematical technicalities wherever possible. One technical matter, however, is central to the very idea of formality: What limits are there (if any) on the size and complexity of formal systems? The crucial issue concerns what it takes "to play the game"—that is, to make and recognize moves allowed by the rules. Roughly, we want to insist that formal games be playable by finite players: no infinite or magical powers are required. On the other hand, our theoretical definition shouldn't be gratuitously parochial: players mustn't be limited to any particular capabilities or resources (such as human or present-day capabilities) as long as they are unquestionably finite. The challenge is to spell this out.

To be able to play a formal game is to be able to follow the rules. But what, exactly, does that involve? In principle, competent players must always (i.e., for any given position) be able to

1. tell, for any proposed move, whether that move would be legal (in that position); and

2. produce at least one legal move (or show that there are none).

Thus, you wouldn't be much of a chess player if you couldn't reliably tell whether your opponent's moves were legal or come up with legal moves of your own. To insist, then, that formal systems be *finitely playable* is to insist that these two necessary abilities be within the compass of finite players. So the question becomes: What can be expected of finite players?

Some operations are manifestly within finite means, essentially because they're trivial. For instance, it doesn't require anything magical or infinite to type a token of the letter *A* on a piece of paper whenever a certain switch is closed. Not only is this clear on the face of it, but we also have an independent demonstration in that (finite, nonmagical) electric typewriters can do it. An ability to identify simple tokens from a standard set is equally mundane in principle, as is shown, for example, by the coin-sorting prowess of common vending machines. Again, it's easy to move, say, a chess piece from one square, indicated by pointing at it, to another; nor is much required to move a pointer to an adjacent square, in a given direction; and so on. It is not important, however, to catalog or even fully delimit these manifestly finite capabilities, as long as it is established that there are some. For they give us a place to start: a finite player is assumed to have some finite repertoire of specific *primitive operations* that it can perform, positively and reliably, any finite number of times.

Primitive operations, of course, are only the beginning. Chess playing requires much more than merely identifying and moving indicated pieces among indicated squares; a player must also determine, for each proposed move, whether it is legal for that type of piece, whether it exposes a king threat, whether it is blocked by intervening pieces, etc. Since such tests typically involve a variety of interrelated factors, they are not altogether simple and trivial; hence, they shouldn't count as primitive. Consequently, finite players must also be capable of operations that are *not* primitive. This is hardly surprising; the task is to define these new, nonprimitive abilities in a way that still keeps them uncontroversially finite.

Players can perform arbitrarily complicated operations by performing ordered combinations of primitive operations. For example, to see whether a king is in check, one might look at each opposing piece in turn and see whether that piece is attacking the king (which might itself involve a combination of still smaller steps). Obviously this sequence of steps is not carelessly or randomly chosen, but explicitly designed for the purpose at hand; moreover, it must be carried out correctly or it won't work. In effect, the particular combination of steps required for a complex operation must be specified by some sort of rule or "recipe," which the player then has to follow to carry it out.

That, unfortunately, is right where we came in: four paragraphs ago we asked what's involved in following rules, and now we find out that it involves following rules. Wonderful! Not all is lost, however, for some rules are easier to follow than others. We need to define a special category of rules that require only primitive rule-following abilities—that is, abilities that are, like the primitive operations themselves, manifestly within finite competence. These special rules can then be used in "building up" both complex operations and complex rule following.

An *algorithm* is an infallible, step-by-step recipe for obtaining a prespecified result. "Infallible" means the procedure is guaranteed to succeed positively in a finite number of steps (assuming each step is carried out correctly). Note that, although the total number of steps must always be finite, there need be no prior limit on how many steps that might be. "Step-by-step" means three things: (1) the recipe prescribes one step at a time, one after another; (2) after each step, the next step is fully determined (there are no options or uncertainties); and (3) after each step, the next step is obvious (no insight or ingenuity is required to figure it out).

Intuitively, algorithms are just mindless "turn the crank" routines that always work (sooner or later). For instance, if you have a ring of keys, one of which fits a certain lock, then trying them in sequence is an algorithm for opening the lock: it's sure to work eventually (no matter how many keys), and "any idiot can do it." Likewise, there are familiar algorithms for sorting arbitrary lists into alphabetical order, for checkmating a lone king with a king and rook, for transposing songs into different musical keys, for multiplying integers (using Arabic numerals), and so on. These algorithms, notice, are specified in terms of an input/output relation: you start with an input of a certain sort (a lock and keyring, a list of names, a songsheet), and the goal is an output related to that input in some determinate way (that lock opened, that list alphabetized, that song transposed).[7]

The simplest kind of recipe is a *straight schedule* of instructions: do A first, then do B . . . and, finally, do Z. It doesn't take much to "follow" such a recipe: basically, the player has to read the current instruction, obey it, and then move to the next one down the list. But, modest as they are, these schedule-following abilities are importantly distinct from the abilities to perform the listed operations themselves (telling what to do is not the same as doing it). A player needs abilities of both kinds to carry out the recipe.

Since there are only finitely many primitive operations in a finite player's repertoire, we may assume that there is for each a unique primitive *instruction*, which the player can reliably obey. Think, for instance, of the separate keyswitches for each of the typewriter's primitive typing operations: closing such a switch is a primitive instruction, which the typewriter can obey. It is equally clear that a finite player can go down a finite list in order; each successive step is fully and obviously determinate. (Consider a typewriter that can be fed a sequence of primitive typing instructions encoded on a paper tape.) Thus we have an initial repertoire of primitive rule-following abilities: (1) obeying primitive instructions and (2) moving to the next instruction in a finite list. Moreover, these abilities are sufficient in principle for following any straight schedule; hence, whenever such a schedule is infallible, it's an algorithm.

The trouble with straight schedules, however, is that they're totally inflexible: exactly the same sequence of steps is prescribed, regardless of the input or any intermediate results. Consequently no recipe with this structure is adequate even for the boring algorithm: try each key in turn, *until* you find the right one. In the first place, the algorithm ought to work for any size keyring (= different inputs); but since a straight schedule has only so many entries, it can go only so far. Second, the algorithm ought to stop when the right key is found (= intermediate result); but a straight schedule just blindly continues, no matter what.

Both deficiencies are remedied by a single, seemingly obvious device, which turns out to be astonishingly powerful: in general, you let the next step *depend* or be *conditional* on the results of preceding steps. There are various ways to achieve this (all quite interesting to mathematicians); but one approach will suffice for illustration. Consider the recipe:

1. Start with any key, and tie a red ribbon on it.
2. Try that key in the lock.
    DID THE LOCK OPEN?
    IF SO, GO TO LINE 4; IF NOT, GO TO LINE 3.
3. Move to the next key on the ring.
    DOES IT HAVE A RED RIBBON ON IT?
    IF SO, GO TO LINE 5; IF NOT, GO BACK TO LINE 2.
4. Quit, triumphant and happy.
5. Quit, frustrated and disgruntled.

A player following this recipe will repeat steps 2 and 3, trying one key after another (no matter how many), until either the lock opens or every key has been tried; thus the behavior varies appropriately, in accord with the input and intermediate results, which is exactly what we wanted.

Clearly the improvement lies in the special directives, written in capital letters. These don't prescribe particular primitive operations (as do the numbered instructions); rather, they serve as explicit signposts, guiding the player around the recipe by specifying which instruction to obey next, depending on what just happened. To carry out the algorithm, two new recipe-following abilities are needed: answering yes/no questions about the previous step and "branching" to one of two specified instructions, depending on the answer. Such conditional directives (this kind is called a *conditional branch*) provide the flexibility lacking from straight schedules of instructions. Thus the first directive above tests the intermediate result and keeps the search from continuing stupidly after the right key is found. And the "loop back" clause in the second directive (GO BACK TO LINE 2) enables the recipe to handle an arbitrary number of keys by repeating two steps an arbitrary number of times.

But what is the point of the red ribbon and of the other clause in the second test? Why not just go around the ring, key by key, until one opens the lock? The problem, plainly, is the unlucky case where the lock never opens; but it's more serious than it seems. Since the input keyring can be arbitrarily large, the algorithm must be able to keep looking (repeating its two-step "loop") *without any limit*; this is precisely what gives it its general power. But to be an algorithm, it must also be guaranteed to succeed, eventually; it cannot be allowed to go on forever, looking for a key that isn't there. Normally the routine quits only when it finds a key that works. But if there may be no such key, then there must be some other successful stopping condition, such as proving that none of these keys works this lock. That's what the red ribbon and the "branch to line 5" clause provide.

Obviously it is possible for a finite player to answer some yes/no questions positively and reliably: the vending machine will make change *if* you insert coins larger than needed. It can also easily "go to" (follow) alternative segments of a finite schedule, depending on the answer: the machine will (follow instructions to) give the correct change, once it has identified your coins. So finite players can, in principle, follow any finite *branched schedule* (i.e., schedule with conditional branches), assuming the branching conditions (the yes/no questions) are suitably primitive. Since such a schedule is also a step-by-step recipe, it will be an algorithm if it's infallible—that is, if it's guaranteed to produce its specified result (and stop) in a finite number of steps. Let's call a branched-schedule algorithm with primitive branching conditions and primitive instructions a *primitive algorithm*. Then we have just established the following conclusion: executing primitive algorithms (positively and reliably) is within the compass of finite players.

This conclusion is remarkably important. In the first place, it gets us off the ground with regard to rule following, since no nonprimitive abilities are presupposed. But second, and more spectacular, it effectively extends the range of what can count as "primitive." Nothing concrete has been said about what's primitive

Box 1
Finitude, Magic, and Mechanism

Suppose someone gives you a simple numeric test and asks: What's the smallest positive integer that satisfies it, if any? For some tests, there might be an analytic (e.g., algebraic) solution to the problem. But let's consider a case with no such solution, where the only approach is brute force: try the test on the number 1; if that fails, try 2; and so on.

If there were a guarantee that at least one number would satisfy the test, then brute force would be an algorithm for finding the smallest one; for, no matter how big that number is, counting will get to it eventually. If, on the other hand, no number will satisfy the test, brute force will *never* establish this fact; for, no matter how high you go, there are still higher numbers you haven't tried yet. When a procedure goes on forever like that, it is called *nonterminating*. In a formal game, the procedure(s) for determining whether a proposed move would be legal must always terminate (yes or no); that's the point of finite playability.

But what if we had an oracle: a crystal ball giving (correct) answers, even to cases that are otherwise undecidable? Would that make the game finitely playable after all? No; and this is the point of adding that no magic is needed to play the game. If magic were allowed, then the restriction to finitude (or anything else) would be vacuous.[8]

Magic, by its essence, is unintelligible. It doesn't follow, however, that everything (presently) unintelligible is magic. For instance, the pioneers of mathematical formal systems were uncertain whether mathematical "insight" and "intuition" might be magical. It's not that they thought these were magic; it's just that no one could be sure because nobody really understood how they work. Indeed, the only certain way to abjure magic is to insist on procedures that are transparently intelligible, such as simple physical mechanisms. That's why typewriters and vending machines are so valuable as examples and also why algorithmic procedures are always "mindless and mechanical."

and what's not, as long as positive and reliable performance is clearly within finite competence. But we just saw that executing primitive algorithms is within finite competence; hence an entire primitive algorithm could legitimately serve as a single "primitive" instruction in a more sophisticated algorithm. In other words, if we think of primitive algorithms as ground level, then second-level algorithms can use simple operations and directives that are actually defined by whole ground-level algorithms; and third-level algorithms could use second-level algorithms as their prim-itives, and so forth.

Our keyring algorithm, for example, could be a single step in a "higher" recipe for trying all the locks around the perimeter of a fortress:

1. Start with any lock, and tie a blue flag on it.
2. Try all the keys in that lock.
    DID THE LOCK OPEN?
    IF SO, GO TO LINE 4; IF NOT, GO TO LINE 3.
3. Move to the next lock around the fort.
    DOES IT HAVE A BLUE FLAG ON IT?
    IF SO, GO TO LINE 5; IF NOT, GO BACK TO LINE 2.
4. Quit, triumphant and happy.
5. Quit, frustrated and disgruntled.

Step 2 involves an arbitrary number of "substeps" (one for each key, no matter how many). But since we have an algorithm for that, we can call it one step and take it for granted. Incidentally, we also see here how important that red ribbon was in the first algorithm: had it been omitted, then this new recipe could never get past the first lock (either that lock would open, or step 2 would continue unsuccessfully forever).

In a similar way, a great algorithmic edifice can be erected on the foundation of chess primitives (identifying pieces and squares, and the like). For out of these we can build algorithms to determine the potential range of any piece, how much of that range is blocked by other pieces, and then which moves would expose the king. Out of these, in turn, we can construct an algorithm to test whether any proposed move would be legal; and then, using that, a straightforward algorithm can generate (list) *all* the legal moves, for any given position. Needless to say, many other fancy and sophisticated algorithms can be constructed from all sorts of simple primitives. It makes no difference how many levels of complication get piled up, as long as it's algorithms all the way down. Only the ground-level abilities need be genuinely primitive—using these bricks, and algorithmic glue, there's no limit to how high we can build.[9]

Complex Tokens

Before turning to automatic systems, we must consider one last "complication": namely, systems in which individual tokens are composed or built up out of simpler tokens. This is a familiar idea: sentence tokens are composed of word tokens, and (in writing) word tokens are composed of letter tokens; likewise, Arabic numeral tokens are strings of digit tokens (maybe with a decimal point). The idea is so familiar, in fact, that it seems inconsequential; but nothing could be further from the truth.

Actually, there are different cases, some of which are more interesting than others. The difference lies in whether the internal composition of the tokens systematically determines how they can be used. For instance, Morse code is totally boring in this regard: though individual letters are composed of "dots" and "dashes," their specific structure has no significance (it matters only that each character type be unique). The alphabetic compositional system, spelling, is more complicated, since it does provide a rough guide to pronunciation. What's important about words, however, is not how they sound but how they are used to say things; and here their spelling is no help at all. So, aside from phonetics, alphabetic composition is basically just as trivial as Morse code.

The point can be illustrated by contrasting spelling with a system that is emphatically *not* trivial: Arabic numerals. When you know the composition of a complex (i.e., multidigit) Arabic numeral, you know everything you need to know about it. Compare, for example, the following lists of compound tokens, composed respectively in the Arabic numeral and English spelling systems:

783	dol
374	edh
662	mho
519	ret
54,912	kylix
99.44	phiz
2,000.2	ootid
0.0043	yagi

Imagine that you happen never to have seen any of these particular numerals or words before, and suppose you were asked to use each correctly in a typical calculation or sentence. What a difference! It's easy to use complex numerals correctly, even the first time you see them, because you can tell what to do from the way they're built up out of digits. But if those words were new to you, you would have no idea how to use them properly—the spelling wouldn't help a bit.

Box 2
Simple and Complex

Here we use 'simple' and 'complex' in their strictly correct senses. 'Simple' means "having but one part; not put together out of several components." 'Complex' means the opposite: "composed or put together out of several components; having more than one part." The classic example is chemical theory, according to which atoms are simple and molecules are complex (put together out of atoms). The example also brings out an important qualification: whether a thing counts as simple or complex depends on how you look at it. From the point of view of chemical compounds, atoms are simple; but from the point of view of atomic physics, they are complexes, made up of simple nuclei and electrons. (Nuclei themselves are composite from the point of view of nuclear physics; but so far electrons have no known structure.)

Awkwardly, however, both these examples cheat: they trade on the *meanings* of the respective tokens. Thus the composition of a numeral tells you what number it stands for, whereas the spelling of a word doesn't tell you what it means. But since formal systems as such are self-contained, nothing about them can depend on meanings. Hence the examples as presented don't really show anything about formal systems. The way out of the trap is to let the *use* of a token be the contribution it makes to the formal position—that is, the difference it makes to what moves would be legal. If the composition of the tokens determines their "use" in this sense, then that composition is formally significant.

With that strategy in mind, we can even fix up the numeral example, by a modest sleight of hand: the trick is to think of arithmetic itself as *purely a game*. To be more concrete, imagine that you learned the rules and moves of multiplication (in Arabic numerals) before you had any idea that these tokens had anything to do with numbers. (Outrageously, I fear, some children do learn arithmetic this way.) Anyhow, the starting position is a pair of tokens written one above the other, aligned at the right, with a line beneath and a sign to the left:

Starting position:	54912	(first token)
	× 783	(second token)

The player then writes one or more new tokens below these, stairstepping all but the last to the left, and draws another line above the last:

54912	
× 783	
164736	(first move)
439296	(second move)
384384	(third move)
42996096	(last move)

I trust this has a familiar look and that there's no need to spell out the rules in greater detail.

But one point about the rules is crucial: I *could* spell them out, without ever mentioning numbers (or anything else "outside" the system): I just tell you which *token* manipulations to make in which positions, all quite formally. Since the moves are clearly also digital, it follows that Arabic numeral "multiplication" can be defined as a completely formal system, which we might call the *formal multiplication game*.

Except, that is, for one little problem: there are infinitely many distinct types of Arabic numeral tokens. Hence formal multiplication has infinitely many distinct, possible positions and moves. But, by definition, a finite player has only a fixed, finite repertoire of primitive abilities. So how can formal multiplication be finitely playable?

The answer is obvious (once you appreciate the question), but it's quite fundamental. Not only are the individual tokens (the numerals, written one per line) complex (put together out of simple digits); but also, and just as important, the rules for manipulating these compounds are expressed as *recipes*. They are specified sequences of simple steps, going through the component digits one by one. This is how the particular composition of the numerals determines what's legal, and it is also how a small repertoire of primitive operations can handle arbitrarily large numerals (by the method of finite but unlimited repetition). Indeed, there is a complete algorithm for Arabic multiplication (obtaining the partial products, writing them a certain way, adding them up, etc.), including various subalgorithms for performing the required steps (digit by digit), and so on. Therefore multiplication is within finite competence.

This is the example we needed: the tokens are complex; their "use" depends on their composition (so the complexity is not trivial); and yet no meanings are involved—the system is purely formal. It also illustrates the incredible power of combining complex tokens with complex recipes. For here we have a system with literally infinitely many different legal positions and legal moves, and yet there is no question that "playing" it remains fully within finite competence. Formalizing multiplication, of course, is not such a big deal; but the same general point holds for the much

Box 3
Unbounded versus Infinite

There are infinitely many distinct finite numbers; hence there are also infinitely many distinct Arabic numeral types, each with only finitely many digits. How can this be? The answer is that, though each of the numbers (or numerals) in question is finite, there is no upper bound or limit on how big they can be; they are *unbounded*. More precisely, for any positive integer, no matter how large, there is a "next" one that is still larger and therefore distinct from every preceding one; you never come to the end of them.

Why does this mean that there are infinitely many? We can construct a proof by trying to suppose the contrary and then showing that that's untenable. So imagine that there were only finitely many finite integers; in that case there would be some particular number of them, say N, and no more. For any positive integer, however, we know that there are exactly that many distinct positive integers up to and including it; thus, there are exactly sixteen distinct integers from 1 through 16, inclusive. So if there were only N distinct finite integers, they would be precisely the integers from 1 through N; in particular, none of them could be larger than N. But for any finite integer, there is always another that is larger (this is where the unboundedness comes in). Hence no finite number can be the number of finite integers—there are always "more." Therefore the number of finite numbers must be infinite.

The conclusion applies as well to Arabic numeral types because every distinct integer has a distinct type of Arabic numeral, with finitely many digits, to stand for it. The notion of "finite but unbounded" is important in other contexts as well. For instance, in algebraic and formal logical systems, the formulae ("sentences") and proofs must all be finite; but there is no upper bound on how long they can be. Similarly, an algorithm must always terminate after finitely many steps; but there's no limit on how many that can be. The same goes in principle for the size of computer memories (such as Turing machine "tapes"; see "Turing Machines and Universality" in chapter 4).

more impressive formalizations of higher mathematics, logic, computer science, linguistics, and so on.

Above all, however, it holds for Artificial Intelligence. For if Hobbes is right that thinking is "computation," it is certainly highly complex computation—far more so, indeed, than Hobbes could ever have imagined. As we shall see (for instance in "Commonsense Stereotypes" in chapter 5), the formal structures that an AI system would have to manipulate, even to have an ordinary conversation in natural English, are enormous and very elaborate. Their detailed internal composition, moreover, is absolutely critical to how they may be used.

Automatic Systems

An *automatic* formal system is a formal system that "works" (or "plays") by itself. More precisely, it is a physical device (such as a machine), with the following characteristics:

1. some of its parts or states are identified as the tokens (in position) of some formal system; and
2. in its normal operation, it automatically manipulates these tokens according to the rules of that system.

So an automatic formal system is like a set of chess pieces that hop around the board, abiding by the rules, all by themselves, or like a magical pencil that writes out formally correct mathematical derivations without the guidance of any mathematician. These bizarre, fanciful images are worth a moment's reflection, lest we forget the marvel that such systems (or equivalent ones) can now be constructed.

The actual playing of a game involves more than just the positions and moves: there must also be one or more players and a referee. The players make the moves, whenever it's their turn. The referee doesn't make any moves but rather determines whose turn it is—that is, which player should move next, and, perhaps, which tokens it should work on. The referee also provides the starting position, decides when the game is over, announces the official results, and so on. For friendly games, we tend to overlook the referee function, since it's often so straightforward that the players perform it for themselves. But strictly speaking, refereeing is always separate from playing (making the legal moves), even when the difference is inconspicuous; and when the cases get complicated, it is essential to keep the distinction clear, on pain of hopeless confusion.

Since an automatic game actually plays by itself, it must include all these elements; in fact, we can think of it as essentially a combination of the player(s), the referee, and the ordinary "manual" game (the tokens). Sometimes, of course, a formal game is only partially automated. For instance, electronic chess sets typically automate only one of the players (plus the referee); the other player is external to the machine—such as the person who bought it. But this makes no important difference to the theory of automatic systems, and we might as well consider all the players as included.

So far we have said what an automatic formal system is: a manual game, combined with automated player(s) and referee. We have not said how they work, what they're made of, or what principles they're based on—because none of that is relevant to explaining what they are. To borrow a wonderful term from engineering, the player(s) and referee are treated as *black boxes*: things you don't look inside of. Thus it is often useful to consider only the "opaque surface" of a component (*what* it does), while taking its inner workings (*how* it does it) for granted. For example, an audio engineer assembling a concert sound system with dozens of microphones, mixers, amplifiers, speakers, etc., can't be worried about how each part does its individual job, as long as it does. The separate components must be treated as black boxes, and taken for granted, in the design of the overall system.

What counts as a black box depends on your point of view; one engineer's component is another engineer's whole system. For instance, an amplifier is itself a complicated system, which some electronics engineer had to design out of still smaller black boxes: transistors, resistors, integrated circuits, etc. The amplifier designer takes these for granted; but, of course, somebody else had to design them too. If you need to know only what something does, then you can look just at its surface (or consult the manufacturer's specification sheet); but if you want to understand how it does whatever it does, then you must look inside (or consult the manufacturer's design staff).

Coming to understand how something does what it does, by considering what it's made of and how it's put together, is called *analysis*. Explaining how a complex system works, in terms of the interactions of its functional components, is one kind of analysis.[10] Suppose, for instance, you are perplexed and amazed by your automatic chess system. You know that it comprises (besides the tokens) two chess-player components and a referee component; and you know that they play legal chess games. Now you would like to understand *how* they do that. In other words, you don't want to treat the components as black boxes anymore; you want to analyze.

One possibility is analysis into smaller automatic formal systems; that is, a single component in the overall system might itself be an entire automatic formal system, with its own private little tokens, manipulated by a group of inner players, guided by an inner referee—all quite distinct from the outer tokens, players, and referee. Take, for instance, one of the "outer" players. It makes a legal chess move whenever the referee indicates a position and says, "It's your move now." What might the "innards" of such a player look like, supposing it were itself a complete automatic formal system?

The answer, of course, depends on the specific design; but here's one design that would work (see figure 1). The tokens of the inner game are a description (or copy) of the current outer position (provided by the outer referee), plus some standard notation for specifying chess moves. There are two inner players: a "move lister" and a "move chooser." The inner referee first indicates the position (inner copy) and signals the move lister, who proceeds to list all the legal moves in that position. Then the referee, indicating the position and list together, signals the move chooser, who proceeds to choose some move from the list. Finally, the referee announces the chosen move as the subsystem's output (that is, the outer player makes this move in the chess game).

That's *one* level of analysis. But there can be many levels: boxes, within boxes, within . . . until the components are so basic that they can't be analyzed further (or perhaps can be analyzed only

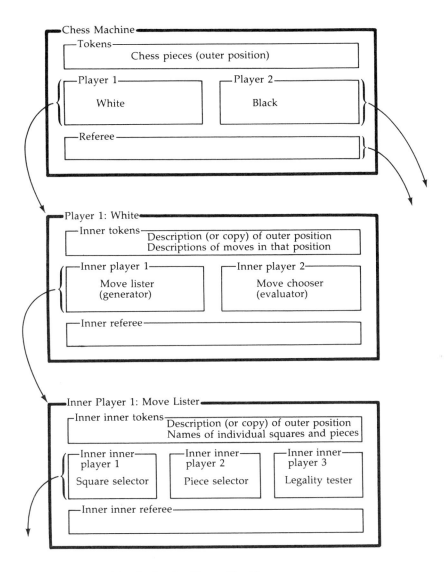

Figure 1   Partial Analysis of a Chess Machine

in some other way). For instance, we might be able to analyze the move-lister and/or the move-chooser components (from the above system) into still smaller systems; the two cases would be quite different, with each illustrating an important moral. (The inner referee might be analyzable too; but this particular one happens to be fairly boring.)

In a deep sense, the move lister is trivial because there is an algorithm for listing all the legal moves in any chess position. What do algorithms have to do with automatic formal systems? In a way, everything. Recall that executing an algorithm requires a fixed, finite repertoire of primitive abilities—both primitive operations and primitive recipe following. So suppose each primitive operation gets assigned a single player, whose sole competence is that operation; and suppose the referee has all the primitive recipe-following abilities. Then, roughly, the referee can follow the recipe, signaling the players in the right order (telling them whose turn it is and what tokens to work on), and the players can then carry out the specified operations. The algorithm can be executed automatically by a system composed of these players and this referee.

But what about those primitive abilities? Well, whenever an ability can itself be specified by an algorithm (in terms of simpler abilities), then that whole ability can count as a primitive in a higher-level algorithm. The only restriction is that all the required abilities eventually get analyzed into ground-level abilities that are *really* primitive—abilities so "mindless and mechanical" that even a machine could have them. This analysis of higher-level primitives into lower-level algorithms precisely parallels the analysis of higher-level components (black boxes) into lower-level systems. Moreover, the ultimate, ground-level primitives are exactly the same—except that, in an automatic system, they not only could be but *are* carried out by primitive machines.

These ultimate primitives (both player operations and referee recipe followings) are the fundamental point at which formal systems meet up with automation. Given this foundation, sophisticated automatic systems can be built back up, black box by black box, in just the way that sophisticated algorithms can be

Box 4
Analysis and Reduction

Many philosophers and scientists believe that nature is unified not only in the fundamental stuff of which it's all made (matter), but also in the fundamental laws in terms of which it can all be explained (physics). Advocacy of this further thesis, sometimes summarized as "the unity of science," is called *physicalism* or *reductionism*—the latter because physicalism (in contrast to mere materialism) amounts to the claim that all other sciences can (in principle) be "reduced" to physics.

The standard example is the reduction of thermodynamics, according to which heat is just an alternative form of energy stored in the chaotic bouncing around of individual molecules. Given this, plus miscellaneous technical breakthroughs, it can be shown that thermodynamic laws are derivable from physical laws—implying that thermodynamics is basically a special case of physics. Such reductions are called *nomological* (from the Greek *nomos* = law).

Many explanations, however, don't appeal to laws; so they can't be reduced nomologically. For instance, when Mr. Goodwrench explains how a car engine works, he doesn't use physics; he appeals instead to the capabilities and functions of the various parts, showing how they fit together and interact as an integrated, organized system. In other words, he analyzes the engine and explains it functionally or systematically.

When an explanation appeals to laws, those laws are not themselves explained but merely used: they serve as unexplained explainers. Reduction is explaining the unexplained explainers of one theory in terms of those of another; hence physicalism is really the view that there are no unexplained explainers, save those of physics. Accordingly, functional/systematic explanations can be reduced too, if their unexplained explainers (essentially the interactive capabilities of the functional components) can themselves be explained in more basic terms.

Analyzing automatic formal systems into ever smaller sys-

tems of interacting black boxes is therefore reductionistic—
not nomologically, but rather in the functional/systematic
sense. Connection to physics is made at (or via) the level of
operations so primitive that they can be carried out by mindless mechanisms.

built up out of ever cruder algorithms, resting eventually on the
ground level. So the essential point may be summed up this way:

AUTOMATION PRINCIPLE: whenever the legal moves of a
formal system are fully determined by algorithms, then that
system can be automated.

This is why automating the move-lister component of the chess-
player component of the chess system is (theoretically) trivial.

The move-chooser component, however, is another story. If
the move lister listed only one legal move, then no choice would
have to be made, and there would be no problem. But chess, like
most interesting formal systems, is *nondeterministic*; that is, in
most positions, any of several different moves would be legal.
Sometimes a particular move is forced because no other move is
legal; but if the whole game were like that, it would just be
oppressive and unbearable—no fun. Algorithms, by contrast, are
always deterministic: by definition they are step-by-step procedures that never permit any options or uncertainties about the
next step. How then can a system allowing choices be automated?

There are a couple of cheap and dirty answers that we might
as well dispose of right way. First, the move chooser might just
choose whatever move appeared at the top of the lister's list
(equally, it could use any other unmotivated principle, such as
selecting the move whose description comes first in alphabetical
order). Second, the chooser might pick from the list randomly;
that is, it could consult some random input (a roll of the electronic
dice, say) and let that determine the choice. These designs would
yield a system that played *legal* chess; thus, in a superficial sense,
they seem to answer the question. But such systems would also

play atrocious chess—so hopelessly crazy and chaotic, in fact, that we should hesitate to call it chess, even though the moves are all strictly legal.

The real problem, then, is to design a chooser that makes good (reasonable, intelligent, wise. . . ?) choices. Unfortunately, there are no known feasible algorithms for telling in general which is the better of two chess moves (let alone for wisdom and the like). Not surprisingly, approaches to this issue begin to involve techniques characteristic of Artificial Intelligence research which we will consider in more detail later. In the meantime, however, a sketch of a chess-move chooser can give a glimpse of what is coming.

Obviously the chooser needn't always find the best move; even the greatest champions don't play perfect chess. The goal, rather, is a system that chooses relatively well most of the time. In other words, an infallible test for the better move (i.e., an algorithm) is not really required; it would be enough to have a fairly reliable test, by which the machine could usually eliminate the worst choices and settle on a pretty good one. Such fallible but "fairly reliable" procedures are called *heuristics* (in the AI literature). Thus heuristics (so defined) are not algorithms because algorithms must be infallible. Intuitively, heuristics are like rules of thumb: rough, generic principles that are not perfectly accurate, but are still accurate enough to be convenient and useful.

There are many rules of thumb for better chess. For instance, other things being equal, it is better to capture opposing pieces while losing none (or only weaker ones); likewise, it is generally preferable to control the center, activate pieces early, keep your king out of the way, and so on. But everybody knows that other things are not always equal: even the best heuristics sometimes fail—as in the apparent blunder ("free" capture) that turns out to be the bait in a brilliant trap. There are various ways to improve the odds, like using lots of heuristics and balancing them off or considering sequences of moves together (looking ahead); and the net results can get pretty good, though still not perfect.

How do heuristics aid automation? Suppose we devise a strict, precise formula for applying and combining various well-defined rules of thumb; the output of this formula is a fallible but relatively reliable estimate of the best move in a given situation. The formula itself is perfectly explicit and unambiguous, so we can well imagine a routine that infallibly calculates its value (i.e., comes up with the exact estimate) for any given position. Is that routine an algorithm? It depends on how you look at it. If the specified goal is to crank through the formula (calculate the estimate), then it *is* an (infallible) algorithm. But if the goal is specified as finding an optimal chess move, then that very same routine is only a fallible estimator, and hence only a heuristic. The punch line is easy: seen as an algorithm, the routine can be automated like any other; but seen as an estimator, the same routine (now automated) can function as a decent move-chooser. In other words, a good but fallible move-chooser can be automated by an algorithm after all.

This strategy of regarding or *redescribing* the very same thing from more than one point of view is essential throughout science. Physicians must learn to see suffering patients as conglomerations of living tissues and living tissues as seething chemical stews. To understand why sonnets are so easily preserved, one must reconceive them as mere strings of digital characters. We shall find that the possibility of adopting multiple viewpoints is particularly important in Artificial Intelligence—analyzing black boxes and automating rules of thumb being but two examples. The most important redescription by far, however, arises in connection with *meaning*—an issue we can postpone no longer.

Are these symbols? What do they mean?

3 Semantics

Meaningfulness

Modern philosophy, as distilled in chapter 1, managed to pose—
but not to answer—the following fundamental question: How is
meaning possible in a physical/mechanical universe? This problem, in turn, may be divided into two basic subproblems:

1. What is compatible with physical mechanism?
2. What is required for meaningfulness?

Chapter 2 assiduously avoided the second subproblem; but, in
so doing, it made important progress on the first. Since formal
systems are (by definition) self-contained, they never permit any
(formal) role for meanings; as a result, traditional mysteries about
meaning cannot infect them. Indeed, even formal rule following
can be fully mechanized, in automatic formal systems. Therefore,
formal systems as such, including automatic ones, are compatible
with physical mechanism. But if this is to be a step toward understanding Artificial Intelligence, not to mention minds, then it must
be combined with an answer to the second problem.

How can we explicate the meaningfulness of thought? According
to Hobbes, thought is inner discourse; and cognitive science, including Artificial Intelligence, is built on much the same assumption: thinking is *like* talking. Hence we can be guided, at
least in part, by what we know about linguistic meaning. Of
course linguistic meaning is derivative (from thought), whereas
mental meaning must itself be *original*. But aside from that one
crucial difference, thought and language could have much in com-

Box 1
Meanings of 'Meaning'

1. When one thing (like a symptom or clue) can help to dis-
   cover or discern another, we sometimes say the first
   means the second.
   —Clouds in the south mean a storm is coming.
   —These broken branches mean a large animal was here.
   —I hope this new desk means I'm getting a promotion.
   (But notice we wouldn't say: "The meaning of clouds
   is . . . .")

2. Saying what (or how much) something *means* is a way of
   indicating its significance, consequences, or importance.
   —Losing millions means little to him.
   —A promotion for me would mean new shoes for the
   kids, and . . . .
   (But, again, not: "The meaning of . . . is . . . .")

3. The *meaning of* something can be its point, purpose, or
   justification.
   —Mystics ponder the meaning of life.
   —What is the meaning of this? [Asks Mother Superior,
   sternly.]
   —Their futile counterattack was a meaningless waste.
   (Here we avoid the opposite paraphrase: "Life
   means . . . .")

4. A person can *mean to* do something, in the sense of in-
   tending or being determined to do it.
   —Mrs. O'Leary's cow didn't mean to burn down Chicago.
   —I deserve that promotion, and I mean to have it.

5. What somebody *means by* something is what he or she
   intends to express, communicate, or say; and, in this
   sense, what the person means is also the *meaning of* the
   expressive utterance or act.
   —Plainly, she meant (by her grimace) that I should shut up.

—The meaning of her grimace was, plainly: "Shut up."
—"That's smart!" he taunted, meaning the opposite.

6. Finally, the *meaning* of an expression or symbol can be what it expresses, represents, or conveys in *standard* usage. This is what dictionaries try to explain, what careful translations try to preserve, and what the present list distinguishes six of.
   —What a surprise that 'meaning' has so many meanings!
   —The German word 'rot' means the same as 'red' in English.
   —Undeciphered, that code looked like meaningless nonsense.
   —Idiomatically, 'kick the bucket' means 'eat the peach'.
   Meaning in this last sense is our present topic; we call it *semantic meaning*.

mon; and so we could still learn a lot from the comparison. Indeed, the more we learn about thought, the better our position will be later for addressing not only the mystery of original meaning, but also the paradox of mechanical reason.

But why would anyone suppose that thinking and talking are similar? It's not just that we sometimes "think in words"; we do, of course, but the theory is meant to cover many more cases than those (which are rather rare, after all). Since this is quite fundamental, it's worth reviewing some of the apparent basic parallels between thought and talk. The most conspicuous relation is that speech acts *express* thoughts.[1] Statements, for instance, express beliefs; but, equally, requests express desires, apologies express regrets, promises express intentions, predictions express expectations, and so on. In this context "thought" and "cognition" obviously include not only conscious deliberations, but also all kinds of hunches, hopes, horrors, wishes, worries, wonderings, etc.—conscious or otherwise. Given that broad sense, nearly all speech acts express corresponding cognitive states or events; conversely, at least a great many thoughts are easy to express in language. Roughly, we can say what we think, and (when we're sincere) we do think what we say.

A deeper similarity between thoughts and speech acts, however, may be the general applicability of a *mode/content* distinction. Consider what the following utterances have in common:

[I assert:]	Fido eats his insects.
[I inquire:]	Does Fido eat his insects?
[I request:]	Please see that Fido eats his insects.
[I apologize:]	I'm sorry that Fido eats his insects.

They all concern Fido eating his insects; or (as philosophers say) they share the *propositional content*

[that] Fido eats his insects.

But each utterance puts that content forward differently—in stating that it's so, asking whether it's so, requesting that it be so, etc. These are differences of *mode*; so the same content can be put forward in different modes. Going the other way, of course, utterances in the same mode can have different contents—that Dinky drinks her milk, that emeralds are expensive, or whatever.

The point is that a parallel mode/content distinction seems to work for thought: I can believe, desire, or regret (= differences of mode) that Fido eats his insects, that Dinky drinks her milk, or that emeralds are expensive (= differences in content). And this suggests a tighter connection between a speech act and the thought it expresses: namely, they should have the *same* content and *corresponding* modes. Thus when I wonder whether Fido eats his insects, I express myself by asking (= corresponding mode) whether Fido eats his insects (= same content); if, instead, I assert that Fido eats his insects or ask whether Dinky drinks her milk, then I express different thoughts. Obviously inquiries correspond to wonderings, assertions to beliefs, requests to desires, apologies to regrets, and so on.[2]

Despite these parallels, it would be extravagant to maintain that *all* thoughts are expressible in words or even that any thoughts are *fully* expressible. Cognitive science, however, is committed to no such view. The idea is rather that all thought is *like* linguistic utterance in some more abstract sense, which still needs to be explained. Such an abstract similarity would be a sameness in some general or structural feature that allowed for various differences of specific detail. For instance, the mode/content distinction *per se* (that is, apart from any specific modes or contents) is just the sort of abstract feature that thought and language might have in common—even if, say, thought is far richer or subtler than language could ever express.

A more important abstract property, however, is being a *symbolic system*. This means two things:

1. the meanings of simple symbols (e.g., words) are *arbitrary;* and
2. the meanings of complex symbols (e.g., sentences) are *systematically determined* by their composition.

The "composition" of a complex symbol depends not only on which simple symbols it's composed of, but also on how they're put together—the "form" or "grammar" of the composite. Clause 2 (above) is sometimes called the *compositionality* of symbolic systems.

Languages are symbolic systems, at least approximately. Word meanings are "arbitrary" in the sense that there is no intrinsic reason for them to be one way rather than another: our word 'squid' could just as well have meant what 'squalid' does, and so on. (Their actual meanings are fixed only by standard usage within the linguistic community.) Likewise, it's hardly news that sentence meanings are, for the most part, built up grammatically out of word meanings. What deserves emphasis is not these mundane observations themselves, but their powerful consequences.

Because sentence meanings are systematically determined by their composition, an ordinary English speaker, with a vocabulary of forty or fifty thousand words, can understand literally trillions of distinct sentences, on countless different topics. You've probably never heard anyone say (let alone define) the sentence "Mongolian lizards avoid strong cheese," yet you understand it easily, just

Box 2
The 'Fido'–Fido Theory

Words and sentences are used to talk about (refer to) things in the world. For instance, the name 'Fido' is used to talk about Fido; the word 'frog' denotes frogs; and the sentence "Fido is a frog" just puts the former among the latter. Moreover, in a seductively clear sense, to say all this is to say what these constructions *mean*: 'Fido' means Fido, 'frog' means (the class of) frogs, and "Fido is a frog" means (the fact or state of affairs) that Fido is a member of the frog class. In general, then, the meaning of a symbol would be whatever it symbolized—the very object or situation itself. This simple view, known as the *'Fido'–Fido theory*, has, however, a number of well-known problems.

First, words and sentences can be meaningul, even if their supposed objects don't exist. For instance, "Santa is an elf" makes perfect sense (adults understand it, children believe it), despite the worldwide dearth of Santas and elves. But if meanings were the very objects meant, then terms and sentences with no objects would have no meanings. So something must be wrong with the theory.

Second, expressions that refer to the same thing can still have different meanings. Thus, 'mile-high city' and 'Colorado's capital' differ in sense, though they designate the same object (namely, Denver). 'Feathered' is clearly not synonymous with 'beaked', but they happen to denote exactly the same things, since (as a matter of biological fact) all and only animals with feathers have beaks (specifically, birds). So, again, the simple 'Fido'–Fido theory gets it wrong.

Finally, some components and features of sentences affect the overall sense, without themselves being "about" anything at all. Consider:

Fido drips.
Does Fido drip?
Fido does not drip.
Fido drips copiously.
Perhaps Fido could drip.

> These are all equally about Fido, and maybe some drippy condition—but that's all. Words like 'does', 'not', and 'perhaps' (not to mention features like word order) don't have "objects"; yet they make a big difference to the meaning. The 'Fido'–Fido theory can't account for such differences.

from knowing the words and grammar. For instance, having no prior experience with that sentence, but only with its components, you could reasonably infer that some dairy products repel some Asian reptiles; and, if you chanced to be harassed by Mongolian lizards, reading the sentence might fund a practical inspiration.

On the face of it, thought seems even more versatile and flexible than language; hence there are many trillions of different thoughts that any one of us might easily have. Given, however, that our brains are limited—only ten billion neurons, more or less—an urgent question arises: How can such a "small" system have such a large repertoire? And a marvelously attractive answer is the very one we have just worked out for language. Distinct thoughts, the line goes, are generally *complex*, constructed systematically (according to their contents) from a comparatively modest kit of atomic constituents; in other words, the versatility of thought is attributed to a combinatorial structure essentially like the compositionality of symbolic systems.

Artificial Intelligence embraces this fundamental approach—to the point, indeed, of arguing that thoughts *are* symbolic. But that doesn't imply that people think in English (or any "language" very similar to English); AI maintains only that thinking is "like" talking in the more abstract sense that it occurs in a symbolic system—probably incorporating a mode/content distinction. Such a system could be vastly different from ordinary languages (in richness and subtlety or whatever) and still have the crucial abstract features of compositionality and arbitrary basic meanings.

Interpretation

Imagine that you (a renowned and crafty explorer) stumble across some alien markings, which you suspect to be symbols. You believe, in other words, that they bear some hidden meaning; and naturally you are aching to figure it out. How do you confirm your hunch and satisfy your desire? That is the problem of interpretation—and the topic of this section.

To *interpret* is to *make sense of*. To interpret a system of marks or tokens as symbolic is to make sense of them all by specifying in a regular manner what they *mean*. The specification typically has two parts: what the simple symbols mean, and how the meanings of complex symbols are determined by their composition (components plus structure). So, loosely speaking, it's like translating a newly discovered language. You give an interpretation by producing a "translation manual," consisting, roughly, of a dictionary and a grammar. The interpretation then "makes sense" of the symbols—makes them understandable—by explaining what they're equivalent to in some other system (like English) that's already understood.

The basic principle of all interpretation is *coherence*: every interpretation must be coherent. There are two sides to the coherence principle, one for what you start with (your "data") and one for what you get (your "rendition" of the data). Specifically: you must start with an ordered text, and you must render it so that it makes reasonable sense. We discuss these separately; but, at root, they are two sides of the same principle.

Ordered text   In a far corner of the galaxy, your intrepid explorations turn up a stunning spectacle: from a certain vantage and angle, the visible stars trace out (with revolting precision) the four letters of an Anglo-Saxon vulgarism. What do you make of it? There seem to be two possibilities: either it's a colossal cosmic coincidence, or it's the work of some higher power (who happens to skywrite in English). If the latter, then the display presumably means something (though, whether as a sinister miracle or an innocent letting off steam is hard to say). But if it's all just a big accident, then it can't mean anything; it isn't even a word, really, but only a curious geometrical happenstance.

Order is the opposite of chaos. An ordered text must have a systematic internal structure that is *not accidental*. A structure that is merely amazing and highly suggestive is not enough (as the example shows); rather, there must be some source or reason for that structure. It is no minor problem to spell out what this means; but at least part of the idea is that there is (or could have been) "more where that came from." Thus if a higher power wrote the oath, you might keep an eye out for further manifestations; but if the pattern were just a coincidence, then sequel seeking would be pointless. (Even after the millionth monkey finally types a sonnet, you don't hold your breath for Hamlet.) Another way to put it is that the actual text is only a sample of the potential text—and the potential text must be consistently interpretable throughout.

In addition, an ordered text must have *enough* internal structure to support interpretation. Suppose we're playing with scrambled-alphabet ciphers (codes in which each letter type stands for another), and I ask you to decipher an urgent message:

Abcd!

You haven't a prayer; it could be "Fire!", "Whoa!", "Egad!", "Nuts!", or any other exclamation with four distinct letters. The fragment is so short that there is hardly any structure to work with: too many alternatives are equally compatible with such meager clues. By contrast, it wasn't easy to find three candidates for the following cryptogram:

A b c d	a e f g	a h f	i j k k g.
D u m b	d o g s	d i g	w e l l s.
C o l d	c a t s	c u t	r i f f s.
R i f e	r a t s	r o t	h u l l s.

The structure is again the type relationships among the given tokens—the first three words begin with the same letter, while the fourth is different, etc. But the longer the text, the harder that constraint is to satisfy and still end up with anything remotely intelligible. I defy anyone to letter-scramble, say, a full page of this book and then find any other sensible solution.

Box 3
What Should We Interpret?

Not everything can be interpreted, of course—at least not symbolically. Most of the symbols in a symbolic system are complexes whose meanings are determined by their systematic composition. Many things in the world are constructed in a regular manner out of standardized components (molecules, electronic circuits, chess positions); but very few of them can be construed as "saying" (asserting, asking, commanding, etc.) anything, by virtue of their respective structures and the "meanings" of their components.

But which ones should we interpret? All we can. Interpretation is discovery; we find coherence—order and sense—where it might otherwise have gone unnoticed or remained indescribable. If it's there to be found, then there's no further question as to whether the tokens are "really" interpretable. Suppose we meet on Pluto some potato-like creatures whose tiny leaf motions turn out to be (consistently and elegantly) translatable conversations—about us, the weather, astrophysics, and what have you. We do not then ask whether Pluto Potatoes can "really" talk but rather congratulate ourselves on having already found out. Discovery of the translation is discovery of the fact.

Interpretation presupposes that the given text is somehow orderly (nonrandom). This does not mean, however, that interpreters must be able to characterize that order or explain where it comes from—apart form being able to identify the relevant texts and say what they mean. Finding a consistently workable interpretation of a consistently distinguishable body of tokens establishes that the text is orderly, even if no one can independently say how or why. Discerning the sense is simply a way of discerning the order; that's why order and sense are, at root, two sides of one principle: coherence.

But suppose we allow fancier codes. Sneaky Nikita, for instance, might have twenty distinct scrambled alphabets, which she applies in rotation (so each one gets used only once every twenty letters). Then a twenty-character cryptogram (like the above example) offers no constraint at all: comparable decoding schemes could equally well "translate" it into any twenty-character sequence you please (because, in effect, the differences among the scramblings mask all internal relationships in the text). In general, the more complicated an interpretive scheme is, the more text will be required to make any success it has nontrivial. So what counts as enough structure in an ordered text depends on how complicated the interpretation has to be to work.

Reasonable sense But what is it for an interpretation to succeed or work? Certainly most conceivable schemes for interpreting given texts would be hopelessly unacceptable, and surely there are "ordered texts" that do not admit any semantic interpretation at all (chess games, for instance, are meaningless—they don't "say" anything—even though they're not random). By definition, to interpret a body of symbols is to make sense of them as symbols. Hence, to a first approximation, an interpretation works for a given text if, as interpreted, that text makes reasonable sense; on the other hand, if the sample comes out gibberish or nonsense under the interpretation, then (other things being equal) the interpretation is a failure.

To an extent, the point is obvious. Why not translate our earlier cryptogram example as:

Z y x w   z v u t   z s u   r q p p t.

or:

V o l t   v i n y   v a n   r u d d y.   ?

Because (assuming we're rendering into English) those aren't interpretations at all. The first is letter salad, the second word salad; and neither makes a whit of sense. If interpretations didn't have to make sense, then any transformation whatsoever could

Box 4
Why Truth?

Why should it matter to an interpretation that what is being interpreted come out (reliably) *true*? Why should truth be a component of sense?

Meanings, in general, are supposed to relate symbols to objects, which they are "of" or "about." Truth discloses— and thereby validates—these supposed connections. For example, one can draw inferences (make predictions) about a symbolic system from knowledge of its objects and likewise draw inferences about the objects from knowledge of the system—*assuming* the system generates truths. If the symbolic arrangements come out generally true under a given interpretation, then there is good reason to assign *these* meanings and objects (rather than some others) to those tokens.

Go back to the astronomical calendar: why "connect" one symbol with, say, a certain date, and another with lunar eclipses? Suppose you wonder whether the moon was (in fact) eclipsed on that date; that is, you want to know something specific about the *world*. Will knowledge of the *symbol* arrangements in the calendar be any help? Yes, under one condition: namely, what the calendar says (as interpreted about eclipses, etc.) is reliably *true*. Given truth, you can learn these particular facts about the objects simply by reading those particular symbols. In other words, there's more than just a whim in assigning the symbols this particular meaning.

It works in the other direction just as well. Suppose a piece of the calendar is missing, but you want to know whether it said there was (or wasn't) an eclipse on a certain night. If you know the astronomical facts, then you can draw a conclusion about the unknown symbol arrangements—but again only on the condition that the calendar is reliable.

count as an interpretation, and the whole topic would be insufferably dull and tiresome. But what is it to make sense?

Deep in uncharted jungle you unearth an enormous stone tablet, covered with apparent hieroglyphs. Your brash assistant proposes a clever scheme, according to which they are an astronomical calendar, recounting various eclipses, equinoxes, planetary positions, etc. Does that make sense? If, as interpreted, the tablet reports several eclipses a night, puts thirty-seven planets by the North Star, and so on, then it's crazy; no "sensible" calendar (on Earth) would say such things. Consequently the interpretation itself is highly suspect. On the other hand, if eclipses were reported on just the right dates, with planets in just the right places, etc., then the tablet would make perfect sense, and the interpretation would be quite convincing.

So telling the truth is a component in making sense (random falsehood is a kind of incoherence). But clearly there's more to sense than truth (see box 4). Sensible people can make mistakes: the authors of our ancient tablet might understandably have omitted eclipses visible only elsewhere on the globe. Furthermore, truth as such is not pertinent to all linguistic acts. The tablet might, for instance, be interpreted as a promulgation of tax laws, a poetic appeal for healthy children, or a list of (unanswered) scientific questions. None of these is strictly true or false; but in each case there is still a difference between sense and nonsense (and, somehow or other, that still has to do with the way the world is).

Making sense of ordered texts—finding coherence—is the foundation of all semantic interpretation. We have a rough, intuitive idea of what it means; but philosophically it is a difficult and murky notion. Closely related issues will come up again in chapters 5 and 6; but nowhere shall we say the last word, rendering sense itself utterly transparent. (It's not clear, indeed, whether that notion even makes sense.) In the meantime, let's proceed on the basis of intuition—for we're nearing a major consolidation in the plot.

Interpreted Formal Systems

Formal systems can be interpreted: their tokens can be assigned meanings and taken as symbols about the outside world. This may be less than shocking news by now; but a century ago the development of interpreted formal systems was a major innovation, with revolutionary consequences throughout logic and mathematics. Moreover, if Artificial Intelligence is right, the mind itself is a (special) interpreted formal system—and the consequences will be even more revolutionary for psychology.

Let's start with some terminology. The general theory of interpretation and symbolic meaning is *semantics*; and the meanings assigned, as well as any relations or characteristics depending on those assignments, are *semantic properties* of the interpreted tokens. For instance, if 'Fido' is a formal token interpreted as a name for a particular frog, then its relation to that frog (reference) is a semantic property. If the complex token "Fido is a frog" is true, then its truth reflects (not only the facts, but) the interpretations of the terms: truth and falsity are semantic properties. When the truth of one sentence would entail that of another, that's a semantic relation between them. And so on.

The opposite of semantics is *syntax*. When discussing formal systems, in fact, 'syntactical' just means formal; but it is typically used only when a contrast with semantics is to the point. Thus it would be odd (though not incorrect) to speak of the "syntax" of a chess position, because chess is not an interpreted system.[3]

Interpretation and semantics transcend the strictly formal—because formal systems *as such* must be self-contained. Hence to regard formal tokens as symbols is to see them in a new light: semantic properties are not and cannot be syntactical properties. To put it dramatically, interpreted formal tokens lead two lives:

SYNTACTICAL LIVES, in which they are meaningless markers, moved according to the rules of some self-contained game; and

SEMANTIC LIVES, in which they have meanings and symbolic relations to the outside world.

The corresponding dramatic question then is: How do the two lives get together?

Athol has discovered a strange game: its tokens are the fifteen letters A–O; a position is a row of letters; a move consists of attaching more letters to the right of the row; and, for each (legal)

Box 5
Numerals and Numbers

Numerals are not the same as numbers: a *numeral* is a standardized symbol, like a proper name, for some particular number. The following are examples of numerals (all, as it happens, naming the same number):

five   cinq   πέντε   5   V   101

The first three are words (in English, French, and Greek); the fourth is an ordinary Arabic numeral; the fifth is a Roman numeral; and the last is in the binary system (which works like Arabic, only in base-2 instead of base-10).

Numerals, like any symbols, must always be understood relative to a specific language or system. Thus, the binary numeral 101 and the Arabic numeral 101 look just alike, but they stand for quite different numbers; similarly, the Latin name for the number six is the word 'sex', which means something else in English. *Numbers*, however, are not relative to any language or system: the number five itself (the number of petals on a petunia) is the same in England, France, Arabia, or ancient Rome—it just has different names.

---

starting position, there is exactly one legal move (after which the game is over). Lest the suspense be excruciating, I hasten to divulge Athol's own daring conjecture: the letters are direct translations of the familiar Arabic numerals and signs for arithmetic; that is, they *are* numerals and signs, but in an alternative notation. How do we tell whether Athol is right?

There are 1,307,674,368,000 different ways to map fifteen letters onto fifteen digits and signs—not all equally congenial to Athol's hypothesis. To illustrate the options, table 1 gives three possible translation schemes, together with the "translations" they would provide for eight sample (legal) games. As you can see, the first scheme generates total gibberish—arithmetic confetti. And so would practically all of the other 1.3 trillion alternatives; they're

Table 1 Athol's Letter Game

I. The eight sample games (untranslated)

	Starting position		Legal move	Starting position		Legal move
	OEO	A	N	MMCN	A	JJ
	NIBM	A	G	OODF	A	OO
	HCHCH	A	KON	IDL	A	M
	KEKDOF	A	F	NBN	A	O

II. First translation scheme

						Sample games as translated					
A	→	1	F	→	6	K → +	= 5 =	1	/	× × 3 /	1	00
B	→	2	G	→	7	L → −	/ 92 ×	1	7	= = 46	1	= =
C	→	3	H	→	8	M → ×	83838	1	+ = /	94 −	1	×
D	→	4	I	→	9	N → /	+5+4=6	1	6	/ 2 /	1	=
E	→	5	J	→	0	O → =						

III. Second translation scheme

						Sample games as translated			
A	→	=	F	→	0	K → 5	9 / 9 =	8	77 − 8 = 44
B	→	+	G	→	1	L → 6	83 + 7 =	1	99 × 0 = 99
C	→	−	H	→	2	M → 7	2 − 2 − 2 =	598	3 × 6 = 2
D	→	×	I	→	3	N → 8	5 / 5 × 90 =	0	8 + 8 = 9
E	→	/	J	→	4	O → 9			

IV. Third translation scheme

						Sample games as translated			
A	→	=	F	→	0	K → 5	1 + 1 =	2	33 × 2 = 66
B	→	/	G	→	9	L → 4	27 / 3 =	9	11 − 0 = 11
C	→	×	H	→	8	M → 3	8 × 8 × 8 =	512	7 − 4 = 3
D	→	−	I	→	7	N → 2	5 + 5 − 10 =	0	2 / 2 = 1
E	→	+	J	→	6	O → 1			

Note: The symbol → means "translates into."

what you would expect by drawing from a hat. Of the few remaining schemes, most would be like the second example, which is superficially better. It puts digits and signs in plausible places, so the results look like equations. Unfortunately, as equations, they would all be false—wildly and preposterously false. In fact, the particular digits and signs in those plausible places seem just as randomly chosen as before; so there's no genuine improvement, after all.

The third scheme, however, is conspicuously different. Its products not only look like equations, they *are* equations: they're true. Obviously this is the scheme that vindicates Athol's brave ideas; consistently true results make the interpretation itself persuasive. The first two cases, by contrast, aren't really interpretations at all: they don't "make sense of" the specimen games in the slightest.

"Formal" calculation, of course, did not revolutionize mathematics; rather, the important discovery was formal *axiomatic* systems. The most familiar axiomatic system is Euclidean geometry (though the treatment in textbooks is seldom rigorously formal).[4] Informally, an axiomatic system consists of a special set of statements (called *axioms* and/or *definitions*), plus a set of *inference rules*, for deriving further statements, called *theorems*. The axioms are conceived as basic and "obvious" and the rules as permitting only valid inferences; hence the derivations of the theorems can be regarded as *proofs*.

As a formal game, an axiomatic system is played by writing out complex tokens called *WFFs* ("sentence" formulae; see box 6). The axiom-WFFs are written first, as the starting position; and the rules then permit other WFFs to be added, depending on whatever's in the position already. Once written, tokens are never modified or removed; so the positions just get bigger as play proceeds. Each new WFF added to a position (or, anyway, each interesting one) thereby becomes a formal theorem of the system; and any game leading up to the addition of a WFF is a formal proof of that theorem.[5]

The idea, obviously, is to design these formal systems so that they can be *interpreted* as axiomatic systems in the intuitive sense. That requires two things of the system (as interpreted):

Box 6
Well-Formed Formulae = WFFs

A common strategy is actually to use *two* formal systems to "formalize" an axiomatic system. The reason is that not every compound of simple tokens is an allowable complex token; so there have to be rules specifying which ones are allowable and which aren't. But it's annoying and confusing to mix these rules up with the inference rules that specify the legal moves. So the two sets of rules are separated into two games.

The tokens of the first game are the simple tokens of the overall system; the rules just allow these to be combined in various ways. The resulting legal positions are the allowable complex tokens: the so-called *well-formed formulae*, or *WFFs*. These WFFs, then, are the tokens of the second game; that is, the *positions* of the first game are the *tokens* of the second. Finally, the rules of the second game allow the complex WFF tokens to be manipulated in the construction of proofs. (Notice that which WFF manipulations are legal at any point is highly dependent on the internal composition of all the WFFs involved; so WFF complexity is nontrivial, in the sense discussed earlier in "Finite Playability and Algorithms").

If that's a little confusing, consider reasoning in English as an analogy. We have various traditional rules for inferring one statement (the conclusion) from one or more others (the premises). For instance, a very useful rule (called the "syllogism in Barbara") permits inferences like the following:

Given:	All frogs are mortal	(premises)
	Fido is a frog	
Therefore:	Fido is mortal	(conclusion)

The three statements (sentences) are, of course, complex symbols built up out of words. But not every sequence of words is a grammatical sentence, and ungrammatical sentences are not allowed. So we can think of grammar as analogous to the first game, for building up allowable complex tokens (sentences) to be manipulated in the second game (syllogistic reasoning, say). In other words, WFFs are like grammatical sentences, and the WFF game is like the grammar of the overall system.

1. the axioms should be *true* (preferably "obvious"); and
2. the rules should be *truth preserving*.

A formal rule of inference is truth preserving (valid) if and only if: for any position containing only true WFFs, any new WFF allowed by that rule will also be true. Hence whenever a system has all true axioms and truth-preserving rules, it is guaranteed that every WFF in every legal position is true as well—the truth of the axioms is "preserved" every step of the way. In other words, the formal *theorems* are all guaranteed true, which is the whole point.

Earlier we noted that *coherence* is the basic principle of *all* interpretation. How does that apply to interpreting formal systems? The "reasonable sense" side of coherence works just as before; in particular, the letter game and axiomatic system examples again illustrate the relevance of truth to sense. (In fact, since both these examples are mathematical systems, they may somewhat overemphasize truth, if only by neglecting any other considerations. But the texts generated by formal systems can make sense in all kinds of ways—as questions, stories, poetry, or what have you— a fact that is crucial to the hopes of Artificial Intelligence.)

The other side of coherence—the "ordered text" requirement— is more interesting: the *rules* defining the formal system introduce an important new factor. Since the text to be interpreted is basically the set of legal games, and since the rules determine what these are, the rules effectively define the entire text. This means, in the first place, that the texts are definitely not random or accidental: whatever structure they exhibit is imposed on them by the rules of the game (the rules are the reason or source of the structure).

And, second, since the entire potential text is well defined at the outset, the interpretation is responsible for all of it. That is, there must be good reason (either empirical evidence or rigorous demonstration, depending on the system) to expect that the scheme would make sense of every legal game.

These two points, however, are mere groundwork for the following: if the formal (syntactical) rules specify the relevant texts and if the (semantic) interpretation must make sense of all those texts, then simply playing by the rules is itself a surefire way to make sense. Obey the formal rules of arithmetic, for instance, and your answers are sure to be true. This is the deep, essential reason why interpreted formal systems are interesting and important at all. Hence it deserves a memorable name and phrase:

FORMALISTS' MOTTO: If you take care of the syntax, the semantics will take care of itself.

Taking care of the syntax is simply playing by the rules; making sense is what "takes care of itself." And that is how the "two lives" of an interpreted formal system get together.

Computers

A *computer* is an interpreted automatic formal system—that is to say, a *symbol-manipulating machine.*[6] This definition has two basic clauses:

1. the referee and (at least some) players of some formal system have been automated—they are black boxes that automatically manipulate the tokens according to the rules; and
2. those tokens are symbols—they have been interpreted, so that the legal moves "make reasonable sense," in the contexts in which they're made.

What an automatic formal system does, literally, is "take care of the syntax" (i.e., the formal moves). Therefore, in accord with the Formalist's Motto (and given the interpretation), the system's semantics takes care of itself—automatically. In other words, a computer is precisely what Descartes said was impossible: a machine that automatically makes sensible utterances in context.

The simplest example is a pocket calculator—an automation of Athol's letter game (but using more familiar numerals). Each new starting position is entered with the buttons; and as soon as the final token is entered (with the = button), the machine automatically writes out (in the display window) the one and only legal move for that position. And that move will be semantically sensible (arithmetically correct) for the same reason as before: namely, the interpretation scheme was acceptable in the first place only because the legal moves all made sense (as interpreted).

The player and referee black boxes are the calculator's electronic guts; what they're like internally, however, is utterly irrelevant to the system's status as a computer. All that matters is that, as black boxes, the components reliably produce the legal moves (i.e., the ones consistently interpretable as correct calculations). The innards of the device could be anything—mystic glowing jelly—and the overall system would still be a perfectly good calculator (we just wouldn't understand how it worked).

Unfortunately, the calculator example is so simple that it obscures an important problem. Even when carried out by hand, arithmetic calculation is fully deterministic: every move is fully determined by the rules alone; the "player" really contributes nothing. But for more sophisticated systems, the rules are almost never deterministic; hence the moves that actually get made are in fact determined *jointly* by the rules and player(s) together— the rules spell out the legal options, and the players then choose from among them. So, in effect, there are *two* sources of order in the resulting text: the rules' constraints and the players' choices.

The principle of interpretation is always coherence: making reasonable sense of ordered texts. If, however, there are two sources of order in the text, then it may be that the interpretation finds sense at two distinct levels—"basic" and "refined," so to speak. The basic sense (if any) would be that intelligibility guaranteed simply by following the rules; the refined sense (if any) would be that further reasonableness exhibited in the players' actual choices (finding *interesting* theorems, *elegant* proofs, or something like that).

Consider, for instance, a simple axiomatization of geometry of high school algebra. The only constraint on its interpretation (as described in the preceding section) is that all theorems—all WFFs legally obtainable from the axioms—must come out true. That's the basic level of sense, in terms of which the interpretation is defensible. But it says nothing about another level of sense, manifested in which theorems are proved and how. Thus it would be less than supremely "sensible" to sit around proving many of:

$$a = a,$$
$$a + a = a + a,$$
$$a + a + a = a + a + a,$$
$$a + a + a + a = a + a + a + a.$$

. . . and so on, *ad nauseam*.

Though these are all perfectly true, checking out more than a few would be gruesomely stupid, and toiling over a dozen or two could win a trip in a padded wagon. A similar point goes for the proofs themselves: absurdly convoluted and erratic demonstrations of the most mundane theorems can be quite valid, though only an idiot or lunatic would dream them up.

In such cases, of course, we distinguish between interpreting the system itself (making its theorems true) and evaluating the player (smart or stupid, sane or crazy, etc.). That is, we apportion responsibility between the two sources of order, thereby recognizing a *division of semantic labor* in accounting for the sensibleness of the actual output. The formal rules (and axioms) are accountable for the basic interpretability of the tokens and steps; the players are accountable for any more refined reasonableness, such as being interesting, goal-directed, clever, or what have you.

The point of saying all this, however, is to take it back—or rather, to emphasize its limitations. The division of semantic labor cannot be taken for granted: in fact, outside a narrow range of cases, it seems to be impossible. When you and your neighbor chat, for instance, the conversation makes sense ("coheres") in a number of subtle ways:

Box 7
Formalization and the Division of Semantic Labor

The division of semantic labor and the corresponding double level of sense depend on finding sufficiently powerful rules to define the legal moves—since the "basic" interpretation must depend on the order imposed by the rules alone. These rules can be neither too loose nor too strict. If they were too loose (too many legal moves), then texts constrained only by them would not exhibit enough order overall to be consistently interpretable. On the other hand, making the rules overly restrictive (too few legal moves) also reduces the usable order by simply curtailing the available text or by making it all the same. (Recall the discussion of brief coded messages in the section on interpretation.)

Mathematicians have found many sets of formal rules that define systems interpretable as containing only truths about some mathematical domain (and, moreover, "enough" truths to support that particular interpretation nontrivially). When such a system is discovered, we say the corresponding domain (or theory) has been *formalized*. Clearly formalization depends on the division of semantic labor. Explicitly developing this conception of strict formalization, with the associated notion of formal system, is among the crowning achievements of nineteenth-century mathematics.

Outside of mathematics and logic, however, sufficiently powerful rules are very hard to find: many important topics of discourse, from politics to engineering, from literature to idle talk, stubbornly resist formalization, or even any decent approximation. That's not to say they will resist forever (one can never tell); but there is little reason to be optimistic. Fortunately, as we shall see, general formalization is not at all required for Artificial Intelligence.

1. there tend to be common topics through groups of utterances;
2. questions and objections tend to be relevant—and get answered;
3. surprises get elaborated, whereas banalities are dropped;
4. suggestions are usually well motivated and apparently feasible;
5. discussion inclines to what's new and interesting (to you);
6. evaluations and judgments more or less fit the evidence offered; *and so forth.*

Oh yes, and your statements tend to be true. But—and this is the point—there is no (known) way to divide up this fabric of coherence so that one part (sufficient to support the interpretation) can be guaranteed by formal rules, while the rest is attributed to the players' intelligence.

For *manual* formal systems, the distinction between the formal constraints and the players' choices is explicit and sharp. Hence interpreting manual systems requires the division of labor: all legal moves must make sense (as interpreted), regardless of who makes them or why. *Automatic* systems, however, are different—or, at least, they can be. An automatic system is an actual physical device, with the game tokens, players, and referee all "built in"; hence its actual net behavior and dispositions constitute a determinate corpus (text), which may well be interpretable as it stands. That is, even if there were no way to apportion responsibility between rules and players so that the rules alone support a basic interpretation, the integrated package as a whole still could exhibit an interpretable order. Consequently, for automatic systems, it may or may not be possible to divide the semantic labor; but, in principle, it's not necessary. Let's compare the two cases.

Type A One can take a previously interpreted formal system and "automate" it. Then its (automatic) outputs will still all abide by the same formal rules and still all make sense according to the same basic interpretation; so the original division of labor remains. Of course these same outputs may also exhibit a more refined order: assuming the system was nondeterministic to start with and assuming it was automated in a sophisticated manner ("good" players), the outputs might be not merely consistently intelligible, but also consistently clever, well motivated, interesting, and all that.

Notice how neatly compatible this picture is with the automatic chess-player sketched out in chapter 2. To be sure, chess tokens are not interpreted, so there's no "semantic" labor to divide. But the problem of making "good" (as opposed to merely legal) moves arises in chess as well; and the solution transfers right over. Thus, imagine that the automated player of our interpreted system is analyzed into two "inner players": one lists all the legal moves in the current position (all of which make basic sense, according to the Formalists' Motto), and the other chooses something interesting or clever from among them. In this simple case, then, the division of labor would be concretely instantiated in the very structure of the machine.

An actual automatic system, however, could be type A even if it were not first conceived as an interpreted manual system and then automated. What matters is whether you can find a set of formal rules that effectively divide the semantic labor: they must be permissive enough to legitimate any move the system would ever make (i.e., the players abide by them), and at the same time resrictive enough to support a basic interpretation. Or (to put it another way) you must be able to distinguish, within the overall interpretable order, some basic level of rule-defined "pure reason" (logical validity, mathematical correctness, or whatever) from a superimposed level of selective wit and insight. (I suspect that science fiction writers may so often depict robots as superrational because they can't see beyond this type-A species of computer.)

Type B   The really exciting prospect, however, is building systems that don't maintain the division of labor and are therefore not restricted to domains where a suitable division (formalization) can be found. A computer that conversed in ordinary English, for instance, would (presumably) be interpretable only as a whole; that is, only when the order implicit in the speaker's choices (of what to say) is imposed on the set of "legal moves" (grammatical sentences, e.g.) does the output exhibit enough structure to sustain interpretation. Not surprisingly, many if not most contemporary AI systems are generically type B.

GOFAI

Despite the name, not just any intelligent artifact would be Artificial Intelligence—not in our sense, anyway. This is not to deny, of course, that there are many theories of the mind, including interesting non-AI mechanisms and computer models. The point, rather, is to maintain conceptual clarity by keeping tight reins on terminology. To mark the intended careful usage, I have capitalized "Artificial Intelligence" throughout; but, lest that not be enough, or if someone else wants these words for another role, we may also speak more explicitly of what I shall call Good Old Fashioned Artificial Intelligence—GOFAI, for short.

GOFAI, as a branch of cognitive science, rests on a particular theory of intelligence and thought—essentially Hobbes's idea that ratiocination is *computation*. We should appreciate that this thesis is empirically substantive: it is not trivial or tautological, but actually says something about the world that could be false. In other words, not every scientific approach to intelligence need accept it; and, in fact, a number of alternative accounts are being actively investigated and developed in various laboratories today. Our concern, however, is neither to explicate nor to evaluate any potential rivals but only to note two consequences implicit in their possibility. First, should any alternative (non-GOFAI) theory of intelligence actually succeed, then it ought to be possible in principle to build an intelligent artifact that works as the theory says; but, by hypothesis, that artifact wouldn't be GOFAI.

Second, and more interesting, given that same theory, it should also be possible (in principle) to *simulate* that intelligence on a computer—just as scientists routinely simulate everything from hurricanes and protein synthesis to traffic jams and the black market of Albania. Here the important point is that the simulating system and the system being simulated do not work according to the same principles: a hurricane is explained through laws of aero- and hydrodynamics, but a computer is not. Rather, the computer would work symbolically, often numerically, carrying out calculations prescribed by those laws, in order to *describe* the hurricane correctly. A simulation of an intellect would likewise "apply" the theory symbolically in order to describe the simulated system's behavior, even though (by assumption) that system itself works some other way (i.e., not symbolically). The thesis of GO-FAI, however, is not that the processes underlying intelligence can be described symbolically (a feature shared by hurricanes and traffic jams), but that they *are* symbolic (which differentiates them utterly from hurricanes and traffic jams).[7] So again the project would not be GOFAI.

More specifically, the claims essential to all GOFAI theories are these:

1. our ability to deal with things intelligently is due to our capacity to think about them reasonably (including sub-conscious thinking); and
2. our capacity to think about things reasonably amounts to a faculty for internal "automatic" symbol manipulation.

Two points follow immediately. First, inasmuch and insofar as these internal symbol manipulations are intelligent thoughts, they must be interpreted as about the outside world (i.e., whatever the system deals with intelligently). Second, in being committed to *internal* symbol manipulation, GOFAI is committed to at least one level of analysis: that is, an intelligent system must contain some computational subsystems ("inner computers") to carry out those "reasonable" internal manipulations.

Alas, the latter sound like homunculi. Have we simply fallen back into the old trap of explaining intelligence by presupposing it? Not quite; but the escape is trickier than it looks. Recall the dilemma: if Zelda's intelligence can be explained only by postulating an intelligent homunculus to manipulate her thoughts, then nothing has been gained. For what explains the homunculus's intelligence? Putting it this way, however, conceals two surreptitious assumptions that turn out to make all the difference. First, it assumes that Zelda has *only one* homunculus, instead, say, of a large team of cooperating specialists. Second, it assumes that the homunculus must be *just as smart* as Zelda herself (or at least that explaining his intelligence would be just as hard as explaining hers). But neither of these assumptions need be true.

It's easy enough to imagine dozens (or maybe thousands) of independent homunculi, all somehow organized and working together, collectively managing Zelda's psyche. And, given that, it's also easy to suggest that each individual homunculus can be relatively narrow-minded—Zelda's net wits emerging only cumulatively from all the separate contributions, plus their systematic organization. Finally, of course, such *homuncular analysis* can be repeated on many levels: each narrow homunculus might itself comprise a team of still straighter colleagues; and so on.[8] Still, this is more metaphor than science. How, one wants to ask, can there be any intelligence at all (narrow or otherwise)? Until that has been answered, nothing has.

Enter computers. We know at the outset that deterministic formal systems are no problem to automate; and, if interpreted, the interpretation will carry right over. We saw in chapter 2 (under "Automatic Systems") how a nondeterministic system (chess) could be automated as a composite of inner deterministic systems. In particular, we saw how one and the same inner system could be regarded from one point of view as performing an algorithmic calculation (e.g., of the value of some formula) and from another point of view as making somewhat clever (though fallible) heuristic decisions (e.g., about good chess moves). Finally, we noted above how that chess-machine structure transfers directly to a type-A computer: the rules support a basic interpretation, and the heuristic decisions superimpose a further "somewhat clever" order on the actual text. Thus we have, or at least appear to have, a machine with *some* intelligence.

This "nose in the tent" settles the issue, on one condition: that homuncular analysis can fill the gap between it and "full" intelligence. In outline the proposed solution is clear: given systems with a little intelligence, we can organize them into coordinated teams with higher and higher intelligence—including eventually type-B computers—as informal and flexible as you please. Unresolved, however, is what counts as "some" (or less or more) intelligence for the purposes of this argument. Homuncular analysis only works if the "inner players" get less and less bright

Box 8
Internal Semantics and Reinterpretation

"One day, Bob's car died. When he couldn't restart it, he opened the hood and poked around. Then he noticed a loose wire. He quickly reconnected it and got back on his way." Bob behaved *intelligently*. Moreover, we can *explain how* he did that by showing how he acted rationally, in the light of various things he saw, knew, inferred, desired, intended, etc. about his car. The GOFAI approach to intelligence is basically inspired by examples like this—though, of course, a full scientific account would mention many more states and processes, including unconscious ones.

Importantly, all the internal cognitive states cited in the account are *about* (mean, refer to) things the system is dealing with—the car, for example. That's crucial in relating the behavior intelligently (i.e., via the reasoning) to the circumstances. Accordingly, it imposes a constraint on how the thought symbols manipulated by the inner players can be interpreted: they (many of them) must be construed as being about things in the outside world.

In a functioning system, however, there could also be other kinds of symbols running around. The cooperating inner players, for instance, might coordinate their activities by sending internal messages about who should do what when. These messages would be symbolic (have meanings), but only about internal business—not about the outside world. (In computer terms, memory addresses, procedure names, etc., would fall in this category.) Interpreting such symbols is *internal semantics*.

The interpretation of a symbol can depend on the level of analysis. For instance, if one inner specialist needs information about spark plugs, she might ask another specialist—the librarian—to look it up for her. We must interpret the symbol she hands him as meaning "spark plug" if we're to understand its role in thoughtful problem solving. But when we analyze the librarian himself, that same symbol has nothing to do with spark plugs: for him it functions only as an (internal) label for the required article. Thus, in changing explanatory contexts, the symbol itself gets *reinterpreted*. (A similar shift occurs when we regard a single procedure as both a heuristic and an algorithm.)

(down to zero); equivalently, building up from the bottom only works if it can get above zero (and then keep going). But by what standard are these judgments made? As near as I can tell, there is only one: *if* a GOFAI analysis of real (human-like) intelligence into primitive computations someday succeeds, *then* that analysis itself constitutes a relevant standard of more and less intelligent— namely, up and down the hierarchy. Until that time, we are stuck with hunches and shaky intuitions.

In other words, we won't really know the answer until we really know the answer. That's not as bad as it sounds: the question as it's now put is entirely scientific. All the old "metaphysical" (i.e., conceptual) homunculus riddles are cleared away, in anticipation of empirical results—and that's progress.

Is GOFAI too narrow? My definition of GOFAI, while leaving lots of room for discovery, variety, and difference of opinion, is nevertheless comparatively strict: it rules out a significant range of contemporary research, including much that relies heavily on computer models and even some that calls itself AI. Yet how dare I legislate? Do I presume—in the worst tradition of philosophy— to tell scientists what to work on? Not at all! I delimit GOFAI only as my own present topic, with no insinuation as to the merits of what does or does not fall within it. I have, of course, motives for this particular choice of topic, including:

1. The great bulk of work called AI over the past quarter-century in fact fits my characterization of "Good Old Fashioned" AI (except that some of it pretends no relation to human psychology).
2. The body of research encompassed and inspired by GOFAI is widely regarded as the most worked out in detail, the

most powerful in theoretical resources, and the most successful in application that psychology has ever known.

3. There are intuitive, long-standing, positive reasons to find the GOFAI framework attractive, even compelling.

4. Finally, the more focused the topic (provided it's not overly idiosyncratic or arcane), the easier it is to say true and interesting things.

None of these means that GOFAI is "right" but only that it's worth discussing; and my only intent in "ruling out" alternatives is to sharpen that discussion.

Paradox and Mystery Dispelled

A GOFAI system has an inner playing field, on which inner tokens are arranged and manipulated by one or more inner players under the supervision of an inner referee. These inner token manipulations are interpreted as the thought processes by virtue of which the overall system manages to make sense and act intelligently. In other words, the overall intelligence is explained by analyzing the system into smaller (less intelligent) components, whose external symbolic moves and interactions are the larger system's internal reasonable cognitions. That's the paradigm of cognitive science.

Since the inner players manipulate meaningful tokens reasonably, they are homunculi. We have defused the traditional infinite-regress objection (homunculi within homunculi . . . forever) by suggesting that the homunculi get dimmer, stage by stage, until the last have no intelligence at all. But that does not yet resolve the more basic *paradox of mechanical reason*: if the manipulators pay attention to what the symbols mean, then they can't be entirely mechanical because meanings exert no mechanical forces; but if they ignore the meanings, then the manipulations can't be instances of reasoning because what's reasonable depends on what the symbols mean. Even granting that intelligence comes in degrees, meaningfulness still does not; that is, the paradox cannot be escaped by suggesting that tokens become less and less symbolic, stage by stage. Either they're interpreted, or they aren't.[9]

A different fundamental strategy is required here: not analysis but *redescription*, seeing the very same thing from radically different points of view and thus describing it in radically different terms. Of course one cannot "redescribe" capriciously; there must be some basis in the phenomena for each mode of description. For instance, a certain procedure is an *algorithm* for computing a certain formula, if it infallibly produces the right answer in finite time; that same procedure can be redescribed as a heuristic for estimating chess moves, if that formula determines (fallible but fairly reliable) move strengths. The redescription depends on this feature of the formula.

Interpretation is redescription grounded in the coherence of a text. For computer interpretation the foundation of semantic redescription is the Formalists' Motto: "You take care of the syntax, and the semantics will take care of itself." In other words, interpretations are legitimate just in case the formal rules suitably constrain the formal moves. The paradox is then resolved by associating its two sides with the two different modes of description. From one point of view, the inner players are mere automatic formal systems, manipulating certain tokens in a manner that accords with certain rules, all quite mechanically. But from another point of view, those very same players manipulate those very same tokens—now interpreted as symbols—in a manner that accords quite reasonably with what they mean. Computational homunculi can have their meanings and eat them too.

Unfortunately, this "solution" is seriously incomplete because, as stated, it works only for type-A computers. Specifically, the Formalists' Motto presupposes the division of semantic labor that defines type-A computers. For that division is just the identification of a set of formal/syntactical rules strong enough to sustain interpretation; and the Motto appeals to just such rules. Consequently, we just go another round and exploit homuncular analysis after all.

Imagine a player, call him Pierre, who is analyzed without remainder into a team of inner players, an inner referee, and a field of inner tokens. Imagine further that each of these inner components is known to be (when described from the right point of view) fully mechanical. Then Pierre too is (i.e., can be seen as) fully mechanical. At the same time, however, these same inner players (seen differently) may also be manipulating Pierre's inner symbols more or less intelligently. Accordingly, they may be contributing more "meaningful order" to the actual inner text than is imposed by any formal rules they all follow—an order that might well be necessary for that text to be interpretable at all. In that event, Pierre is a type-B computer, but still redescribable as fully mechanical, via the analysis.

This of course leaves open the question of whether *all* type-B computers—native English speakers, say—are so analyzable, and if so, how. Devising and testing such analyses is bread and butter, workaday AI; it's what the scientists do. The extent to which they will succeed cannot be told in advance; but, as with homuncular regress, the conceptual, philosophical problem is now solved by rendering it empirical and scientific: mechanical reason is paradoxical no more.

The *mystery of original meaning*—Hobbes's problem in telling minds from books—is older and deeper. In this chapter meaning has been introduced entirely in terms of semantic interpretation and the principle of coherence. The basic idea works equally well for ancient inscriptions, secret codes, foreign languages, formal systems, and (presumably) brains: if an ordered text consistently comes out making reasonable sense, then the interpretation is vindicated. Notice that this is perfectly neutral between original and derivative meanings. Thus, suppose some special brain symbols had *original* meaning and all other meaningfulness derived therefrom. Still, *interpreting* these would be no different in principle from any other interpretation. To be sure, it would be conceived as a *discovery* process, figuring out meanings that are already there (like "cracking" somebody else's language or code), and not as an act of stipulation (like "giving" an interpretation to a new notation or code). But the canon of success is essentially the same whether the meanings are original or derivative.

The questions remain: Which symbolic systems have their meanings originally (nonderivatively) and why? These are related. If we understood why brain symbols have original meaning (assuming they do), then we could better tell which other symbols (for instance, those in GOFAI systems) might have original meaning too, and vice versa. Hence we can pursue our interests in both AI and philosophy by asking more closely about minds and books.

The most conspicuous difference between book symbols (printed words) and brain symbols (thoughts) is that book symbols just sit there, doing nothing, while thoughts are constantly interacting and changing. But that by itself can't be the crucial difference, since book-like symbols can also be interactive and variable. Imagine printing individual word tokens on thousands of tiny floating magnets or on the backs of busy ants. The resulting physical symbols would interact vigorously and form various amusing combinations; but their meanings would still be just as derivative (from us) as those of any lines inked quietly on a page.

Nevertheless, this may be on the right track. Consider writing the following premises on a piece of paper:

All frogs eat insects.
Fido is a frog.

Nothing much happens. More revealing: if we set them out on magnets or ants, then plenty of activity might ensue, but most likely nothing interesting about frogs or insects. In sum, the behavior of such symbols (independent of our manipulations) is quite unrelated to what they mean. By contrast, if we got those premises into somebody's head (say, in the form of beliefs), then a new complex symbol would very likely appear—and not just any new symbol, but specifically a valid conclusion about Fido and insect eating:

Fido eats insects.

And that's exactly the sort of fact that inclines us to suppose that people *understand* their thoughts, whereas paper and floating magnets are utterly oblivious.

So the important difference is not merely that thoughts are active, but that their activity is directly related to their meanings; in general, the changes and interactions among thought symbols are semantically appropriate. Accordingly, I say that thought symbols are *semantically active*, in contradistinction to printed or magnetic symbols, which are *semantically inert* (even if they're "active" in other ways that are semantically irrelevant). The only times when the meanings of semantically inert symbols make any difference are when they interact with users (e.g., people writing or reading them). Such symbols have no effect at all, as meaningful entities, apart from the way users take them to be meaningful; and that, surely, is why their meanings seem only derivative.

Furthermore, semantically active symbols are prima facie candidates for original meaning. For when they interact with one another, they do so independently of any outside user; yet their interactions remain consistently appropriate to what they mean. And that suggests that those meanings are somehow "there," in the active symbolic system itself, regardless of whether or what anyone else takes them to be.

Of course calling the *symbols* active is a literary conceit. Expressed more carefully, "active" symbols are the interpreted states or parts of an integrated system within which they are manipulated automatically. Thus thought symbols could only be appropriately active in the context of numerous brain processes that respond to them, affect them, and generally mediate their relations in various standard ways. Only if we hide all such processes backstage do the thoughts look active all by themselves.

Now, however, the plot thickens, for we have just described a computer. In the context of the overall system, the interpreted tokens interact with one another—leading to and constraining changes in subsequent positions—all entirely automatic and semantically appropriate. The player and referee components can be hidden backstage or brought into the limelight, as the occasion demands. But, in either case, the system as a whole manipulates the tokens in ways appropriate to what they mean, with no intervention from outside users; and that's semantic activity.

Does this mean that the mystery of original meaning is resolved? It's hard to say. Let's close the chapter by comparing two examples from opposite extremes of interpreted automatic systems. The first is our tiresome pocket calculator: it automatically manipulates numerals in a way that is semantically appropriate, since it always gets the right answers. But it would be tough to maintain that this crude and limited device manages to refer to numbers all by itself—quite apart, that is, from how *we* use it. In some intuitively compelling sense, it "has no idea" what numbers are. It can't count; it can't explain anything it does; it can't tell a proper fraction from a buffalo chip; and it doesn't care. *All* it can do is crank through four mindless algorithms, depending on which buttons are pushed. A number of considerably more elaborate systems, such as automatic bank tellers, word processors, and many computer games, belong in essentially the same category.

The opposite example is the GOFAI system of fondest fiction. By hypothesis, such systems are ensconced in mobile and versatile bodies; and they are capable (to all appearances anyway) of the full range of "human" communication, problem solving, artistry, heroism, and what have you. Just to make it vivid, imagine further that the human race has long since died out and that the Earth is populated instead by billions of these computer-robots. They build cities, conduct scientific research, fight legal battles, write volumes, and, yes, a few odd ones live in ivory towers and wonder how their "minds" differ from books—or so it seems. One could, I suppose, cling harshly to the view that, in principle, these systems are no different from calculators; that, in the absence of people, their tokens, their treatises and songs, mean exactly nothing. But that just seems perverse. If GOFAI systems can be developed to such an extent, then, by all means, they can have original meaning.

What lesson do we draw from these cases? The quick and dirty (but not necessarily false) surmise would be that they are the ends of a continuous spectrum: calculators have quite minimal semantic activity and a correspondingly minimal amount of original meaning, whereas our super robots have a full complement of each. A variation on that simple theme would be to accept the continuum but require a certain minimum threshold of semantic activity before acknowledging any original meaning at all. Both versions take "originality" of meaning to come in degrees and then more or less abandon the issue to a dubious "slippery slope."

A more interesting prospect might be this: only semantic activity of certain sophisticated or advanced kinds, or with certain distinctive characteristics, can suffice for genuine original meaning.

In that case both philosophical and scientific questions would still want answers: What are these special kinds or characteristics, what makes them so special, and can we build GOFAI systems that have them? In chapters 5 and (especially) 6 we will explore several aspects of intelligent systems that may bear on the first and second of these questions; but the third question mostly remains open. Thus a final option regarding the above examples is flat rejection: perhaps the robot scenario is in fact impossible, and something quite different from semantic activity is required for original meaning.

The mystery of original meaning, evidently, is battered but not down. The notions of semantic activity and automatic computation make it seem a whole lot less mysterious; yet the uncertainty in identifying just what makes the difference, and why, leaves the matter somewhat unsettled. This much, however, is clear: we shall get no further without additional conceptual and factual tools. We now turn to a more specific review of the structures and kinds of computers, followed by a survey of actual research and discoveries in Artificial Intelligence.

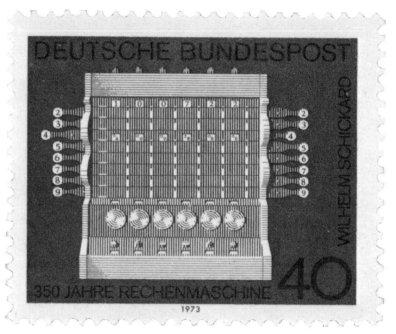

Postage stamp depicting Schickard's calculator on its 350th anniversary

4   *Computer Architecture*

Babbage and His Analytical Engine

People too often assume that computers are all essentially alike and then they can imagine only one basic design for Artificial Intelligence (or the mind). But computers differ dramatically from one another, even in their fundamental structure and organization. In this chapter we will sample several different general *architectures*, savoring just enough of each to bring out its own special flavor. The point is not to canvass candidate psychological arrangements—we're not yet contending for that lofty honor—but rather to illustrate how much machines can vary and to see what some of the theory is like.

As far as we know, the automatic digital calculator was invented around 1623 by an obscure German astronomer named Wilhelm Schickard (1592–1635). I say "as far as we know" because nobody knew about Schickard's invention until recently, and who knows what else may still be lost. The first publicized calculator was built some twenty years later by the French philosopher Blaise Pascal (1623–1662), after whom a popular programming language is now named. His device caused quite a stir, even though it could only add and subtract, and only clumsily at that. Predictable improvements followed in due course—most notably multiplication and division, introduced in the 1670s by the German philosopher Gottfried Leibnitz (1646–1716)—but nothing very exciting happened for a couple of centuries.[1]

England's Charles Babbage (1792–1871), history's first computer scientist, was also a classic eccentric genius—notorious, among other things, for an obsessive hatred of organ grinders. Trained as a mathematician, and for nine years Lucasian professor of mathematics (Newton's chair at Cambridge), Babbage never actually taught a course, or even moved to the university from London. Intellectually, he was as versatile as he was pioneering, making original contributions not only in mathematics, but also in precision metalworking (his shop was among the finest in Europe) and in what we now call operations research (he wrote one of its earliest systematic treatments). But, above all, Babbage is remembered for his calculating engines.

In fact, he designed two quite different machines. The first (ca. 1823–1833), called the *Difference Engine*, is not terrifically important, though it was certainly innovative and potentially useful. Many components and even prototypes were built, but no Difference Engine was ever actually completed, for several reasons. First, critical tolerances made construction very expensive (hence the fine machine shop); second, Babbage kept improving the design, requiring constant modification and rebuilding; and third, sometime around 1833 his imagination was seized by a more elegant and far grander scheme.

The new *Analytical Engine* occupied Babbage for the rest of his life and was his crowning achievement. Its design incorporates *two* utterly profound and unprecedented ideas, which together are the foundation of all computer science:

1. its operations are fully *programmable*; and
2. the programs can contain *conditional branches*.

Like the Difference Engine (and for similar reasons), the Analytical Engine was never finished, although nearly a thousand technical drawings, timing diagrams, and flow charts were prepared, along with six or seven thousand pages of explanatory notes. Moreover, quite a number of parts were made, and a substantial model was under construction when Babbage died (at age seventy-nine).[2]

For many years, however, the only published account of the new Engine was a little "memoir" with an engaging history of its own. In 1842 L.F. Menabrea, an Italian engineer, published (in French, but in a Swiss journal) a summary of some lectures

Babbage had given privately in Naples. The following year Ada Augusta, a gifted young protégé of Babbage's (and later Countess of Lovelace), translated it into English—adding, with the master's encouragement, a few explanatory footnotes. These "notes" turn out to be three times longer and considerably more sophisticated than the original article. Though Babbage probably supplied some of her material, it seems certain that Lady Lovelace understood his work better than did anyone else in his lifetime; the powerful new language *Ada* has been named in her honor.[3]

The Analytical Engine has three major components: the *mill* (an arithmetic unit), the *store* (data memory); and a sequencer/controller unit, for which Babbage provided no name. The tokens manipulated in the system are signed numerals, and the playing field is essentially the store. The mill can perform the four standard arithmetic operations, using any indicated locations in the store for operands and results. Thus, using our earlier terms, we can think of the mill as a team of four rather limited "inner players," one for each primitive ability. And the controller, then, is the inner referee, never manipulating tokens itself, but only telling the players when and where to exercise their respective talents; that is, it calls on them, one at a time, saying which numerals to work with and where to put the answer. Every move is fully determined.

But what "game" does the Analytical Engine play? What are the rules? What determines the instructions that the referee issues to the players? These are all the same question, and the answer is the key to the whole brilliant concept. Within certain limits, the Analytical Engine will play whatever game you tell it to. That is, you specify the rules (in a particular manner), and the referee will see that the players abide by them. So just by handing the referee different "definitions," you can make the Analytical Engine be any automatic formal system you want (within its limits).

This remarkable exercise, *making* a specific automatic system, simply *by describing* it appropriately for a general purpose system, is called *programming*. It is one of the most powerful ideas in the history of technology, and Babbage invented it all by himself.

Compare an ordinary calculator. It can perform the same four operations, but you have to enter each command manually, each

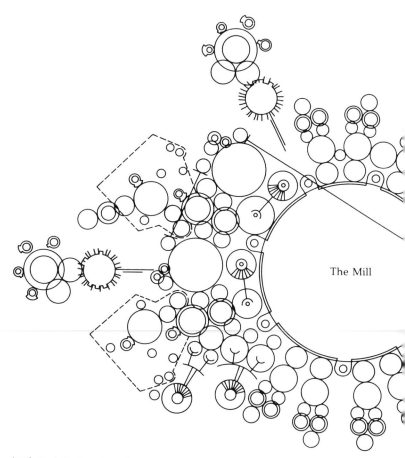

Analytical Engine, top view

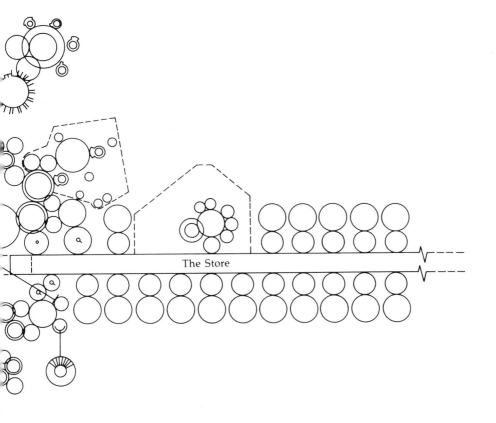

The Store

step of the way. If you want to evaluate $3(x + y) - 5$, for given x and y, you must first add the two data, then multiply their sum by three, and finally subtract five from the product. If you need the value for various givens, you must go through the whole sequence, step by step, every time. A calculator is essentially just four independent special-purpose devices, each of which can do only one thing; any combination or repetition of operations must be done by hand. One could, of course, build a more complicated special-purpose machine to compute not the sum or product of two numbers, but (say) five less than triple their sum; but that would be weird and ugly.

A much better plan would be a machine for which you could prespecify *any arbitrary sequence* of basic operations (on any specified variables). Such a machine could evaluate any formula you like, given the appropriate specifications; and, given those specifications, it would act exactly like a special-purpose machine custom made for that formula. For all intents and purposes, it would *be* that special machine—until the specifications were changed. Needless to say, this is how the Analytical Engine works: the "specifications" are the program.

The second great invention in the Analytical Engine is the *conditional branch*: a directive to the referee to move to another part of the program, depending on the result of some test. We have already seen the importance of conditional branches, in our key/ lock algorithms; in fact, Babbage's programs are essentially branched schedules, just like those algorithms. Such branches are required for many numerical calculations, as Babbage was well aware (see box 1 for an example). Conditional control is crucial also in other general symbol manipulators, including those that matter in Artificial Intelligence.

Inasmuch as the Analytical Engine is an automatic formal system, it is strictly medium independent. But 150 years ago physical realization was a major obstacle, and Babbage's amazing design is worth a brief description. Numerals are forty decimal (not binary) digits, plus a sign. (He seems to have had several different ideas for keeping track of fractions, but none settled.) Each digit is represented by the rotation of a brass gear, roughly the size of a

Box 1
Sample Program for the Analytical Engine

The user programming facility is the least well defined aspect of Babbage's design. The following is a rough compromise between his informal notation and the format we used for algorithms in chapter 2.

Locations in the store have names: V1, V2, V3, etc. The instruction: "V1 + V2 → V3" means "get the numbers stored in V1 and V2, add them, and put the sum in V3." You can think of it as the referee instructing the addition specialist to "do his thing" using these locations. Directives to the referee are printed in capital letters. The conditionals (IF . . .) test whether a certain number is greater than zero: if so, the referee branches; if not, she just continues to the next instruction. (Note that the branch directions don't tell the referee what line to go to, but rather how many lines to move from where she is.)

The sample program computes the value of: $ar^m - r^n$.

Before starting, load storage locations with initial values as follows:

V1 with *a*, V2 with *r*, V3 with *m*, V4 with *n*, and V5, V6, and V7 all with the constant *1*.

Program	Explanation
START	
V5 x V2 → V5	Multiply V5 by *r* (to be repeated *m* times)
V3 − V7 → V3	Subtract 1 from *m* (i.e., count loops)
IF V3 > 0, GO BACK 2 LINES	Repeat above ("loop") *m* times—compute: r^m
V1 × V5 → V5	Multiply by coefficient *a*

```
    V6 × V2 → V6              Compute: rⁿ (by repeated multiply-
                             ing again)
      V4 − V7 → V4
IF V4 > 0, GO BACK 2
LINES
      V5 + V6 → V8           Add the two terms
PRINT V8                     Print the final results
STOP
```

doughnut, with the forty gears for each numeral stacked a few inches apart on a brass rod about ten feet high.

The mill consists of more than a hundred such columns, arranged in a circular pattern four or five feet across. The store contains another hundred or so columns in a double row extending out to one side of the mill. All of this, of course, is riddled with levers and ratchets, pinions and interlocks, making sure everything turns when (and only when) it should—including sophisticated precautions against wear and backlash. Recent analyses suggest that the parts being manufactured in Babbage's shop were both accurate and strong enough for a working Engine. Completed, the whole thing would have been about the size and weight of a small railway locomotive, though far more complicated and expensive.

Programs for the Analytical Engine are not kept in the store but are encoded on sequences of punched cards, strung together with ribbons. The ribbons enable the machine to back up and repeat a group of instructions over and over, which is essential for implementing loops. This basic arrangement was inspired by a system used to control the brocaded patterns woven by Jacquard looms, and that fact, in turn, inspired Lady Lovelace to a famous simile:

We may say most aptly, that the Analytical Engine *weaves algebraic patterns* just as the Jacquard-loom weaves flowers and leaves.

And just so does a mind weave general symbolic patterns—if Artificial Intelligence is right about us.

Turing Machines and Universality

Alan Turing (1912–1954), like Babbage an English mathematician (but not so cranky), is prominent in the history of computing on several counts. We have already reviewed the famous "Turing test," which he proposed in 1950 in an influential discussion of machine intelligence. Prior to that, during and immediately after the second world war, he made major contributions to the pioneering British development of electronic computers.[4] And most important, before the war (while still a graduate student, in fact), Turing produced the first mathematically sophisticated theory of computation, including some astonishing and profound discoveries about machine capabilities.[5]

Crucial to these theoretical findings was the invention of a new kind of computer—a new basic architecture—comprising what are now called *Turing machines*. There are infinitely many (possible) specific Turing machines, no one of which is terribly significant by itself; what matters are the overall category of such devices and various general theorems that Turing proved about them.

Before proceeding, we might mention that, like his predecessor, Turing never actually built any of his machines; but the reasons are entirely different. The Analytical Engine is extraordinarily large and complicated, near the limits of what could be understood, let alone constructed, in its time. Turing machines, on the other hand, are amazingly simple; moreover, though they can be arbitrarily large, they are typically fairly small. Beneath this surface contrast lies a deep difference in essential goals. Whereas Babbage intended his Engines to be useful for practical purposes, Turing was interested only in abstract theoretical questions. Therefore Turing's designs are elegant to describe and convenient to prove things about, but utterly impractical to use. Hence building one, though easy, would be pointless.

A Turing machine consists of two parts: a *head* and a *tape* (figure 1). The tape is just a passive storage medium: it is divided along its length into squares, each of which can hold one token (from some prespecified finite alphabet). We assume that the number of tape-squares available is unlimited but that only a finite segment of them is occupied at any one time; that is, all the rest are empty

Figure 1   *Diagram of a Turing Machine*

or contain only a special blank token. The tape is also used for input and output, by writing tokens onto it before the machine is started and then reading what remains after it halts.

The head is the active part of the machine, hopping back and forth along the tape (or pulling the tape back and forth through it) one square at a time, reading and writing tokens as it goes. At any given step, the head is "scanning" some particular square on the tape, and that's the only square it can read from or write to until it steps to another one. Also at each step, the head itself is in some particular *internal state* (from a prespecified finite repertoire of states). This state typically changes, from one step to the next; but under certain conditions, the head will enter a special "halt" state, in which case the machine stops—leaving its output on the tape.

What the head does at any step is fully determined by two factors:

1. the token it finds in the square it is scanning; and
2. the internal state it is currently in.

And these two factors determine each of three consequences:

1. what token to write on the present square (replacing whatever was previously there);
2. what square to scan next (the same one, or the one immediately to the right or left); and
3. what internal state to be in for the next step (or whether to halt).

So the entire functioning of a Turing machine (i.e., of the head) can be specified in a single, two-dimensional chart, with one row for each token that the head might find and one column for each state that it might be in. Each entry in the chart simply specifies the above three actions, as determined by that token and that state. (See box 2 for examples.)

Turing machines are easy to describe as "automatic games." The tape, clearly, is the playing field, and the tokens on it are the game tokens. The various internal states correspond to inner players, each of whom is very narrow. A player can read the current token, and, depending on what she finds, replace that token with another (of the same or a different type), and then tell the referee which way to move the tape, and which player to call on next. The inner referee is even dimmer: he merely starts with player 1 and then moves the tape and calls on players as they themselves request—until somebody says HALT.

With the idea of a Turing machine, we can describe a milestone of mathematical history—a proposal put forward in various ways by Turing and others around 1936. Recall the problem of finite playability: in a formal system, the rules must be "followable by players that are indisputably finite." Unfortunately this condition is somewhat vague; so it's not perfectly clear just which systems or rules satisfy it. In the mid-thirties a number of mathematicians were worried about this question, and several quite different criteria were suggested. Each was gratifyingly rigorous and intuitively plausible; moreover, it was soon established that they are all theoretically equivalent—hence the plausibility of each augments that of all the others. Moreover, every plausible criterion since proposed has also been proven equivalent.

As a result, essentially all mathematicians now accept *Turing's thesis* that these mutually supporting criteria do rigorously capture

Box 2
Two Simple Turing Machines

In the charts below, the states are numbered across the top, and the alphabet is listed down the left. Corresponding to each state and token is either a three-character entry in the chart or the word "HALT." The first character is the token to be written; the second character is an L or an R, for move left or move right; and the third character is the number of the next state.

Example 1   ARTHUR:

	1	2
__	__R2	HALT
A	AL1	BR2
B	BL1	AR2
C	CL1	CR2

ARTHUR has three types in his alphabet (besides the blank, which is indicated by an underscore: __). We assume that he starts in state 1, scanning some square in the midst of a string of A's, B's, and C's. First, he just moves to the left, not changing anything on the tape (state 1). But when he gets to the left end of the string (the first blank), he switches to state 2, and starts moving right, converting all A's to B's and B's to A's (while leaving C's alone). At the right end of the string, he stops.

Example 2   BERTHA:

	1	2	3	4	5	6	7	8	9
__	HALT	HALT	__L5	AR7	__R1	__R1	AR8	AL9	__R1
A	AR2	AR3	AR4	AR3	*L6	AL5	AR8	AL9	AL9
*	*R1	*R2	*R3	*R4	*L5	*L6	AR8	AR9	*L9

BERTHA is more complicated but also more fun to figure out. We assume she starts in state 1, at the left end of a string of A's and asterisks. First, she moves to the right end of the string, not changing anything, but keeping track of A's. If she found one or no A's along the way (states 1 and 2), she halts. Otherwise, if she found an even number of A's (finishing in state 3), she goes back to the beginning, converting every second A to an asterisk (states 5 and 6), and starts over; but if she found an odd number of A's (finishing in state 4), she puts three more A's on the right end of the string (states 4, 7, and 8), before returning and starting over (state 9).

Now check this: if the number of A's in the initial string happens *not* to be a multiple of 3, BERTHA will methodically eliminate all but one of them and halt gracefully; otherwise she will land helplessly in an infinite loop, and never rest.

the intuitive idea of finite playability.[6] There are, of course, as many ways to spell this out as there are explicit criteria; we sketched one in our discussion of algorithms. Another (and more rigorous) formulation is as follows:

TURING'S THESIS: For any deterministic automatic formal system whatever, there exists a formally equivalent Turing machine.

In other words, no automatic formal system can do anything (nonrandom) that Turing machines can't do; in principle, Turing machines are the only automatic systems we ever need. Note that this is called a "thesis" (and not a "theorem") because it is not amenable to proof; strictly, it is a proposal about what "deterministic automatic formal system"—especially the "finite playability" clause—really means.

So far we have not mentioned programming, but some Turing machines can be programmed so as to mimic others. The gist of the idea is to encode a description of the machine being imitated and use that as (part of) the input for the imitator. The latter will read this description, do a lot of computing, and, from time to time, make a move (in a reserved part of its tape) exactly equivalent to the next move that the former would make. (The equivalence may involve some transliteration, of course, if the two machines don't happen to use the same alphabet.) The encoded description of the first machine is then functioning as a program for the second.

Suppose, for instance, that the tape of some machine, say MOM, has squares tinted alternately pink and light blue. (These are only for our convenience; MOM herself is color-blind.) We then encode the description of some other machine—call it BABY—into a sequence of pink squares only. This description is essentially just BABY's two-dimensional chart (as discussed above), stretched out into a single line, with a little punctuation thrown in to avoid confusion. So exactly what BABY would do for any given state and scanned token is *explicitly listed* somewhere in this sequence on MOM's pink squares. The blue squares are reserved as a surrogate for BABY's own tape. Now all MOM has to do is keep track of BABY's successive tape positions and internal states (she uses some extra pink squares as a scratch pad for this purpose), read the corresponding blue square, look up BABY's response in her list, and then go do it.

Of course, we have yet to show that any machines can really be such MOMs. Turing, however, did even better: he proved that some Turing machines are *SUPER-MOMs*—or, in his more decorous terms, *universal machines*:

TURING'S PROOF: There exist universal Turing machines that can mimic, move for move, any other Turing machine whatever.

If you have just one universal Turing machine (and divine patience), then, in principle, you never need any other Turing machine for any other purpose. For, suppose there were some other Turing machine you needed: you could just take its standard description (chart), transliterate the alphabet, code it up for your SUPER-MOM, and then pay attention to only her blue squares. The moves being made on those squares are *exactly* the moves

Box 3
Minsky's Universal Turing Machine

"Most" Turing machines (including, e.g., those in box 2 are *not* universal. Still, there remain indefinitely many designs that are universal, and the question arises: Which design is "simplest"? Defining 'simple' is, of course, hard; but for Turing machines a widely accepted measure is the product of the number of internal states times the number of token types in the alphabet. (This is because there are easy technical tricks for reducing either, at the expense of increasing the other.) By this measure, the simplest universal Turing machine known was discovered by an American computer scientist, Marvin Minsky (1927–). It has four symbols (including the blank) and seven states—for a winning product of twenty-eight. Here it is.

	1	2	3	4	5	6	7
Y	__L1	__L1	YL3	YL4	YR5	YR6	__R7
__	__L1	YR2	HALT	YR5	YL3	AL3	YR6
1	1L2	AR2	AL3	1L7	AR5	AR6	1R7
A	1L1	YR6	1L4	1L4	1R5	1R6	__R2

Not surprisingly, the proof that this astonishingly simple chart defines a truly universal machine is itself fairly difficult and lengthy; the reader is referred to Minsky (1967, section 14.8) for the details. I present it here purely as a work of art.

(as transliterated) that the other machine would have made on its tape—so, in effect, you have that other machine already.

Needless to say, Turing's thesis and Turing's proof complement one another splendidly. According to the former, Turing machines are the only automatic formal systems we ever need; and, according to the latter, we only ever need one Turing machine—a universal one. Put these ideas together, and our one SUPER-MOM can do the work of all possible (deterministic) automatic formal systems. You might suppose that such powerful, general-purpose systems would have to be quite complicated; but that's not true (see box 3 for a specimen). What they are is *slow*. The encoded description of a Turing machine (e.g., BABY) is really just a transcription of a number of primitive rules into a very regimented form. So all MOM needs is a few basic abilities enabling her to decode and follow arbitrary rules in this specific form—and lots of time.

Since Turing's original proof, it has been discovered that there are many other possible architectures for universal formal systems, including, in fact, Babbage's. In the remainder of this chapter, we will look at three more universal programmable architectures, each quite different from the others (and from Turing machines) and each widely used in practice today.

The Ubiquitous von Neumann Machine

Although John von Neumann (1903–1957) was born and educated in Hungary, he moved to the United States as a young man, which nicely symbolizes several transitions in our story. So far our main characters have been Europeans, but from now on they'll be Americans; moreover, von Neumann's own interest in computers blossomed at about the same time as U.S. domination of the field, basically after World War II. This period also saw the earliest *practical* general purpose computers, a development in which von Neumann (and the U.S.) played a major role. Finally, those were the days when computer science itself began to mushroom, with dozens and soon hundreds of people all working more or less together. As a result, associating particular ideas with particular individuals becomes more tenuous and difficult. Babbage, for instance, was truly a lonesome hero, whose ideas are his alone; and Turing machines are wholly the invention of one man, even though several contemporaneous systems turned out to be mathematically equivalent. What is now called "the von Neumann architecture," on the other hand, actually evolved over some years, with numerous individual contributions that are not always clearly separable. This trend will become more evident as we proceed.

Von Neumann, like most computer pioneers, was trained in mathematics; but unlike the others, he always remained primarily a mathematician. (Though he did manage to squeeze in some brilliant, original work in quantum mechanics and economics— the famous "theory of games"—along the way.) His involvement with computers began almost accidentally, as a consultant for the ENIAC project, which, at the time, was easily the largest computer in the world. Reflection, by von Neumann and others, on ENIAC's weaknesses culminated in the IAS (Institute for Advanced Study) computer, which, though smaller, was more powerful and much easier to program and which proved to be the basis of many subsequent designs.

Crucial to a von Neumann machine is a large memory that can be accessed in either of two different ways: relatively or absolutely. *Accessing* memory is finding a particular location in it, so that any token there can be read and/or replaced. The two modes of access are analogous to two ways of specifying a particular building in a city. *Relative access* is specifying a new location in terms of its relation to the current one. Thus, in giving directions to a stranger, we often say things like: "Go down two blocks, make a left, and it's the second door on your right." That tells the person where the place is from here, that is, relatively. Similarly, in computer memory, you can specify the next location to use (read or write) in terms of its relation to one you've just finished using. For instance, a Turing machine tape is accessible (only) relatively: the next square to be scanned is always specified relative to the present square (it's the same or right next door). Notice that, for relative access, the memory locations must all be organized in some regular way (such as the linear ordering of a Turing tape), and at each moment the machine must be "at" some particular location (e.g., the square now being scanned).

Absolute access (also called *random access*) is specifying a particular location with a unique name (or number). The post office, for example, identifies buildings by unique addresses (1234 Main Street or Cathedral of Learning, Pittsburgh); similarly, phone calls are routed absolutely, with unique phone numbers. Absolute access does not require any organized structure or "current" location, as long as each possible target can be reached reliably by name. The store of Babbage's Analytical Engine, for instance, is accessible (only) absolutely; the variable columns all have individual names (which happen to be numerals), but they are not related to one another in any usable manner.

The main memory of a von Neumann machine is not only accessible in both these ways, but is also used for two quite different jobs; and this is surprisingly important. First, the memory holds the tokens to be operated upon: initial data (if any), intermediate values, and then the final results, ready for output. Thus if the system were programmed to sort lists alphabetically, the memory would first be loaded with the original list, subsequently contain partially alphabetized lists, and end up holding the final list. This is just like Babbage's store, except that the latter was designed primarily for numerical data and didn't allow relative access. Relative access is useful if the data itself is structured (like a list or an array): the machine can go (absolutely) to the beginning of the data and then move through it item by item (relatively).

The other use of the same main memory is to hold the program that the machine is executing. Von Neumann programs are branched schedules, basically like Babbage programs, except that the latter were encoded on strings of punched cards rather than held in the store with the variables. Those cards could be accessed (only) relatively; that is, the string could be advanced or backed up by so many cards (e.g., for repetitive loops), but there was no way to access an arbitrary card by name. A von Neumann machine also generally accesses its program relatively, either step by step in a straight schedule or back and forth by specified numbers of steps (in loops).

Where the von Neumann architecture really shines, however, is in the use of absolute access to implement subroutines. A *subroutine* is a "mini-program" that a larger program can invoke at any point *as if it were a single step.* Suppose, for instance, that your main program (a big record-keeping system, say) needs to alphabetize various lists at various times. One possibility is to insert a complete alphabetizing routine into the program at each point where it might be needed; but that's clearly wasteful. A much better strategy is to include only one copy of the routine, at some agreed location where it can always be found. Whenever the main program needs to alphabetize something, it just branches over to this handy subroutine, which then branches back when it's done.

The trick, of course, lies in these two branches, especially the second. Since the subroutine itself remains at a fixed (absolute) location but gets *called* (branched to) from all different parts of the program, it is most easily called by name (address). Just as important, when the routine is finished, it must *return* (branch back) to wherever it was called from so that execution can resume where it left off. But this raises a delicate question: how does the subroutine know where to branch back to, given that it might have been called from anywhere? The answer is to use another prearranged location to store the return address. Then whenever the program calls a subroutine, it puts its own current address in this special place before branching. When the subroutine is finished, it automatically gets the program address from that prearranged place and uses it to branch back (absolutely). (See box 4 for further details.)

Babbage's Analytical Engine cannot use this clever subroutine technique, for two different reasons. First, it can access portions of its program (the strings of cards) only relatively; but the above subroutine branches use absolute access. Second, the return addresses have to be different on different occasions (because the subroutines can be called from different places in the program). That means they have to be alterable (rewritable) by the machine during execution of the program. But Babbage's cards were permanently punched; programs could be changed only by punching new cards and stringing them together again manually. Other early systems (e.g., the ENIAC) were like Babbage's in this regard. But a von Neumann machine can read, write, and use *addresses* (not just data) that are stored in main memory and that, therefore, are easily altered by the machine itself while the program is running. Consequently, absolute subroutine calls (and returns) are feasible and convenient; in fact this is the primary architectural advance of von Neumann's design.[7]

When Babbage and Turing machines are described as automatic formal games, the role of the inner referee is fairly trivial. But von Neumann machines have a more elaborate structure, and the referee therefore has more to do. His job is to tell the inner players whose turn it is and which tokens they can play with—that is, which primitive operations to carry out when and what they

Box 4
The Return-Address Stack

The return-from-subroutine problem is subtler than it looks. In the first place, if there is only one prearranged location to store the return address, then only one subroutine can be called at a time; in particular, one subroutine couldn't in turn call a further "sub-subroutine," which would often be very convenient. A partial solution (and the standard approach in von Neumann's day) is to set aside a separate location for the return address for each subroutine; then each can find its way back independently of the others.

This is still limiting, however, because any given subroutine can still be called only once at a time; that is, a subroutine cannot call *itself* as a sub-subroutine. (That may sound like a bizarre idea, but it's actually quite feasible and useful; compare the discussion of *recursion* in the next section.) A general solution of the problem (invented in the mid-fifties by Allen Newell and Cliff Shaw) is to use a special kind of memory, called a *stack*. This is a "last-in-first-out" memory, like a stack of letters on your desk that you access only from the top. Thus every time you get a letter that needs to be answered, you throw it on top of the stack; and every time you get a chance to answer letters, you take them from the top of the stack. For correspondence this may not be a wonderful method, because the poor guy who wrote you first gets answered last. But it has an important advantage for subroutine returns.

Here's how it works. Whenever a portion of your program calls a subroutine, it first puts its return address on the top of the stack and then branches. Whenever any subroutine finishes its job, it removes whatever address is on top of the stack and branches back there. The result is that any subroutine always returns automatically to the most recent call that has not yet been answered. Since each return address is removed from the stack as it is used, the return address that remains on top of the stack (if any) is automatically the one put there previously for the subroutine that called the sub-

subroutine that just finished. Thus subroutine calls can be *nested* (subroutines calling sub-subroutines and so on) arbitrarily and without restriction. (Notice that the stack memory itself uses a particular sort of relative access.)

should operate on. Since branching directives (including subroutine calls and returns) control the sequence of execution, they are the province of the referee. In other words, branches are not operations (token manipulations) that players perform, but shifts that the referee makes in determining which player to call on next. In these terms, then, it is the referee's business to keep track of all subroutine calls and returns and to see that execution resumes where it left off; hence the special return-address storage (the "stack") is actually a private little memory belonging exclusively to the referee.

Subroutines are important not only because they are efficient, but also because they allow programs to be more *modular*. That is, once a subroutine for a particular task has been written and "debugged" (corrected and made to work right), then it can be used at any time without further ado. As a result, the problem of writing a large program, composed mainly of lots of different subroutines, can be broken down into a number of smaller and more manageable subproblems—namely, getting each of the various subroutines to do what it's supposed to do separately. Furthermore, once useful subroutines have been written and debugged for one program, they can then be borrowed wholesale for use in other programs, without the headache of writing and debugging them all over again.

This idea is in turn the foundation of another, which is perhaps the backbone of all modern programming: *higher-level machines* (so-called "programming languages"). A general selection of widely useful subroutines can be collected together to form a sort of "library," which any programmer can then draw upon whenever necessary; it saves a lot of work. Then all you need is an automatic librarian to take care of the calls and other miscellaneous bookkeeping, and the subroutines themselves are tantamount to new primitive operations, any of which can be invoked with a single instruction (they become new "players" in a fancier game). In effect, you have a new and more powerful computer. This is the essence of such familiar systems as BASIC, Pascal, FORTRAN, COBOL, etc.

These particular *virtual machines* ("languages") all happen to be roughly von Neumann in architecture: their programs are all branched schedules, with loops, named subroutines, and so on. But that's just a coincidence. It's equally possible to write sub-routines and librarian/referees that give the new machine quite a different architecture. For instance, one could easily write a von Neumann machine program that exactly simulated a Babbage or Turing machine. Then, for all practical purposes, that new machine would be the one you worked with—writing programs for it, etc.—if, for some odd reason, you wanted to. This is precisely the situation we encountered earlier with SUPER-MOM Turing machines; in fact, von Neumann machines (with unlimited memory) are also universal machines, in exactly the sense that (some) Turing machines are.

Von Neumann universality, however, is far more important (in the real world) than Turing universality. For one thing, von Neumann machines are much easier to program; for another, they are much faster—they don't have to search back and forth along the tape, one square at a time. And it turns out that von Neumann architectures are easy to build out of basic electronic components. This last point is less a comparison with Turing machines (which are almost trivial to build) than with certain other universal ar-chitectures, which, though easy to program and fast enough, are hard to build. The upshot is that virtually all (programmable) computers in current production have a basically von Neumann architecture at the hardware level.

In the next two sections, we will look at two quite different architectures that are widely used in Artificial Intelligence work. Theoretically, of course, it doesn't matter how they are built or implemented as long as they always make legal moves in legal positions (medium independence again); but it gives some pause to remember that (at present anyway) they are all actually being simulated on von Neumann SUPER-MOMs.

McCarthy's LISP

In our survey of computer architects, John McCarthy (1927–) is the first native American and the last trained mathematician. Professionally, however, his interests soon focused on computer automata; and by 1956 he had coined the term "Artificial Intelligence" and had organized the fledgling field's very first scientific conference.[8] In 1958 he and Marvin Minsky founded the AI Lab at MIT and in 1963 he set up another out at Stanford. Both are now world centers of AI research. In the meantime, he also developed the first "time-sharing" operating systems—the ingenious (and now common) arrangement by which one central computer can simultaneously support many independent users.

Our topic, however, is McCarthy's invention, in 1959, of a whole new kind of computer, named *LISP*.[9] McCarthy machines— as LISP systems might also be called—have a simple and elegant structure that is remarkably flexible and at the same time remarkably different from either Turing or von Neumann machines. Compared to these predecessors, LISP is distinctive in two main respects: its *memory organization* and its *control structure*. Though neither development is difficult to understand, each is peculiar enough to merit some explanation.

Memory Imagine a long line of tin cups strung on a chain and a plentiful supply of atomic tokens to put in the cups, one token per cup. Obviously it's a "memory" device. It works just like a Turing machine tape, if we assume that cups can be specified only by relative position and that the head can move down the chain only one cup at a time. On the other hand, if each cup also has a unique label ("address") and if the processor can jump any distance in a single step, then we have a von Neumann memory.[10] Notice that the two memories are organized just alike and differ only in the additional access mode of the von Neumann machine; in particular, the structure of each is:

1. LINEAR: the chain has no forks or junctions;
2. UNITARY: there is only one chain; and
3. FIXED in advance: the chain is always the same.

Are these structural features essential to computer memory? Not at all.

Imagine, in place of the tin cups, a huge stock of Y-connectors, piled loose in a heap. A *Y-connector* is a Y-shaped device with a base or plug on one end and two sockets set at angles on the other. One common variety allows you to put two light bulbs in a single fixture; and there are different kinds for joining garden hoses, electric cords, and so on. The important point is that the base of one Y-connector can be plugged or screwed into a socket on another; and this process can continue as long as you please, building up bizarre Y-connector *trees*. Each such tree will have one exposed base at the bottom (its *root*)[11] and any number of empty sockets around the top and nestled among the limbs. So just imagine labels on the roots of all the trees and atomic tokens plugged into all their empty sockets (like "leaves"), and you have the basic idea of LISP memory.

The Y-connectors (joints) in a LISP tree are called *nodes*. The atomic symbols in a tree's terminal sockets are also nodes (specifically *terminal* nodes); in fact, an atomic token all by itself can be a single-node tree (like a seedling, with one leaf and no branches). No socket in a LISP tree can ever be empty; but there is a special atomic token, *NIL*, that serves as a "blank" or "nothing" when necessary. One critical deviation from our analogy is that LISP nodes are not symmetrical: the branches (sockets) are explicitly designated "left" and "right," respectively. Hence any node in any tree can be specified by a combination of absolute and relative access: name the tree and then give a path—a sequence of left and right turns—to that node from the root.

Distinguishing left and right branches also makes it possible to define *lists* as special trees built as follows: take as many Y-connectors as there are items to be listed, line them up in a row and plug each into the right socket of its predecessor, plug the list *elements* into all the left sockets (in order, starting from the base), and plug NIL into the last right socket. (See figure 2.)

The contrasts with cup-chain memories are striking. LISP trees clearly aren't linear (though lists can do duty for linear structures, whenever necessary). Moreover, since many trees can be alive at once, the overall structure isn't unitary either. But, most important, the "shapes" of LISP trees aren't fixed in advance: they are built to order as needed (and thrown back on the heap when no longer needed). This has two subtle but significant consequences. First, since trees are not all the same shape but vary from case to case, the shapes themselves must be part of what the system "remembers." Thus cup-chain memories store only the contents of the cups; but LISP trees store not only their terminal tokens, but also the particular connections among all their nodes. Hence they are especially convenient for keeping track of complex structural relationships. Second, since the trees are built to order as the program runs, there's no need to know ahead of time exactly what they'll be like or even how big they'll grow; such details can be resolved on the spot, as the situation develops. Consequently, LISP programs can be extraordinarily flexible in response to widely differing conditions.

Control   To explain the distinctive control structure of LISP, we must shift analogies. *Control* is determining who does what when. Consider serving me breakfast: chilled orange juice and two fried eggs, please. Basic cooking skills ("primitive chefs") are not the issue here, but rather how they might be organized. In other words, we're mainly interested in the executive chef, the kitchen referee. In von Neumann's kitchen, the referee calls on specialists according to a schedule:

ORANGE
JUICE that orange;
CHILL that juiced stuff;
EGG
EGG
CRACK those eggs;
SKILLET
FRY those cracked things in that skillet;
SERVE that chilled stuff and those fried things.

Capital letters indicate which specialist to call on: the first line activates ORANGE, the orange-getting specialist; the second line then tells JUICE, the juicing specialist, to do his thing (on whatever

Figure 2   Examples of LISP Trees

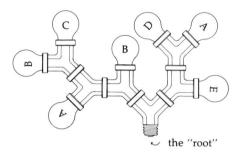

This is a simple Y-connector tree.

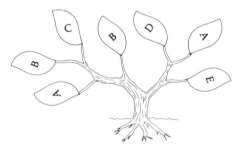

Here's the same tree, looking somewhat more botanical.

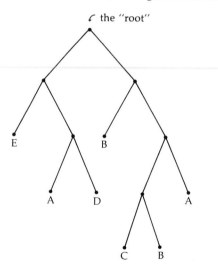

Here it is again, as a computer scientist would draw it. (For dark reasons of their own, computer scientists always draw trees upside down.)

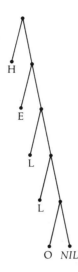

This is a special sort of tree, called a "list." (The NIL just plugs up the last right socket; it's not one of the items listed.)

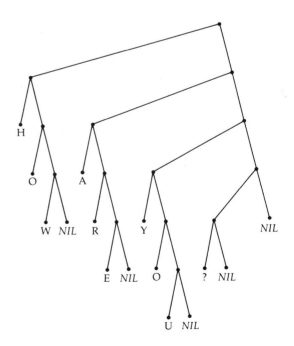

This is also a list; but the items listed happen to be lists themselves—so we have a list of lists.

ORANGE got); and so on. Notice that the routine is basically linear and that its order reflects priority in time.

What happens in McCarthy's kitchen? The same primitive actions are performed in the same order; but they are arranged, so to speak, from the opposite end. The McCarthy referee always starts from a required result and works back to prerequisites. Thus she begins by telling SERVE to serve chilled orange juice and two fried eggs and then waits to see if he needs anything. Predictably, he does: namely, orange juice from CHILL and two eggs from FRY. So she accepts these as new (subsidiary) requirements and calls in turn on CHILL and FRY—waiting now to see what they might need (orange from JUICE, eggs from CRACK, etc.).

So far everybody's just passing the buck, and nothing is actually getting done. But when (at JUICE's behest) ORANGE finally gets called on, the buck stops: ORANGE is a simple stockboy who requires no preparations; he just gets an orange and hands it over. When that happens, however, the referee can start fulfilling prior requests: thus, remembering who wanted the orange, she gives it to JUICE, who can now perform and return the orange juice. Then, remembering who wanted that, she passes it to CHILL, and so on, until, eventually, SERVE has everything he requested and can bring ME breakfast. This is the essence of LISP control.

Notice that the structure is not basically linear but hierarchical and that the primary ordering is not by time but by results and prerequisites: when a specialist is engaged, he can't deliver his product without first engaging others to prepare his materials. Two dimensions show it best:

$$
\text{SERVE} \begin{cases} \text{CHILL} \begin{cases} \text{JUICE} \begin{cases} \text{ORANGE} \end{cases} \\ \\ \text{FRY} \begin{cases} \text{CRACK} \begin{cases} \text{EGG} \\ \text{EGG} \end{cases} \\ \\ \text{SKILLET} \end{cases} \end{cases} \end{cases}
$$

The order of engaging is left to right, and the order of delivery is then right to left; vertical columns just list the engaged preparers, when there's more than one.

In mathematical terminology, specialists who interact in this way are called *functions*, their prerequisites (if any) are called *arguments*, and the results they return are called *values*. Functions that require no arguments are *constants*; they always return the same value. Mathematicians allow the arguments and values of functions to be anything at all, as long as the following essential condition is met:

FUNCTIONS: For each allowable argument (or combination of arguments), there is *one and only one* (permanently assigned) value.

For instance, MOTHER[x] is a perfectly acceptable function (taking people as arguments) because each person has exactly one (permanent) mother. But UNCLE[x] is not an acceptable function because some people have no uncles and others have many. LISP primitives (and programs) are all functions, but they differ from their mathematical counterparts in two basic respects: they are active players who automatically evaluate themselves when called upon, and their (uninterpreted) arguments and values must always be LISP trees.

Whenever a LISP function gets an argument, it assumes that the argument is actually specified via another function, which therefore ought to be evaluated first. In the kitchen we called this "passing the buck"; but a symbolic example will illustrate the real point:

THIRD LETTER OF [SECOND WORD OF [THIS BOOK'S TITLE]]

What is the value of that function for that argument? Well, the argument is:

SECOND WORD OF [THIS BOOK'S TITLE]

Is its third letter C? No, because the actual argument is not that very expression but rather what it specifies: namely, the *value* of the function *SECOND WORD OF*[ ], when applied to the argument:

THIS BOOK'S TITLE

So is the intended word *BOOK'S* (with third letter *O*)? No, for the same reason: *THIS BOOK'S TITLE* is also a function, specifying a value. Fortunately, however, it's a *constant* function, with no arguments. Therefore, unlike the first two functions, this one can be evaluated straightaway, without evaluating anything else first. (The third letter of the second word of its value is *T*.)

How do you program a LISP machine? Certainly not by writing out a sequential schedule, as for a von Neumann machine. Instead, you program it by *defining* new functions in terms of other functions that are already defined. The general idea is familiar from algebra; for instance, the square of a number can be defined in terms of multiplication:

SQUARE[x]   = def   TIMES[x,x]

Or, back in the kitchen, a BREAKFAST function could be defined in terms of SERVE, FRY, SKILLET, etc. Defined functions are "management" specialists: like all functions, they return values for given arguments, but they do it entirely by telling the referee who else to call on, making no (other) contribution of their own.

Obviously not all functions can be defined in terms of others; there have to be some primitive functions to start with. Real-world LISP systems provide lots of convenient primitives, including many (naturally interpreted as) standard arithmetic functions, etc. But quintessential LISP, out of which all the rest can be constructed, comprises only six primitive functions:

LEFT[x]   RIGHT[x]   JOIN[x,y]
EQUAL[x,y]   ATOM[x]   IF[x,y,z]

Each of these functions takes only LISP trees as arguments and returns only LISP trees as values (remember that single atomic tokens count as "seedling" trees). With these primitives, it is possible to manipulate (build, modify, destroy) LISP trees of arbitrary complexity, in any algorithmically specifiable way; hence it is possible to define a single complex function that will return any such transform as its value, for any input. LISP is therefore universal.

The first three primitives are used for assembling and disassembling arbitrary trees. The value of LEFT[x] is whatever is screwed into the left socket of the Y-connector at the very base of (the value of) x; in effect, it returns the left half of its argument. If the argument doesn't have a left half (because it's only an atomic seedling), then LEFT[x] reports an error and quits. Needless to say, RIGHT[x] is just the same, except that it returns the right half. JOIN[x,y] takes two arguments, and, not surprisingly, puts them together; more specifically, it gets a new Y-connector, plugs (the values of) its first and second arguments into the left and right sockets, respectively, and returns the new tree thus constructed.

The other three functions provide LISP's alternative to testing and branching. EQUAL[x,y] returns the special token TRUE if (the values of) its two arguments are the same; otherwise it returns FALSE. ATOM[x] returns TRUE if (the value of) its argument is a single atomic token; otherwise FALSE. IF[x,y,z] might be clearer if we wrote it as IF[x, (THEN)y, (ELSE)z], because what it does is return the value of either its second or its third argument, depending on whether (the value of) its first argument is TRUE or FALSE. Thus IF[__, __, __] does not "branch" LISP around to different parts of a schedule of instructions (there is no such schedule to branch around in). Rather, it determines which functions actually get evaluated by asking the referee for the value of either its second or its third argument (but not both).

LISP is distinctive in its dynamic, tree-like memory organization and its function-application control scheme. Moreover, these are related in a beautiful inner unity: the hierarchical structure of functions applied to arguments which are themselves functions, etc. is essentially a *tree*. More specifically, LISP represents functions with their arguments as *lists*, with the function name as the first element of the list and the arguments following in order. Since those arguments in turn are function calls, they too will be represented as lists, and so on—making the whole structure a list of lists of lists . . . which is to say, a tree. In other words, LISP programs and LISP memory units ("data structures") have exactly the same underlying form.

Box 5
Recursion and Universality

Inasmuch as LISP machines have the power of *universal* Turing machines—the power, that is, to mimic any other computer—they must be able to repeat a specified process over and over (an arbitrary number of times) until some condition is met. Von Neumann machines accomplish this with loops and conditional branches. McCarthy machines rely instead on *recursive definitions*: in defining a function, that function itself can be used, as long as there's an escape clause that eventually stops the regress. To put it somewhat paradoxically, it's okay for a definition to be "circular" as long as it's not circular forever.[12]

Suppose, for example, you needed to count the atoms in LISP trees. This task is naturally conceived recursively: the atom count for any tree is either 1 (if the whole tree is just a single atom) or else the sum of the atom counts for its left and right halves. So we can define a simple function:

COUNTATOMS[x] = def
IF[ATOM[x],
(THEN) 1,
(ELSE) COUNTATOMS[LEFT[x]] + COUNTATOMS[RIGHT[x]]]

This definition is recursive, because the function COUNTATOMS[__] is not only being defined, but also being used in that very definition.

But notice how it works: if the given tree is atomic, then the function returns 1 immediately; otherwise it calls (repeats) itself for each half of the argument. Moreover, it can keep recalling itself (for ever smaller halves of halves, etc.), an arbitrary number of times. Sooner or later, however, there won't be any smaller halves: every branch ultimately ends with terminal atoms. Then COUNTATOMS[__] does not call itself again but simply returns 1 to its predecessor; and when the predecessors start getting numbers back, they can start re-

> turning sums to their own predecessors, until, at last, the original call to COUNTATOMS[__] gets back a value.
>
> What keeps this "circular" definition from being vicious? Two things: first, every time COUNTATOMS[__] turns around and calls itself, it does so with a simpler argument; and second, the arguments eventually get so simple that COUNT-ATOMS[__] can handle them directly, without calling itself again (that's the necessary escape clause).

Newell's Production Systems

Allen Newell (1927–   ) considered a career in mathematics, but reconsidered. The Rand Corporation, a high-flying "think tank" out of California, seemed a lot more exciting than graduate school in New Jersey; so off he went.[13] There he met Cliff Shaw, a farsighted computer pioneer (who had joined Rand the same year, 1950), and Herbert Simon, a rising star in economics and management science (who visited from Carnegie Tech in the summer of 1952). By 1955 the three of them had more or less invented general symbol manipulators, heuristic search, and Artificial Intelligence.[14] It was not until the 1960s, however, after Simon had lured him back to academia, that Newell's thoughts turned to *production systems*—the distinctive computers that might fairly be called "Newell machines."[15]

The active players in a production system—the chefs in Newell's kitchen—are called *productions*. Like their Turing and von Neumann counterparts (but unlike LISP functions), productions all act on a common linear memory, called the *workspace*. But they differ from their colleagues in determining who works where when. Each Newell chef constantly surveys the entire workspace, looking for a certain *pattern* of prerequisite ingredients; whenever he finds his particular pattern, he goes there and performs his specialty (with those ingredients). For instance, one modest expert might look exclusively for a pint of whipping cream, flanked by a whisk and a cold copper bowl. Unless and until that appears, he does nothing; but as soon as it does, he rushes over, whips the cream in the bowl, and discards the whisk. Most such actions modify the patterns in the workspace, which may then "satisfy" some other specialist, such as the cake decorator, who has been waiting patiently for a bowl of whipped cream. And thus the processing continues.

Two things are remarkable about this procedure. In the first place, locations in the workspace are not specified either absolutely (by "name") or relatively (how to get there from "here"); rather, they are identified by their *contents*, that is, in terms of whatever is currently stored there. So if the paradigm of absolute access is a city address (1234 Main Street) and that of relative access is directions (go north six blocks, and east two), then the paradigm of content-based access would be a description of the destination: find a yellow brick split-level with pink curtains, wherever it may be. In a production system, of course, these described contents are nothing other than the patterns for which the various specialists are looking.

Second, nobody tells productions when to act; they wait until conditions are ripe and then *activate themselves*. By contrast, chefs in the other kitchens merely follow orders: Turing units are nominated by their predecessors, von Neumann operations are all prescheduled, and LISP functions are invoked by other functions. Production system teamwork is more laissez-faire: each production acts on its own, when and where its private conditions are satisfied. There is no central control, and individual productions never directly interact. All communication and influence is via patterns in the common workspace—like anonymous "to whom it may concern" notices on a public bulletin board. Accordingly, overall direction emerges only as the net effect of many independent decisions—reminiscent of an open market, guided by Adam Smith's "invisible hand."

Fastidious readers may have noticed a couple of loose ends. What happens, for instance, if two productions find their conditions satisfied at the same time? Assuming they can't both act at once, some arbitration procedure (referee) is needed. The simplest solution is to rank order the players and then always select the petitioner with highest priority. Imagine them all standing in line: the first one checks for his pattern and acts if he can; otherwise the second one gets to check; and so on. After any production is satisfied and acts, they start over again at the head of the line. In a similar vein, what happens if some chef's pattern actually occurs twice in the workspace? Which one should he use? Again, the easiest solution is a prior ordering: for example, the productions could always scan the workspace left-to-right, stopping at the first satisfactory pattern.[16]

How do you "program" a production system? By *constructing* (defining) productions; the productions themselves are the program. An unprogrammed production system is just an empty workspace, a referee, and a kit of primitives, out of which productions can be built. The programmer's job, then, is to put together a set of productions—each able to perform a certain action in certain circumstances—whose collective behavior will be that of the desired system. The "primitives" in the kit correspond roughly to von Neumann primitive operations or LISP primitive functions, but the way they're assembled into a composite system is entirely different.

Every production has two basic parts: a *condition* and an *action*. The definition of a production is essentially a rule (imperative) that says:

WHENEVER ⟨condition⟩ IS SATISFIED, PERFORM ⟨action⟩

or, more schematically:

⟨condition⟩ → ⟨action⟩

The condition is a pattern that might appear in the workspace, and the action is usually some modification of that pattern (but sometimes it's external output). Thus the primitive abilities needed are for various kinds of pattern recognition and then for modifying the patterns recognized.

For example, a system to simplify algebraic equations might contain a rule like the following:

"A + B = C + B" →   replace with: "A = C"

Here the quote marks indicate what's in the workspace itself, with the capital letters (A, B, and C) understood as placeholders for arbitrary strings of actual workspace tokens; hence the equation

$$2x + 4y(z - 14) = w - 3 + 4y(z - 14)$$

would reduce to

$$2x = w - 3$$

in a single application of the rule. This example presupposes some fairly classy recognition and matching capabilities—for instance, the ability to match the complex expression "$4y(z - 14)$" with "B" on both sides of the equation. But such facilities are common in production systems; and with them, many useful productions (including other algebraic simplifications) are easy to design and easy to understand.

In one way, Newell machines are throwbacks to Turing machines. For unlike LISP or von Neumann machines, Turing and Newell machines use no explicit "IF . . ."; rather, they have conditionalization built right into the architecture: *every* step is conditional. Thus which successor a Turing unit nominates always depends on which token it found on the tape; likewise, a production will self-activate only on condition that it finds its special pattern in the workspace. The point can also be put in terms of sequencing: von Neumann and McCarthy machines don't *need* to make a decision at each step because they have a "natural" order of execution "built in." A von Neumann machine automatically follows its schedule, and LISP automatically evaluates the arguments of each function before evaluating the function itself. Hence conditionals are needed only occasionally, to redirect the flow at critical junctures. Turing and Newell machines, by contrast, have no predisposed flow, so an explicit decision must be made for each step.

But Newell machines are far from just Turing machines warmed over: the basic spirit is entirely different. Turing's intent was to make the machine itself as simple as possible (just a few very

Box 6
Repetition in Production Systems

The production architecture, like the others we've discussed, is universal: for any symbolic algorithm, some production system can execute it. Hence production systems must be able to repeat arbitrarily, until some condition is met. In fact, repetition comes naturally to production systems; the hard part is stopping or avoiding it. Consider, for example, a system with just one production:

any integer, N $\longrightarrow$ increment: N

(Incrementing a number means increasing it by one.) If this system ever finds an integer to get started on, it will just sit and increment till the cows come home. Yet there is nothing (no branch instruction, loop, recursive definition, etc.) that tells the system to repeat; it just does. On the other hand, if you want it ever to stop (say, when it gets to 100), then you have to tell it, by adding another production, with higher priority:

any integer greater than 99 $\longrightarrow$ stop

(Alternatively, the test could be incorporated into the condition clause of the original production.)

As another illustration, imagine a workspace that can hold LISP-like trees, and a kit of primitives allowing tree manipulations. Then the following simple production system does the same job as the COUNTATOMS[___] function from box 5:

any atomic tree, A,
    and integer, N $\longrightarrow$ delete A and increment N
any tree, T $\longrightarrow$ replace with: LEFT[T] & RIGHT[T]
anything at all $\longrightarrow$ stop

The workspace initially contains the tree to be counted and

the numeral 0. The middle production repeatedly cuts trees in half, until it reduces them to their terminal atoms; meanwhile, the first production constantly sweeps up and discards those atoms, incrementing the counter each time. Notice again that the "recursion" or "looping" just takes care of itself—the "invisible hand." The last production never gets a chance until the first two have completely chopped up the original tree, counted the pieces, and swept them all away; then it stops the system.

primitive units, operating only on atomic tokens) and then let its programs be numbingly large and tedious. Production systems, by constrast, tend to have very powerful and sophisticated "primitives"—such as automatic finding and matching of complex patterns (with variable constituents)—which go naturally with pattern-based access and self-activating players. Accordingly, Newell programs are comparatively brief and elegant: each line does a lot.

Production systems promote a degree of "modularity" unrivaled by other architectures. A *module* is an independent subsystem that performs a well-defined task and interacts with the rest of the system only in certain narrowly defined ways. Thus the tape deck, preamp, etc. of a "component" stereo are modules. In LISP, user-defined functions serve as separate program modules; but they are not as independent as individual productions.[17] For any LISP function to evaluate, it must be called explicitly; and the caller must know not only when to call that function, but also its name, what arguments to provide, and what sort of value to expect back. Or rather, the programmer must keep track of all this for each situation where any particular function could (or should) be invoked.

A production, on the other hand, will activate itself when and where conditions are right, regardless of what any other production knows or decides. The point can be illustrated with a fanciful example. Suppose we're designing a robot taxi driver and everything is in place, except that we forgot about sirens. So now we have to add a feature: whenever the robot hears a siren, it should pull over until the danger is past. Depending on the architecture, that would involve a new subroutine, function, or production that checks memory for a SIREN report (from the "ears") and outputs a PULL OVER signal when it finds one.

How can this new unit be integrated into the rest of the system? Presumably the driver should respond to a siren (if any) before entering an intersection, before pulling out from a parking place, before changing lanes, and so on, as well as while driving along the road. Hence in a von Neumann or McCarthy machine, the routines or functions that perform all these activities would *each* have to be modified, so that they call on the new SIREN unit at appropriate moments. In a Newell machine, on the other hand, the SIREN production merely has to be added to the lineup, with a suitably high priority; no existing productions need be touched. The new one will just sit there quietly, doing nothing and bothering no one, until a siren comes along; then it will issue the PULL OVER signal all by itself.

Counterbalancing the obvious advantages of production modularity, however, are two limitations. In the first place, not every task is conveniently divisible into components that can be handled autonomously; that is, sometimes the subtasks must be explicitly coordinated, with particular information or instructions being directed to particular units at particular times. Such organization, while not impossible in production systems, is distinctly awkward compared with "centralized" subroutine or function calls. Second, production modularity is single-level; that is, in a production system, you don't build high-level modules out of lower-level modules, built out of still lower ones, and so on. All the productions are on a par, except for priority. LISP definitions, by contrast, are inherently hierarchical, and von Neumann programs often are.

Our primary goal in this chapter has been a broader view of what computers can be. Too often people unwittingly assume that all computers are essentially like BASIC, FORTRAN, or even Turing machines. Once it is appreciated that equally powerful (i.e., universal) architectures can be deeply and dramatically different, then suddenly the sky's the limit. Artificial Intelligence in no way claims that the mind is a Turing machine or a BASIC program—or any other kind of machine we've considered. It is true that, for reasons of convenience and flexibility, most AI programs happen to be written in LISP. But the virtual machines thus concocted are not LISP machines; in principle, they could be anything. It is also true that some workers suspect the mind itself may be organized rather like a production system, though one much more elaborate and sophisticated than the elementary structure reviewed here. The important point, however, is this: the mind could have a computational architecture all its own. In other words, from the perspective of AI, *mental architecture* itself becomes a new theoretical "variable," to be investigated and spelled out by actual cognitive science research.

The ENIAC, stretching in a large U around three walls of a room

5 Real Machines

Pre-AI

Computers have always been impressive. The Analytical Engine, with its clockwork precision and locomotive proportions, would have been a wonder of the world. ENIAC, the original electronic behemoth, had a front panel a hundred feet long, contained 18,000 vacuum tubes, weighed thirty tons, and took two and a half years to build.[1] That same period (mid-1940s) also saw a one-hundred-ton Differential Analyzer boasting a million feet of wire and a 760,000-part gear and ratchet monster (named "Bessie") that would have made Babbage weep for joy. These marvels were not only huge, but also "ultra-fast." ENIAC, the speed king of 1946, could do thirty-eight nine-digit divisions in a single second; indeed, it solved in just two hours a problem that allegedly would have taken a skilled person a hundred years. Small wonder the wide-eyed press resorted to phrases like "superhuman brain," "custom-built genius," and even "robot Einstein."[2]

Today, of course, you can buy the power of ENIAC for a few hours' wages and take it home in a paper bag. Recent "super-computers" are roughly a million times faster, with a million times as much main memory—all for about six times the price (in constant dollars).[3] Either way it's a performance/cost improvement of about 100,000 to 1. As a vivid comparison, if air travel had improved at the same rate over the same period, we would now hop from city to city in minutes, for less than a dollar.

In the early years the prospect of unprecedented computing power was thoroughly dazzling: it seemed that machines capable of all that people can do (and more) must be right around the corner. Scale alone, however, is not enough, as can be illustrated by reviewing a pair of false starts from the 1950s. The most celebrated is "systems" or "control theory," also dubbed *cybernetics* by mathematician Norbert Wiener (1948a,b). Consider a system, S, that is supposed to produce a certain output, O. In the real world, of course, S will be imperfect, which is to say the output will contain some error (it will not be exactly O). There are two basic ways to reduce this error:

1. build S better in the first place, with more accurate parts, more careful calibration, etc.; or
2. build S so that it measures its own output, detects any errors therein, and then automatically compensates for them.

Contemporary Cray 1 "supercomputer"

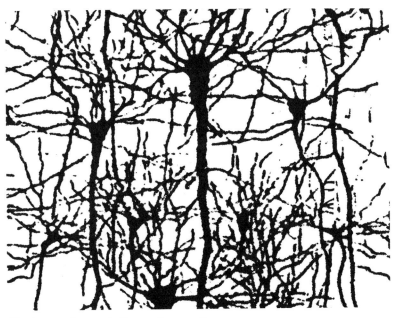

The human "computer": neural connections

Box 1
Brains Are "Big" Too

An adult human brain weighs only about three pounds, but it is extraordinarily complex. It contains approximately ten billion separate neurons. (These are the cells that do the real "work"; there are perhaps ten times as many other cells that hold everything together and take care of the housekeeping.) The neurons are highly interconnected, by means of tiny fibers reaching out and touching one another; though individual cells vary widely, they average something like a thousand interconnections each. That gives ten *trillion* neural connections per brain (plus or minus a few trillion, but who's counting?).

Comparing these numbers with computer hardware, however, is not at all straightforward. A single neuron can't do anything like 64-bit floating-point arithmetic; but, with a thousand connections, it "stores" far more than 64 bits of information. Moreover, this storage is of two sorts: the relatively permanent information structure implicit in which neurons are connected to which, and the more transitory storage in the changing operational state of the cell and its fibers. Though current computers have quite a bit of explicit, transitory storage ("memory"), there is, by comparison, exceedingly little information implicit in their structure.

Furthermore, all contemporary computers are *serial* processors, or nearly so; that is, only a comparative handful of components are actively doing anything at any one time—the rest are just waiting passively. But there is every reason to believe that brains function massively in *parallel*; millions or even billions of processes go on simultaneously. On the other hand, advanced semiconductors operate roughly a million times faster than neurons; and there is at least an approximate trade-off between speed and degree of parallelism.

Despite these difficulties in comparison, I think it safe to say that the brain is many orders of magnitude more complex than any present artifact. In one respect, this makes the project of Artificial Intelligence all the more daunting. But in another respect, it is reassuring, for it means that the limitations of current programs may not be fundamental; they may just show that we need more raw power to catch up with the brain.

Both approaches are potentially expensive; but, in fancy complicated systems, the second is much more effective.

The theory of self-compensating (or self-regulating) systems is the central topic of cybernetics; and its fundamental principle is *negative feedback* (essentially a highbrow name for "compensation," but see box 2 for more details). Feedback is a general and deep concept, with instances everywhere. Perhaps the most familiar is a thermostat, which keeps the temperature of a house approximately constant by monitoring the temperature and turning on the heat (or cooling) when it gets too cold (or hot). There are also numerous biological regulators, controlling various bodily pressures, potentials, concentrations, and so on.

Negative feedback is seductively analogous to *purpose*, in the following way. When we aim for a certain result and some intrusion throws us off, we try to adjust. Thus if constant temperature were my goal, I would tend to start the furnace when the room cooled off, just like a thermostat. And, superficially, the point seems to generalize: your garden falls behind in its battle with the insects, so you compensate by adding a little insecticide or switching to resistant varieties of plants. Those modifications tend to redress the output imbalance, so they seem like negative feedback. Then it's but a short step to seeing cybernetics as the science of all human action. "Of course," one piously acknowledges, "people are far more complicated than mere thermostats. But the essence of life is goal-seeking, and *that* is now explained by negative feedback."

Except it isn't. Cybernetics, as science, is a mathematical theory relating quantitative input and output displacements, affecting one another to known degrees with known delays, all expressed in differential equations as a function of time. Take away those equations and little remains but handwaving and amusing par-

Box 2
Negative Feedback

Let the *output* of a system be the variable or result that is of concern (e.g., the temperature); let the *input* be those external factors that affect the output (e.g., heat transfer through the walls and from the heating/cooling equipment). Then *feedback* is taking some part or consequence of the output and using it to modify the input (e.g., in response to the temperature, the thermostat turns the equipment on or off).

Feedback is *positive* if it tends to exaggerate output changes, thereby driving the value to an extreme. Feedback is *negative* if it tends to cancel output changes, thereby maintaining the value at some intermediate point. Thermostats, for example, are almost always connected for negative feedback: if the temperature falls, the heater comes on (bringing it back up); but if it rises, the refrigeration will cool it back down. One could, of course, connect a thermostat for positive feedback: if the temperature drops, the refrigeration comes on (making it even colder); whereas, if it rises above some value, the furnace drives it hotter still. Positive feedback is used, for instance, in designing switches: they tend to "click" all the way to the nearest stop and to avoid intermediate positions. But negative feedback is the most important concept.

I will give two examples, one abstract and elegant and the other more nitty gritty. Consider three balls: one resting on a flat, level surface; one resting at the bottom of a rounded valley; and one resting at the top of a rounded hill. All three are in *equilibrium*—that is, perfectly balanced—but they will behave differently if slightly perturbed. The first is in *neutral* equilibrium: if it rolled a little, that would introduce no new forces (no feedback). The second is in *stable* equilibrium: if it rolled a little, gravity would tend to pull it back down where it was (negative feedback). The third is in *unstable* equilibrium: if it rolled a little, gravity would accelerate its motion and roll it all the way off the hill (positive feedback).

A highway speed regulator ("cruise control") on a car is a

perfect example of negative feedback in action. If the car slows down (say from going uphill), the regulator gives the engine a little more gas; and vice versa, if the car speeds up. But here we can also see how some of the finer points come in. How much gas should the regulator add to (or take away from) the engine? If it weren't enough, then the system wouldn't be very effective. But suppose the regulator overdid it—too much gas too fast? Then a slight hill would make the car speed up wildly, whereupon the regulator would compensate the other way, and it would slow down wildly, whereupon . . . and so on. This undesirable behavior (another kind of instability, in fact) illustrates why the exact mathematics of cybernetics is quite important.

allels. Sure, you can imagine insectostats switching on the spray when the bug readings get high; but gardeners don't work that way. A person will notice the damage, figure out the pest from the symptoms (perhaps consulting a book), find out what techniques are safe and effective (check the book again), take account of what supplies are handy, make a plan, and follow it.

There are no equations for life or gardening. The relevant "variables"—perceptions, inferences, knowledge, plans—are not quantitative magnitudes; they can't be specified with numbers or vectors. Trying to explain thought and reason in cybernetic terms is as hopeless and misguided as trying to explain it in terms of conditional reflexes or Hume's gravity-like association of ideas. No doubt there is association, conditioning, and negative feedback in all of us; but none of these is the key to psychology.

A different pipedream of the 1950s was *machine translation* of natural languages. The idea first gained currency in 1949 (via a "memorandum" circulated by mathematician Warren Weaver) and was vigorously pursued in the United States, England, and Russia for at least a dozen years. Basically, the problem was conceived in two parts: grammar and vocabulary. The grammar part covered all those routine things you hated to memorize in French 1A— declensions, conjugations, word order, etc.—which nevertheless

had to be converted to keep the translation from sounding ridiculous (or getting distorted). The vocabulary task, meanwhile, was
superficially simpler: find an equivalent term in the target language
for each word (or idiom) in the original text by, for instance,
looking it up in a mechanical dictionary.

The problem is that many ordinary words are ambiguous, and
the ambiguities are seldom the same from language to language.
For example, the English noun 'suit' means one thing in a law
court, another in a card game, and still a third at a tailor's. The
German word *Klage* means lawsuit (and also a lament), but nothing
to do with cards or clothes. *Farbe* is the German for suit of cards
and also the normal word for color and paint (but not lawsuit or
dress suit). Finally, an *Anzug* is a man's suit, or else a kind of
approach or beginning (but none of those other things). Clearly
there is no German "equivalent" for 'suit'.

A translating machine will have to deal with this issue, on pain
of producing nonsense. Weaver actually proposed a *statistical*
solution based on the N nearest words (or nouns) in the immediate
context. Thus if 'card' or 'club' appeared near 'suit', that might
increase the likelihood of *Farbe* being right, whereas a nearby
'judge' or 'case' might favor *Klage*. But of course nothing that
simple could ever work: tailors and lawyers have business cards
(and clubs), and anyone can judge the color of a suit in a display
case. Might a more sophisticated "statistical semantics" (Weaver's
own phrase) carry the day? Not a chance.

In 1951 Yehoshua Bar-Hillel became the first person to earn a
living from work on machine translation.[4] Nine years later he was
the first to point out the fatal flaw in the whole enterprise, and
therefore to abandon it.[5] Bar-Hillel proposed a simple test sentence:

The box was in the pen.

And, for discussion, he considered only the ambiguity: (1) pen
= a writing instrument; versus (2) pen = a child's play enclosure.
Extraordinary circumstances aside (they only make the problem
harder), any normal English speaker will instantly choose "playpen" as the right reading. How? By understanding the sentence

Box 3
Statistical Semantics

The most amazing thing about statistical semantics (and MT in general) is the lack of effort to *understand* the text being translated. This approach is so incredible in retrospect that we might well ponder why smart people ever thought it made sense. Three factors contributed, I think.

First, enormous progress was made on (statistical) cryptography during the war. Weaver recounts a case in which a message encoded from Turkish was successfully decoded back into Turkish (using statistical methods) by someone who knew no Turkish (in fact, the decoder didn't recognize the result as a message and believed he had failed). So why not, Weaver asks, just regard Chinese as English that has been encoded into "Chinese code" and then proceed to decode it? Second, the development of many diverse but equivalent notations ("encodings") for various *formal* languages had to be fresh in every mathematician's mind, and such systems can be "intertranslated" quite mechanically (algorithmically).

Natural languages, of course, are not precisely formal; nor is translation as regular and methodical as decyphering. Still, languages often seem to approximate formal regularity, as if they really were formal systems deep down but somehow defective or cluttered up in practice. That brings us to the third point: Weaver himself (along with Claude Shannon) was also a pioneer in statistical "information theory," one of the prime concerns of which is reliable transmission through noisy, distorting channels (notoriously, without any attention to meaning). Thus, pressing the analogy, a proper formal language (or an exact codebook) could be regarded as a pure limiting case, like a theoretically perfect transmission channel. But the real world, including natural language, is always imperfect; so that's where approximation and statistics come in—all very hard-headed, modern, and scientific (or so it must have seemed).

and exercising a little common sense. As anybody knows, if one physical object is *in* another, then the latter must be the larger; fountain pens tend to be much smaller than boxes, whereas play-pens are plenty big.

Why not encode these facts (and others like them) right into the system? Bar-Hillel observes:

> What such a suggestion amounts to, if taken seriously, is the requirement that a translation machine should not only be supplied with a dictionary but also with a universal encyclopedia. This is surely utterly chimerical and hardly deserves any further discussion. (1960, p. 160)

In other words, a "mere" translator is impossible: any system capable of genuine, accurate translation must know what people know and must apply its knowledge sensibly. That is, for simple and basic reasons, mechanical translation presupposes full-fledged Artificial Intelligence. Now whether AI is "utterly chimerical" remains to be seen, but it certainly deserves further discussion.

Heuristic Search

Artificial Intelligence, conceived at Carnegie Tech in the autumn of 1955, quickened by Christmas, and delivered on Johnniac in the spring, made a stunning June debut at the conference from which it later took its name. The proud parents were a prolific team of three: Allen Newell, Cliff Shaw, and Herbert Simon. When they presented their *Logic Theorist* at McCarthy's Dartmouth Summer Research Project on Artificial Intelligence, they stole the show from a field that was otherwise still expecting.[6] The essential difference between Newell, Shaw, and Simon (hereafter NS&S) and earlier work in cybernetics and machine translation was their explicit focus on *thinking*.

More specifically, they conceived of intelligence as the ability to *solve problems*; and they conceived of solving problems as finding solutions via *heuristically guided search*.[7] Though the early programs concentrated on puzzles and games, it's easy enough to cast ordinary activity, or even conversation, as a series of *mental quests*: "find" a way to start a car, "look for" (think of) something to say, etc. Of course NS&S had more in mind than an easy metaphor: they had a concrete account of what intellectual search amounts to and how to implement it on a machine.

Every search has two basic aspects: its *object* (what is being looked for) and its *scope* (the region or set of things within which the object is sought). For actual system design, each aspect must be made explicit, in terms of specific structures and procedures. For instance, a system cannot seek an object that it couldn't recognize: it has to be able to "tell" when it reaches its goal. Consequently, the design must include a practical (executable) *test* for success, and that test then effectively defines what the system is really seeking.

The designer must also invent some procedure for working through the relevant *search space* more or less efficiently. For instance, if I have lost my keys somewhere in the house, then there's no point looking out in the yard; but it would be equally foolish to look only in one room or in the same places repeatedly. The search space should be the whole house, and I should scour it according to some thorough, nonredundant pattern. More generally, any well-designed searcher needs a practical *generator* that comes up with prospective solutions by slogging methodically through the relevant possibilities; and again, the generator itself then defines the effective search space.

Given a concrete system with procedures for generating and testing potential solutions, the basic structure of search becomes an alternating cycle: the generator proposes a candidate, and the tester checks it out. If the test succeeds, the search is finished; if not, the system returns to the generator and goes around again (at least until the space is exhausted).

So far we haven't mentioned thinking; but we also haven't mentioned how *hard* search can be. Consider chess: its rules define a tree-like search space, in which each node (joint) is a possible board position and each branch growing out of a node is a legal move in that position. Thus the starting (or current) position can be the trunk, with main limbs leading to whatever positions could result after one move; then smaller branches lead from those to each possible next position; and so on, until you reach checkmates and draws, at the tips of the twigs. In this search space it's straightforward to tell whether the game is over, and if so who won. Moreover, there is a mechanical procedure, called *mini-maxing*, for converting these ultimate tests into an optimal choice for the current move. You work backwards from the end, assume your opponent never makes a mistake, and ruthlessly prune off every branch that results in a loss or tie; whatever lines remain are then forced wins (therefore optimal).

Unfortunately this rosy theoretical analysis is utterly and absurdly infeasible. Here's why. In a typical chess position, a player has thirty or thirty-five legal options; and for each of these, there will be comparably many legal replies. Hence looking ahead one full move (each side gets a play) involves about a thousand alternative possibilities. By the same reasoning, looking ahead a second move would involve a thousand ways of continuing from each of a thousand possible beginnings, for a million combinations overall. Three moves ahead gives a billion combinations, four moves a trillion. Extrapolating to a complete game (say forty full moves) an exhaustive search would have to generate and test 10^{120} different combinations (that's a one followed by 120 zeros). Such a number is not merely "astronomical," it's preposterous: there haven't been 10^{120} distinct quantum states of all the subatomic particles in the entire history of the known universe. Thus I boldly predict that no computer will *ever* play perfect chess by means of exhaustive search.

This difficulty is called, picturesquely but vividly, the *combinatorial explosion*. It haunts not only chess, but also any search in which each node leads to numerous alternative nodes, and so on, for a number of levels—in other words, almost every interesting case. In one way or another, controlling or circumventing combinatorial explosion has been a central concern of Artificial Intelligence from its inception; the issue is broad and deep.

In general, therefore, search must be *selective*, that is, partial and risky.[8] The crucial insight, however, is that the selection need not be random. Newell, Shaw, and Simon propose that problem-solving search always follows *heuristic* guidelines (recall "Automatic Systems" in chapter 2), thereby dramatically improving the odds; they even suggest that the degree of improvement (over random chance) is one measure of a system's intelligence. Applying such heuristics, then, is what it means to *think* about a hard problem, trying to find a solution. And the challenge of designing an intelligent machine reduces to the chore of figuring out and implementing suitably "powerful" heuristics for it to employ.

For instance, after the Logic Theorist, NS&S worked on a program, modestly named *General Problem Solver* (GPS), in which they developed a species of heuristic reasoning called *means-ends analysis*. To see what this means, think about problems abstractly. You always start with:

1. a specified initial state (premises, position, data . . .);
2. a specified goal state (or states); and
3. a set of operators, for transforming one state into another.

The task is to find a sequence of operations that will transform the initial state into the goal state. If there are many different states and operators, the search space will explode combinatorially; so the problem is hard.

Now suppose a system is supplied with heuristics of two sorts:

1. procedures to detect salient differences between specified states (perhaps indicating how "important" the differences are); and
2. rules of thumb about which operations typically reduce differences of which sorts.

Then the attack can proceed as follows: detect some important difference between the given and goal states, and then apply some operator that typically reduces such differences. If the resulting state is the same as the goal state (no differences remain), the job is done; otherwise try the same strategy again, taking the new state as given.

That's basically how GPS works, but it can also handle two important complications. First, an operation sometimes has unwelcome side effects making the new problem harder rather than easier; when that happens, GPS can back up to an earlier state, look for a different salient difference, and work on that instead.

Second, operators generally have preconditions on their applicability, and often enough a given state won't quite meet those conditions. In that case, GPS can specify an intermediate state that does meet the conditions and set up a "subgoal" of transforming the given state into the intermediate one. Thus the search process can back away from dead ends and even plan ahead a little in fitting pieces of the solution together.

This is "means-ends" analysis because the operators are means, and the goal and subgoals are ends. The system is "general" in that the basic apparatus for means-ends analysis is separate from any particular set of heuristics and operators; hence the latter can easily be changed to suit various kinds of problems. The underlying intuition is simple but profound: means-ends analysis—reflecting on what you need and how to get it—is fundamental to all thoughtful problem solving; therefore a system designed on these principles should move intelligently and naturally through all kinds of search space.

NS&S intended their systems to solve problems in just the way that people do; indeed, they took program design to be a new and better way of formulating *psychological* theories. Accordingly, to test their hypotheses, they had to compare machine and human performance, which they did in a series of *protocol analysis* experiments. Some unsuspecting undergraduate is asked to solve a problem, "thinking out loud" all the while; then the same problem is given to GPS in "trace mode." The respective transcripts (protocols) are compared to see whether the student and machine tackled the problem in similar ways. The results, though not perfect, were quite remarkable and impressive at the time. (See box 4 for an example.)

Implicit here is a valuable side lesson about computers and logic. In popular fiction, intelligent computers tend to be supremely, even frightfully "logical"—as if rational inference were as trivial for them as addition is for a calculator. Yet GPS, running on a big machine, barely manages to bumble through elementary logic at novice level. The point isn't that GPS is a primitive program, but that general problem solving is a far cry from calculation, even if the reasoning is logical. GPS is supposed to *think* a problem out, by trying various combinations that look plausible and seeing

Box 4
GPS as Logician

The problem, given both to a college student (not experienced at logic) and to GPS, is to transform the logical expression $(R \supset \sim P) \wedge (\sim R \supset Q)$ into the simpler expression $\sim (\sim Q \wedge P)$ by repeated application of twelve prespecified rules. Below are the protocols of both for the first few steps (leading, as it happens, to a temporary dead end). (Adapted from Newell and Simon, 1961.)

STUDENT
Well, looking at the left-hand side of the equation, first we want to eliminate one of the two sides by using rule 8. It appears too complicated to work with first. Now—no,—no, I can't do that because I will be eliminating either the Q or the P in that total expression. I won't do that at first. Now I'm looking for a way to get rid of the horseshoe inside of the two brackets that appear on the left and right sides of the equation. And I don't see it. Yeh, if you can apply rule 6 to both sides of the equation, from there I'm going to see if I can apply rule 7.

WRITES: $(\sim R \vee \sim P) \wedge (R \vee Q)$ [applying R6 to both sides of given]

I can almost apply rule 7, but one R needs a tilde. So I'll have to look for another rule. I'm going to see if I can change that R to a tilde R. As a matter of fact, I should have used rule 6 on only the left hand side of the equation. So use rule 6, but only on the left hand side.

WRITES: $(\sim R \vee \sim P) \wedge (\sim R \supset Q)$ [applying R6 to left side only]

Now I'll apply rule 7 as it is expressed. Both—excuse me, excuse me, it can't be done because of the horseshoe. So— now I'm looking—scanning the rules here for a second, and seeing if I can change the R to $\sim R$ in the second equation, but I don't see any way of doing it. (Sigh.) I'm just sort of lost for a second.

GPS

Goal 1: Transform L1 into L0	[Given problem = main goal]
Goal 2: Delete R from L1	
Goal 3: Apply R8 to L1	[delete right half]
Produces: L2 = R ⊃ ~ P	
Goal 4: Transform L2 into L0	
Goal 5: Add Q to L2	
Reject	
Goal 2	[again]
Goal 6: Apply R8 to L1	[delete left half]
Produces: L3 = ~ R ⊃ Q	
Goal 7: Transform L3 into I	
Goal 8: Add P to L3	
Reject	
Goal 2	[again]
Goal 9: Apply R7 to L1	
Goal 10: Change connective to ∨ in left L1	[needed for R7]
Goal 11: Apply R6 to left L1	
Produces: L4 = (~ R ∨ ~ P) ∧ (~ R ⊃ Q)	
Goal 12: Apply R7 to L4	[still pursuing goal 9]
Goal 13: Change connective to ∨ in right L4	
Goal 14: Apply R6 to right L4	
Produces: L5 = (~ R ∨ ~ P) ∧ (R ∨ Q)	
Goal 15: Apply R7 to L5	[still pursuing goal 12]
Goal 16: Change sign of left right L5	[i.e., R to ~R]
Goal 17: Apply R6 to right L5	[undoes goal 14]
Produces: L6 = (~ R ∨ ~ P) ∧ (~ R ⊃ Q)	[same as L4]
Goal 18: Apply R7 to L6	[still pursuing goal 15]
Goal 19: Change connective to ∨ in right L6	
Reject	[we've been here before]

[and so on]

what it can find. The hope is: if we solve problems that way, then potentially machines can be as versatile and clever as we are. But by the same token, machines that think like us won't find logic especially trivial, any more than we do.

GPS was a dream come false. Its ideal of generality rested on several unfulfilled assumptions, of which two are most noteworthy. First, the basic plan presupposes that, under the skin, all problems (or at least all solutions) are pretty much alike. Thus once a problem is suitably formulated, it should succumb to the same general techniques—means-ends analysis or whatever—as any other. The only variations are in the initial statement of conditions and goals, plus a few further hints about the particular problem space (e.g., the heuristics for noticing differences and selecting operators).

Alas, powerful and general techniques proved hard to come by, whereas special purpose methods, tailor-made for specific problem domains, often paid off handsomely. This fostered, by the mid-sixties, a trend towards *semantic* programs, so called because of a new emphasis on "domain specific" information and procedures.[9] In effect, it was found that programs with more particular "expertise"—in the form of idiosyncratic data structures, peculiar heuristics, and other shortcuts—perform better. These improvements, however, are purchased at a price: the resulting systems tend to be brittle specialists, *idiot savants* that shine at one narrow task but are helplessly inept at everything else. A way was needed to reap the advantages of detailed knowledge without the penalties of overspecialization.[10]

The second unfulfilled assumption undermines not only GPS, but heuristic search in general, including the "semantic" phase. It is that *formulating* a problem is the smaller job, compared to solving it once formulated. Given this assumption, it was legitimate for experimenters to optimize the formulation themselves and assign only the solution part to the computer. Unfortunately, choosing a good search space (not to mention good heuristics to move around in it) turns out to be both quite difficult and quite important; by comparison, the actual search, though tedious, is just routine. In other words, much (perhaps most) of the intelligence exhibited in problem solving is needed at this "preliminary" stage—leaving only the busywork to mop up by heuristic search.

In one sense, of course, a problem is already formulated as it is posed. (We neglect, for now, yet another aspect of intelligence: knowing when there is a problem.) But the formulation required for posing a problem (in English, say) and that required for solving it by heuristic search are two different things. The classic example is the mutilated checkerboard. Consider a set of dominoes, each exactly large enough to cover two adjacent squares on a certain checkerboard; then, obviously, the entire checkerboard (all sixty-four squares) can be exactly covered with thirty-two of the dominoes. Problem: suppose two squares, at diagonally opposite corners, are removed from the checkerboard; can the resulting "mutilated" board (with only sixty-two squares) be exactly covered with thirty-one dominoes?

Well, try a few layouts and see if you can do it. That suggests one way of formulating the problem: let the space be all the ways of distributing thirty-one dominoes on a checkerboard, and search for a distribution that leaves opposite corners uncovered. It will be a long haul! There is, however, a simpler formulation. Since the opposite corners of a checkerboard are the same color, there are two possibilities: either the mutilated board has thirty red squares and thirty-two black, or vice versa. Let these two possibilities be the entire search space. Since each domino covers one red square and one black, any board covered exactly by thirty-one dominoes must have thirty-one red squares and thirty-one black. Can we find such a board in our new search space? It doesn't take long to find out.

Either of these formulations could easily be programmed for computerized search. Adopt the first, and the answer will never be found (not in our lifetimes, anyway). Adopt the second, however, and the problem is already solved; there's nothing left for the machine to do. In other words, the "real" challenge is not to find the solution, given a fully articulated formulation, but rather to come up with a good formulation (small search space, efficient tests, etc.), given the "informal" statement of the problem in English.

The idea of using explicit selection heuristics to tame the combinatorial explosion is a major intellectual milestone. It was perhaps the crucial element in actually launching the field of Artificial

Intelligence, and it has been a conceptual mainstay ever since. The early programs may now seem crude and easy to fault, but we must remember what they accomplished. The Logic Theorist (interpreted as such) was not algorithmic: rather, it pursued a symbolically specified goal by making sensible symbolic explorations, guided by symbolically coded knowledge. Thus it was the first human artifact plausibly describable as solving problems by *thinking* about them; its inventors were justly proud.

Micro-Worlds

A *micro-world* is a contrived, artificial domain in which the possible objects, properties, and events are all narrowly and explicitly defined in advance. Chess, for instance, is a micro-world: there are only a handful of pieces and legal moves, and they are all clearly spelled out by the rules. Unlike a real medieval warlord, a chess strategist never has to worry about plague, excommunication, rumors in the ranks, or Cossacks on the horizon—because nothing can happen in a micro-world that isn't expressly permitted in the specification. Similarly, Monopoly is a crisp micro-caricature of the real estate business.

By 1970 micro-worlds were all the rage in AI, especially the so-called *blocks-world* developed at MIT.[11] It contains a few (imaginary) "blocks" strewn about a flat surface, sometimes one atop another. They can be of various sizes and simple shapes, but always have perfectly flat surfaces. Sometimes they are colored or cast shadows, but they are never made of any particular material and never have any determinate mass or texture. Needless to say, these blocks can't get lost, chewed by the dog, traded for water pistols, or burnt wistfully on a cold winter night—the blocks-world includes no such "complications."

Why bother with a fake little "world" like that? The primary motive, ironically, is *generality*. The collapse of (pre-AI) machine translation revealed, above all, that language-using systems must understand what they're saying; they have to *know what they're talking about*. Of course, heuristic problem solving (early AI) is based, in a way, on knowledge, conveniently encoded in well-chosen heuristics and problem spaces. But such predigested "expertise" gives no hint of what a question is really "about": a system could solve missionary/cannibal problems, for example, and still not know a cannibal from a bowling ball or where to pass the ketchup if a missionary has a heart attack. Genuine intelligence calls for a fuller, more versatile familiarity with the objects and events within its ken.

A micro-world can be known (represented) thoroughly; and that can be taken as a first approximation to common sense. To be sure, the phony blocks-world is remarkably unlike any bona fide toy chest; still, it does mimic the spatial properties that are in some sense basic. More important, the domain is not tailor-made for any particular ability or task. There are blocks-world studies of perception, planning, action, talking, learning, and so on; and since they all inhabit the same world, they could presumably be integrated into a single comprehensive system. Thus the artificial simplicity of micro-worlds is just a temporary expedient: a way of cutting through the distracting details of reality, to expose the basic principles of general intelligence—much as the early physicists ignored friction and deformation to get at the underlying universal laws of motion.

The best known and most impressive blocks-world program is Terry Winograd's (1971) simulated robot SHRDLU, designed primarily for communication in natural language (namely English). SHRDLU can carry on surprisingly fluent conversations, including complex noun phrases and ambiguous pronouns, as long as we talk only about the blocks on a particular table (see figure 1). He will often figure out what an unclear sentence must mean by considering what was said earlier or how the blocks are presently arranged. Moreover, SHRDLU is not all talk: if we ask him to move or build something on the table, he will tirelessly comply, right before our wondering eyes (on a video screen, of course). Further, if our request entails that something else be done first, SHRDLU will take care of that all by himself; and if we then ask why he did whatever it was, he will politely explain. Finally, we can also add to SHRDLU's modest vocabulary at any time, merely by telling him what a new word means; and he will then use it correctly in both conversation and action (see box 5 for a sample dialogue.)

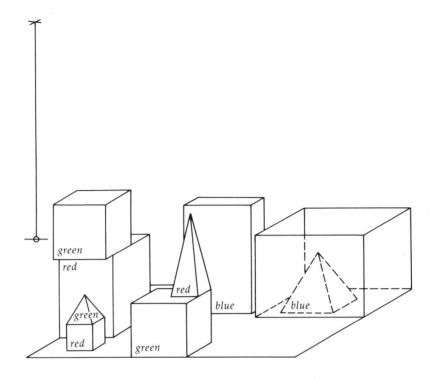

Figure 1   SHRDLU's "World"

This is SHRDLU's micro-world (Winograd, 1972). The little circle dangling at the upper left is his "hand." Note that there is no actual tabletop with blocks on it, of which this is a picture; all SHRDLU really "inhabits" is a computer data structure *describing* a blocks-world situation. (That data structure can be connected to a video driver and screen, producing a drawing like the above for the amusement of spectators—but that's nothing to SHRDLU.)

Box 5
A Conversation with SHRDLU

The lower-case lines with "arrows" were typed in by a person; SHRDLU's responses are capitalized. The italicized paragraphs are explanatory comments added by Winograd 1971, pp. 35–55.

→ Pick up a big red block.
OK

> *The system answers "OK" when it carries out a command. In order to pick up the red block, it had to clear it off by finding a space for the green one and moving the green one away.*

→ Grasp the pyramid.
I DON'T KNOW WHICH PYRAMID YOU MEAN.

> *There are three pyramids in the scene, so the program does nothing.*

→ Find a block which is taller than the one you are holding and put it into the box.

> *The system has to figure out what is meant by "one" and "it", as well as using deduction to decide which block it is holding.*

BY "IT", I ASSUME YOU MEAN THE BLOCK WHICH IS TALLER THAN THE ONE I AM HOLDING.

> *Printed out to keep us informed.*

OK.

> *The hand has to set down the red block to pick up the taller blue one.*

→ What does the box contain?
THE BLUE PYRAMID AND THE BLUE BLOCK.

→ What is the pyramid supported by?
> *Earlier the system responded to "the pyramid" by saying "I don't know which pyramid you mean." Now, it*

> *knows that we must mean the one which was just mentioned.*
>
> THE BOX.
>
> → Does a steeple . . .
>
> SORRY, I DON'T KNOW THE WORD "STEEPLE".
>
> *The system interrupts immediately when it sees a word it can't figure out*
>
> → A "steeple" is a stack which contains two green cubes and a pyramid.
>
> *The quote marks indicate that we are defining a new word.*
>
> I UNDERSTAND.
>
> → Are there any steeples now?
>
> NO.
>
> *The new definition is used as a description to recognize steeples.*
>
> → Build one.
>
> OK.
>
> *The description given in the definition is enough to deduce a plan for building new objects as well as recognizing them. The word "one" means "a steeple", and the plan is carried out.*

SHRDLU's "natural" versatility and reasonableness are amazingly captivating. Lest anyone get swept away, therefore, let's note a few of his more obvious deficiencies right off the bat. First, he never initiates anything but only responds. In fact, SHRDLU has no motivational or purposive structure whatever, except for the goals (and subgoals) introduced by questions and requests from the outside. Second, he has no sense at all of conversational coherence or continuity; he is not bothered in the least by gratuitous shifts from "Pick up a big red block" to "Grasp the pyramid" to "Find a block which. . . ." A person, on the other hand, might well get testy and suggest you "make up your damn mind." Third, all the hard problems of perception and action involve the interface between *symbolic* cognitions and *nonsymbolic* objects and events. But Winograd's system solves none of these, even by simulation: SHRDLU's "world" is symbolic already—just a blocks-world description elsewhere in the computer—so he can "interact" simply by invoking handy little read/write routines.[12]

To dwell on these shortcomings, however, is to miss the fundamental limitation: the micro-world itself. SHRDLU performs so glibly only because his domain has been stripped of anything that could ever require genuine wit or understanding. In other words, far from digging down to the essential questions of AI, a micro-world simply eliminates them. Neglecting the tangled intricacies of everyday life while pursuing a theory of common sense is not like ignoring friction while pursuing the laws of motion; it's like throwing out the baby with the bathwater. A round, frictionless wheel is a good approximation of a real wheel because the deviations are comparatively small and theoretically localized; the blocks-world "approximates" a playroom more as a paper plane approximates a duck.

To see why, we need a clearer sense of how much SHRDLU is really missing. Let's ignore the fact that the blocks are only imaginary and see what happens if we propose a deal:

→ Trade you a squirtgun for a big red block.
SORRY, I DON'T KNOW THE WORD "TRADE".

Oops, a vocabulary snag. Fortunately, SHRDLU can learn new words; Winograd taught him about steeples, and now we'll tell him about trades (and squirtguns).

→ A "trade" is a free exchange of property.
SORRY, I DON'T KNOW THE WORD "FREE".
→ A "free" act is done willingly, without being forced.
SORRY, I DON'T KNOW THE WORD "ACT".
→ "Acts" are what people do on purpose, and not by accident.
SORRY, I DON'T KNOW THE WORD "PEOPLE".
→ Sorry, I thought you were smarter than you are.
SORRY, I DON'T KNOW THE WORD "SORRY".

Needless to say, SHRDLU also doesn't know 'property', 'force', 'accident', 'smart', or any of the other (perfectly ordinary) words we used.[13] Worse yet, he completely lacks more fundamental notions such as wanting, having, agreeing, and the like, without which trading can make no sense at all.

This problem runs deeper than just vocabulary: the concepts required for trading would be quite unintelligible in the blocks-world, even if they could somehow be added to SHRDLU's dictionary. Hence the domain itself must be enriched, and not only the robot. So why not expand the blocks-world, turn it into a larger "blocks-and-trading" micro-world? This, it turns out, is the crucial question; and the answer is that it can't be done.

The world of trading cannot be "micro." Unlike chess strategy or block geometry, trading cannot be separated from the rest of everyday life and treated by itself; there are no plausible, non-arbitrary boundaries restricting what might be relevant at any juncture. Try to imagine, for instance, that instead of crashing on the first word, SHRDLU would give our offer a typical, ordinary response:

I ALREADY HAVE A WATER PISTOL, BUT I'LL GIVE YOU
TWO BLOCKS AND A PYRAMID FOR YOUR SLIMY OLD
FROG.

Childishly simple, no doubt; but look at how much is presupposed:

1. SHRDLU appreciates that a second squirtgun would be less valuable than the first; presumably, this means he knows how to play with them, can visualize the awkwardness of shooting two-handed, etc.
2. Further, he *expects us to know* all that (and know that he knows it), so we can tell that he is giving a reason for not wanting our gun and hence that the offer is being declined.
3. Still, he sees that we want a block badly enough to part with something important; moreover, he recognizes that blocks (unlike pistols) are valuable in quantity.
4. Not taking any chances, he tries to soften our reluctance, by demeaning the frog (so he must assume that slimy, old things are less desirable); clearly, he hopes to strike a bargain and is prepared to haggle.

And these but scratch the surface; with the hang of it, you can spin out a "simple" negotiation involving pretty much any aspect of common sense or mundane familiarity. Such unbounded potential relevance is exactly antithetical to the basic idea of micro-worlds; therefore, a micro-world of trading is impossible.

So what? Who cares whether a robot's world is really "micro," anyway? SHRDLU cares (or would if he could): for everything about him depends on it. He could not begin to act or converse intelligently in a more realistic environment, even if it were spoon-fed to him (in a "simulation") and even if he had plenty of vocabulary. The reasons are not temporary loose ends nor mere limitations of size, but are built in to the very structure of the program and essential to its operation.

For instance, SHRDLU remembers everything that ever happens in his world (until he is "restarted," and then he remembers nothing). This is feasible only because the world is so small and the sessions short. Any remedy, however, would require *selective* memory, including some sense of what's worth remembering (important, interesting, relevant, useful), of which SHRDLU hasn't a clue. On the other hand, SHRDLU remembers nothing of the present situation (e.g., where the blocks are); his world is so tidy and accessible that he simply checks anew whenever he needs any current information, even if he just checked seconds earlier. Here he is spared not only memory selection, but also memory updating, particularly in deciding how a modification in one belief entails changes in others. As we shall see later in this chapter, memory updating is a profound difficulty, unless you dodge it entirely by living in a micro-world.

Even more telling, SHRDLU has no sense of situation. He can get away with this because there is only one thin topic in the blocks-world; hence nothing can depend on what's going on. In the real world, by contrast, sensible behavior is strongly conditioned by circumstance. Consider, for instance, the different (reasonable) responses to "Block the big red pick-up" uttered in a rowdy singles bar, at an auto repair shop, during football practice,

Box 6
Expert Systems

At the beginning of this section, we noted how narrow and contrived chess "battles" are compared to real medieval warfare. The main point, or course, is that most of the real world is *not* a micro-world. The example, however, cuts both ways: some domains within the world actually are "micro" — chess itself being conspicuous among them.

But games aren't the only genuine micro-worlds. Recent developments in "applied AI" — so called "expert systems" — depend on the discovery that many domains may be treated as micro-worlds, at least for certain decision-making purposes. Several things are required to make this practical:

1. The relevant decisions must depend entirely on a well-defined (and not too large) set of variables or factors.
2. The values of those variables must be known (or discoverable), and there must be a way to specify or express them articulately.
3. The exact way in which the results (decisions) depend on the values of the variables must be known and "computable," at least to a decent approximation.
4. The interrelations among the factors in determining the result should be complex enough to make the project worth the effort.

These conditions are stringent and rule out the bulk of ordinary life; but some specialized, technical domains fill the bill nicely, including:

1. Diagnosis (and recommended chemotherapy) for certain classes of infectious disease. Classic symptoms, standard blood tests, etc., constitute the input factors, while various bits of medical lore provide the known dependencies.
2. Geological analysis of bore samples from drill rigs for de-

termining types of strata and estimating the likelihood of petroleum deposits.

3. Optimizing microscopic layouts and dimensions for integrated circuit chips, subject to constraints imposed by heat dissipation, propagation delays, interference between adjacent channels, etc.

These particular domains happen to have enough economic value to command research and development resources; but surely other areas will emerge, when costs come down.

Expert systems, while obviously important in practical terms, should not be confused with GOFAI or cognitive science. They are designed only to get a carefully limited job done; hence the theoretical shortcomings of micro-worlds can't bother them. By the same token, however, they have little or nothing to contribute to our understanding of common sense or general intelligence.

or in a spy adventure. SHRDLU would, of course, be quite helpless—and not just because he lacks the relevant notions of 'block' and 'pick-up' (and 'bar' and 'shop' and . . .). Even if he had all those concepts, he wouldn't know how they relate to one another or which ones make sense in which situations; that is, he wouldn't really understand them at all. But, by the same token, he doesn't understand the words he already has either—a fact that is conveniently masked by the artificial restriction to the blocks-world.

My conclusion about micro-worlds, therefore, is rather negative: as a device for exploring the underlying principles of general intelligence and common sense, they are thoroughly misguided. Any investigation, of course, must begin somewhere; and that means simplifying or ignoring various "complications" in order to concentrate on the essentials. The micro-world strategy was conceived in this eminently reasonable spirit. It turned out, however, that the broad interconnectedness and situation dependence of common sense are not at all incidental, but central and crucial to its nature; to disregard them is not to home in on but to evade the fundamental issues. The apparent successes of SHRDLU (and other micro-world programs) are, in effect, gimmicks: they are not modest manifestations of intelligence in modest environments, but demonstrations that on a suitably contrived stage, with clever baffles and mirrors, you can give a startling impression of something that isn't there. SHRDLU can no more speak English than Houdini can saw his assistant in half—but it makes a great show.

This cold assessment, it should be acknowledged, is possible only through the marvels of 20-20 hindsight; no criticism whatever is intended of Winograd or his coworkers. On the contrary, it was they who faithfully pursued a pioneering and plausible line of inquiry and thereby made an important scientific discovery, even if it wasn't quite what they expected. Just as the machine translation failure established that language competence requires understanding, so the micro-worlds effort may be credited with showing that the world cannot be decomposed into independent fragments.[14] Realizing this amounts to a fundamental insight into common sense and mundane intelligence—and therefore points the way for subsequent AI.

Commonsense Stereotypes

Pleads pious Pat:

We bought the boys apples, because they were so hungry.

"No," counters cagier Chris:

We bought the boys apples, because they were so cheap.

The two rationales are exactly alike, word for word, until the last. Yet that little difference changes everything: whereas Pat defends the snack by saying something about the boys, Chris defends the purchase by saying something about the apples. Thus the pronoun 'they' (which is grammatically ambiguous) must refer to the boys in one case but to the apples in the other.[15] Native speakers, however, understand such sentences so quickly that they usually don't even notice any ambiguity. One question is: How do they do that?

Obviously, it's just common sense. Assuming that boys and apples are the only options, the reasoning is trivial: if hungry, they must be boys—because boys eat and apples don't; but if cheap, they must be apples—because apples have a price and children don't.[16] Plausible enough; but from the perspective of Artificial Intelligence, that leaves all the crucial questions unanswered. How, for instance, would it "occur" to a system to reason in just this way? Why consider these particular facts, as opposed to countless others that everybody knows—about the stripes of tigers, the use of knobs, the Queen of England, or whatever? Of course, prices and eating are *relevant* in this context, whereas queens and knobs are quite beside the point. But to say that is merely to rename the issue: How does a cognitive system determine what's "relevant" in any given situation?

Common sense ranges fast and wide. Almost any bit of general knowledge can turn out to be pertinent in almost any ordinary conversation; yet most of the time we talk glibly and easily, as if there were nothing to it. In computer terms neither the raw speed nor the raw size is especially overwhelming: micro-second, mega-word memories are commonplace. The trick is efficient access: finding what you want when you want it, without much tedious search. That's what seems to happen when people realize "instantly" that Chris is talking about the price of apples, not boys—let alone tigers or tea in China.

Think of memory as a vast storehouse of knowledge, a super filing system, in which zillions of mundane facts are stashed conveniently at our mental fingertips. In a conventional filing system, there's nothing complicated about having tons of cabinets, even buildings full; and any idiot can open a drawer to pull out a folder. The challenge is to keep track of it all so that when the boss wants a particular item (years later, naturally), nobody has to sift through thousands of individual files. The standard solution is clever organization, including indexes, hierarchical categories, and lots of cross-references. Hence, if common sense really is analogous to a filing system, the key to its efficiency should lie in its organization (which must be very clever indeed). In AI this is called the *knowledge access* or *knowledge representation* problem.

By 1975 representing knowledge in *linked stereotypes* was an idea whose time had come.[17] Stereotypes are general descriptions, in some conventional format, of familiar objects, events, and situations. They are like elaborate "definitions," except that they are far more encyclopedic than ordinary dictionary entries, and they must be painfully thorough and banal. By contrast, published reference works can take up where common sense leaves off: they needn't say much about tying shoes, walking sticks, or getting wet in the rain. But if common sense is itself an "encyclopedia," it must start from zero, with extensive articles on all sorts of humdrum trivialities.

Let's see how stereotypes could handle the example that shot down mechanical translation:

The box was in the pen.

Recall that, in Bar-Hillel's (1960) view, disambiguating sentences like this would require a mechanized encyclopedia, which, he maintained, was utterly hopeless. A decade and a half later nearly everyone accepted his diagnosis and therapy—but not his despair. Imagine a system with one stereotype apiece for 'box' and 'in', and two for 'pen' ('inkpen' versus 'playpen'). The entry for 'in' will specify a relation between two objects, spelling out such details as: the second object surrounds some hollow or cavity, where the first is located. Especially prominent, however, will be an *explicit prerequisite*: the first object must be smaller than (the cavity in) the second. Having this requirement "prominent" means that the system will deal with it right away. And, thus alerted, it will promptly look up the size specifications in the other three stereotypes, and resolve the ambiguity without further ado.

Several significant gains are illustrated here. First and most obvious, only four stereotypes (indexed directly by words in the sentence) are ever looked at; the needed information is found and identified quickly, without wasting any effort dismissing knobs or stripes. The essential point is that the system does not first consider tigers (etc.) and then notice that they are irrelevant; rather, it never considers them at all. Most of the far-flung facts known to the system never even come up in situations where they don't matter, and this alone yields a huge saving in search effort. Moreover, like a good filing system (or encyclopedia), the efficiency is achieved through prior *organization* of the information stored. Stereotypes organize knowledge *by topic*, with related facts stored together or cross-referenced; hence discerning pertinent topics (from words or context, say) automatically brings relevant information to the fore quickly.

Equally important is the use of *constraints*: some stereotypes (notably those for predicates) impose conditions on how others may be conjoined with them. Thus 'inside of' requires a pair of objects obeying a relative-size restriction, and we just saw how that can be exploited for a swift disambiguation. Similar constraint-driven processing might well work with our opening example: the hungry boys and cheap apples. For surely the 'is hungry' stereotype will stipulate that its subject be animate or capable of eating—characteristics that should be easy to recover from the 'boy' stereotype but not the 'apple' one, and so on.

A third gain emerges if we vary the situation:

"Listen carefully," whispered Agent Orange, breathing hoarsely, "do you see that pen on Raoul's desk? Your films are sealed in a tiny box, and the box is in the pen." Alas, before she could explain. . . .

Everyone knows that boxes come in many sizes, so some might fit in writing pens after all. How can our system accommodate this complication without forfeiting its ability to solve the Bar-Hillel case? The answer is both simple and powerful: features listed in a stereotype are attached with differing (modal) *qualifications*. Thus the size entry under 'box' would be qualified as "typical," and given as a range; for example, boxes are typically between a few inches and a few feet on a side. This achieves two goals: it provides useful information that the system can rely on, other things being equal; but it also allows that information to be overridden in unusual circumstances, such as when a sentence explicitly says "tiny" box. Such cancelable specifications are called *default assignments*; they act like provisional assumptions that the system can take for granted unless something else rules them out.

Default assignments are crucial to the suggestion that stereotypes capture common sense.

Qualifications in stereotypes, however, include much more than just typical defaults. Frogs, for instance, are *always* four-legged (*unless* defective), *usually* brown or green (*except* poisonous species, which tend to be brightly colored), *occasionally* kept as pets, *never* ferocious, and so on. Thus if you mention a frog (and before you say anything else), I will assume that it's brown or green; but I will be prepared to learn otherwise and will fear poison if I do. On the other hand, I will be highly confident that it's a mild-mannered quadruped; and though I won't expect it to be a pet, I won't be surprised if it is.

The frog example also brings out a fourth and final advantage of organizing knowledge by stereotypes: namely, *cross-referencing*. We all know that frogs are cold-blooded, smooth-skinned vertebrates that hatch from eggs and later metamorphose from aquatic larvae into air-breathing adults. We know the same things about toads and salamanders, and for the same reason: they are all amphibians. Therefore it's economical to store the common facts (and default assumptions) about amphibians in a single stereotype, which is then cross-referenced by the more specific frog, toad, and salamander entries. Often this extends to a *hierarchy* of generic knowledge. Thus frogs resemble not only toads, but also eels and elephants, in having an internal skeleton, a heart, and a spinal cord—characteristics common to all vertebrates.

Unlike micro-worlds, stereotypes are not an attempt to evade the intricate tangles of daily life; quite the contrary, the goal is to duplicate the organization and operation of common sense in all its irregular glory. As even a brief account shows, it is a profound idea, with considerable intuitive appeal and formidable theoretical power. Still, not all is well; stubborn difficulties emerge that not only provide continuing research puzzles, but may yet again undermine the larger enterprise. Here I will sketch three, which I call the selection, no-topic, and tunnel-vision problems, respectively.

An effective organization of common sense must provide efficient access to relevant stereotypes since the whole point is to avoid costly search or problem solving. Thus in our overly slick

Box 7
Sketch of a Stereotype for "Cocker Spaniel"

The following is very sketchy; a real AI stereotype has far more structure than this and is also far less cavalier in its use of categories and relations. In the appropriate spirit, however, indentation below is meant to indicate hierarchical subordination, initial words specify conceptual categories, parenthesized words insert modal qualifiers, and capitalized words refer to other stereotypes.

COCKER SPANIEL:
  Subclass of: (always) DOG
    Specifies: (always) BREED
  Has as part: (always) COAT
    Equals: (always) FUR, HAIR
    Location: (almost always) entire SURFACE
     (except) EYES, NOSE, PAWS
    Color: (usually) BLOND or BLACK
    Care: (needed) BRUSHING
      Frequency: (ideally) twice a WEEK
      On pain of: (inevitably) SHEDDING, MATTING, STINKING
  Has as part: (always) TAIL
    Location: (always) TOP REAR
    Type: (almost always) STUBBY
    State: (usually) WAGGING OBSEQUIOUSLY
  Adult size: (almost always) MEDIUM (for a DOG)
                      SMALL (for a SPANIEL)
    Height: (typical) 15 INCHES
    Width: (typical) 9 INCHES
    Length: (typical) 30 INCHES
    Weight: (typical) 25 POUNDS
  Good habits: (typical) LOYAL and PLAYFUL
  Bad habits: (too often) BARKS and JUMPS
             (sometimes) hard to HOUSEBREAK
             (whenever possible) STEALS FOOD
  Examples   (known)   AUNT MAUD'S BOWSER III
                      The ROBINSON'S GOLDEN LADY

The BLACK one who CHASES our CAT
(heard of) AUNT MAUD's BOWSER JUNIOR
AUNT MAUD's BOWSER WOWSER
(metaphor) AUNT MAUD's HUSBAND, CALVIN
Miscellaneous:
(definitely) POPULAR
(presumably) GOOD with CHILDREN
(allegedly) PUPPY MILLS are WRECKING the BREED

treatment of Bar-Hillel's example, the required knowledge structures were directly indexed by words in the given sentence. In
real discourse, alas, such convenient cues are not always so handy.
The *selection* problem then is: How are needed stereotypes picked
out, in the absence of explicit pointers? Consider, for instance,
the following exchange:

SWAG: Where is Johnny's toy box?
MANDY: I don't know, but try his pen.

Awkwardly, the word 'in' is missing; so although the size relationships are readily available, nothing prompts the system to
worry about them. (What is "trying" a pen, anyway?) Alternatively,
'box' might be omitted:

The brown rectangular object labeled
"INDIA INK—48 BOTTLES—HANDLE WITH CARE"
was in the pen.

Trouble is, the system doesn't have a typical size for "brown
rectangular objects," and nothing tells it to check out boxes. In
sum, sentences don't always contain (useful) surface cues to guide
stereotype selection; yet without them, the scheme loses much
of its beguiling facility.

Like encyclopedias, stereotypes organize knowledge around coherent subjects or topics. The assumption is that a reader understands a general topic first and then can use that as a guide in

looking up relevant further details. But how many "topics" are there for common sense? The following sentence is roughly similar to our earlier examples:

I left my raincoat in the bathtub, because it was still wet.

Does 'it' refer to the bathtub or the raincoat? To the raincoat, obviously, because:

1. a raincoat's being wet is an intelligible (if mildly eccentric) reason to leave it in a bathtub, whereas
2. a bathtub's being wet would be no sensible reason at all for leaving a raincoat in it.

But where are these reasons to be "filed"? They hardly seem constitutive of the general, commonsense concepts of either raincoats or bathtubs (let alone wetness); nor are they part of some other concept, for which there just doesn't happen to be a word in the given sentence. Thus the difficulty is not in finding or selecting the relevant stereotype, but rather that there doesn't seem to be one, because there isn't a natural topic under which the relevant information would plausibly be filed. Accordingly, I call this the *no-topic* problem.[18]

Finally, even assuming a crop of relevant stereotypes has been gathered, it still must be winnowed; that is, unworkable combinations must be sorted out, basically by testing for constraint satisfaction. This works well enough for single clauses (apples don't get hungry, etc.) but deteriorates rapidly as contexts widen:

When Daddy drove up, the boys quit playing cops and robbers. They put away their guns and ran out back to the car.

When the cops drove up, the boys quit their robbery attempt. They put away their guns and ran out back to the car.

Despite the large overlap, these stories differ entirely in tone and sense. Did the boys "quit" happily or out of fear and failure? When they "put away" the guns, were they tidying up or concealing their weapons? Could 'ran' be paraphrased by 'scampered' or 'fled' (or 'jogged')? Such distinctions, though subtle, are easy for people to make and essential to understanding the text. Yet local constraints are powerless to make them since they depend on an overall appreciation of the situation. The *tunnel-vision* problem is just this difficulty of making stereotype selection sensitive to broader circumstances.

What do these problems show about commonsense stereotypes? As usual, it's hard to tell. One way to formulate the larger issue is: How is knowledge brought to bear *in context*? Thus the system "knows" a lot about typical sizes and relationships; the trick is to employ that information effectively, in the context of Johnny's toy box, Orange's microfilms, or what have you. Stereotypes work smoothly and well when the context is small: a single predigested and explicitly identified topic with local constraints. But as soon as the text opens up—as soon as anything like a genuine grasp of context is required—all that elaborate machinery lurches and stumbles. Though it's certainly too soon to pass final judgment on knowledge organization as an account of common sense, the showing so far is disquietingly reminiscent of micro-worlds: clever equipment and staging permit a startling impression of something that isn't there.

The Frame Problem

Once upon a time, there were three Boxes: Papa Box, Mama Box, and little Baby Box. Papa Box was resting on the floor in the middle of their modest cottage, with Baby Box perched up on his back; meanwhile, Mama Box was sitting quietly on a chair over by the door. Suddenly, in rolled Goldiwires, bent on problem solving. She looked around and then carefully pushed Papa Box across the room to the opposite wall.

IQ TEST for Goldy (or reader):
—How many Boxes are there now?

Well, what's so hard about that? As any fool can see, the number of Boxes doesn't change; hence it must stay at three. But how, exactly, can the robot "see" that the number of Boxes stays the same? This question is trickier than it looks, as three more stumpers reveal:

—Where is Papa now?
—Where is Mama now?
—Where is Baby now?

Presumably Goldy knows where Papa went because she herself pushed him there (on purpose), and she might well suppose that Mama and Baby remain where they were, since she never touched them. Unfortunately, moving Papa has a *side effect*: Baby (though not Mama) comes along for the ride. Individual side effects are hard to anticipate, because they follow only incidentally, depending on the details of each particular situation; for example, Baby (but not Mama) happens to be atop Pop. On the other hand, checking explicitly for all conceivable consequences would be out of the question. (Did opening the door break the window, let out the cats, or change the number of boxes?) Hence the real problem—the so-called *frame problem*—is how to "notice" salient side effects without having to eliminate all the other possibilities that might conceivably have occurred had the facts somehow been different.[19]

The frame problem is superficially analogous to the knowledge-access problem. In both cases the basic issue is how to ignore (selectively) almost everything that the system knows or can imagine; that is, how to home in on relevant factors without spending an enormous effort ruling out alternatives. In other words, the underlying difficulty is not how to decide, for each potential consideration, whether it matters or not, but rather how to avoid that decision in almost every instance.

But the two problems are not the same. The knowledge-access problem concerns primarily "generic" information: common knowledge that could be relevant any time, anywhere. But the frame problem arises with knowledge of the current situation, here and now—especially with keeping such knowledge up to date as events happen and the situation evolves. The fundamental difference, therefore, is *temporality*. By contrast, our stereotype treatment of the box in the pen was essentially timeless: the facts used, about sizes and prerequisites, are all constant (the system needn't reconfirm that pens are still less than a centimeter thick). But when things start moving and changing, "knowledge" of the current situation may not stay valid: Baby won't still be in the middle of the room, for example. It seems, then, that the system's knowledge must be divided into (at least) two categories: *perennial* facts that stay the same and *temporary* facts that are subject to change at any moment and therefore must be actively kept up to date.

The constant flux of the here and now makes the frame problem harder than the (plain) knowledge-access problem, in two related ways. First, when updating temporary knowledge, the system must find its way around the knowledge base (selectively and efficiently) not according to what's stored where, but according to how all the entries are *interdependent*—that is, how each might be affected by changes in various others. In other words there's another whole level of combinations to keep under control. But second (and worse), the relevant interconnections and dependencies are themselves *situation bound*; that is, the actual side effects of any particular event are quite sensitive to the happenchance details of the current circumstances. Thus Baby rides along this time, but next time may be different. Hence, update decisions can't be worked out in advance; each new situation must be handled on the fly, as it comes.[20]

Standard approaches to the frame problem can be divided into two main camps, which I call the "cheap test" and "sleeping dog" schools. The difference between the two turns on how seriously they ignore alternatives. The *cheap test* strategy looks over the entire situation (as represented) quickly, to tell at a glance most of what's irrelevant to a certain event and won't be affected. The basic intuition is easy to see: when Goldy pushes Papa, she realizes this may alter the locations of various things (Papa included). But she also knows it won't change what color they are, or their size, or shape, or weight, because (under normal conditions) location, color, shape, weight, and so on are independent properties. All she needs is a prior classification of events and facts, based on which types of event affect which types of fact. Then each fact-entry in her current situation model can wave a conspicuous "flag," indicating the type(s) of event that might affect it. For instance, all facts likely to be affected by movements could fly bright red flags; then, whenever the given event is a movement, Goldy could quickly bypass (ignore) all facts not flying red flags because she already knows that they needn't be updated.

In a similar spirit, Goldy (or her designers) might reasonably assume that an event can only influence things in its immediate vicinity—no action at a distance, in other words. Thus moving Papa could easily affect Baby because Baby is actually touching Papa; but it won't bother Mama or her chair because they are clear across the room. In this version, then, the "flags" would represent not which properties might interact, but which objects might interact, according to some measure of causal proximity. Either way, however, the system must scan the entire situation (= temporary knowledge), relying on some easy sign to rule out most entries quickly; that's what I mean by a "cheap test."

The trouble with cheap tests is that the real world isn't so conveniently compartmentalized. The above might work for SHRDLU; but down in Philadelphia, Mama will quite likely be affected if Goldy shoves Papa against a wall—and the ensuing changes may well include her color and shape. Moreover, the potential for these effects to ramify throughout the situation— say to the contents and velocity of a frying pan—is computationally breathtaking. Further examples abound. Of course, the tests could be made more discriminating, with numerous conditions and qualifications; but then they're no longer cheap, which defeats the whole point.

The alternative, the *sleeping dog* strategy, is to let things lie, except when there's some positive reason not to. That is, in the absence of some positive indication that a particular fact may be affected, the system will totally ignore it (without even performing any cheap tests). This is a satisfying suggestion on the face of it; but it raises formidable design questions about how to get the needed positive indications for all the important side effects. How, for instance, will it occur to the system that it better worry about Baby's future position (though not Mama's or the number of Boxes) when it starts moving Papa? I will outline two approaches that have some currency and power.

One proposal is to divide all temporary facts further into *basic* and *nonbasic* facts, such that:

1. basic facts are all independent of one another, and
2. nonbasic facts are all derivable from basic facts.

The essential idea is that since basic facts are independent, a change in one will not affect the others. Hence there are no side effects among basic facts and therefore no "basic" frame problem. In other words, side effects and the frame problem are confined to nonbasic (derivative) facts. On a chess board, for example, the locations of individual pieces (and whose move it is) are the only basic facts.[21] Everything else about the board—like who's winning, which pieces are threatened, what moves would be good, etc.— is derived from these. So when one piece moves, there's no problem updating the positions of others (they're unaffected); all that needs updating are nonbasic inferences about current threats, opportunities, and the like.

Derivative facts, in turn, can be divided again into two subgroups:

1. conclusions that the system (at some given moment) has already drawn—that is, consequences it has *explicitly* derived; and
2. conclusions that the system has not yet drawn (though it might)—that is, consequences that so far remain merely *implicit*.

Any decent set of basic facts will have untold numbers of tedious logical consequences, and no robot in its right mind would actually derive all (or even very many) of them. So most nonbasic facts remain implicit, and these are no problem: no sooner are the basic facts updated than all their implicit consequences are updated too, at the very speed of logic. At least some nonbasic facts, however, must be inferred explicitly, for only then can the system take account of them in its decisions and actions. But each such explicit conclusion lives in danger of having its rug pulled out whenever a basic fact is updated, and this is where the frame problem reappears. One brutally direct response is simply to discard all previous conclusions whenever anything is updated; but that's clearly wasteful. A subtler approach associates with each basic fact all the explicit inferences that depended on it; then the system can tell which beliefs are in jeopardy at any update and safely ignore the rest.

Alas, this approach faces similar difficulties. Computer scientists (like philosophers before them) have had trouble picking out just which facts are "basic." If Mama's and Papa's locations are basic, for example, then moving Papa won't affect Mama; and the changing distance and direction between them will be nicely derivative (just like on a chess board). But, by the same reasoning, Baby's location should be basic too, in which case it won't be affected by Papa's move either; so when Papa goes, Baby stays behind, awkwardly suspended in thin air. Why not make each object's position basic relative to what supports it? Then Baby's location relative to Papa would remain unchanged when Papa moves, which seems right. But what if Baby is also tied to the doorknob with a rope? What if, instead of sliding sideways, Papa tips over? Then Baby's position relative to Papa doesn't seem so basic after all. Other suggestions have analogous problems. Moreover, the Boxes' frugal cottage isn't much different from a microworld; delineating basic facts in, say, an army field hospital would be distinctly messier.

The other main variant of the sleeping dog strategy wants to capture typical side effects—all those interdependent "what ifs"—in elaborate *stereotypes* for situations and their changes. Thus the "move something" stereotype would have a clause saying that anything supported thereby will come along for the ride . . . unless it's roped to the doorknob, assuming the support doesn't tip over, as long as there are no low bridges, and so on. Of course these hedges will themselves have to be qualified, in case Baby is also glued to Papa, the doorknob is glued to Papa, or whatever. Such stereotypic definitions could get very hairy—raising the worry that the frame problem is not so much resolved as relocated, in the problem of finding one's way around the stereotypes.

Box 8
On Being Jerky

In the frame problem we see a phenomenon that also haunts Artificial Intelligence. Special cases aside, AI "intelligence" seems oddly inconstant. A typical system, for instance, will cruise along smoothly, doing (or saying) sensible enough things; and then, out of the blue, it will bumble and blunder ridiculously, as if it had no sense at all. I call this curious pattern the *JERK problem* in AI. The question is: What (if anything) does it show?

Gleeful opponents are quick to claim the imposter has been unmasked—just a clockwork orange after all, any semblance of sense being mere illusion. Meanwhile embarrassed designers are quickly patching up the oversight (or pointing out that they could) by adding another clause or qualification to cover this particular unanticipated quirk. "Nothing fundamental," they say, "just a little trip up." Unfortunately, it keeps happening, leaving spectators to wonder when it will ever end— or whether.

AI systems seem to lack the flexible, even graceful "horse sense" by which people adjust and adapt to unexpected situations and surprising results. So it's tempting to suppose that adding more "clauses" merely postpones the inevitable; like greasing a rusty bearing, it doesn't address the underlying problem, but at best hides it a little longer. In this view, then, graceful and jerky differ not in degree but in kind—and never the twain shall meet.

Always beware the swift dismissal. Several familiar analogies suggest the jerk/grace gap may not be as wide as it looks. For instance, if you run a movie slowly, the images lurch clumsily from posture to posture; but speed it up a little and those ungainly leaps blend into lovely, fluid motions. Similarly, at a certain threshold of resolution, the angular black grains of a photograph vanish into delicate contours and tonalities. In other words, the stark contrast between smooth and jumpy often disappears completely, if only the jumps are "small" enough.

Why couldn't that happen for AI? Just as our smooth visual

experience is somehow based in a "grainy" retina, perhaps our own easy, flexible good sense is ultimately based in (sufficiently fine-grained) rules and stereotypes.[22]

We can pursue that worry by thinking a little further about "typicality." Consider horses and living rooms. With rare exceptions, horses all have legs, ears, and tails; they contain blood, bones, and stomachs; they can be used for riding and pulling plows. Living rooms, likewise, have many things in common: by and large they have walls, windows, and ceilings; they typically contain soft chairs, low tables, and rugs; they can be used for loud parties or quiet conversations. It looks as if we have stereotypes for each.

But the cases are not really comparable. Horses not only have legs, they have exactly four legs, which, moreover, are a matched set, attached in standard locations; their bones are always arranged in a specifically equine skeleton; and there are, after all, rather few ways to ride a horse. Living rooms, by contrast, can have any number of windows, in any number of locations; the furniture, not to mention its arrangement, varies enormously from one room to the next, and it often doesn't match; finally, there are all kinds of ways to have a loud party or a quiet conversation. The point is that living rooms differ far more than horses do, particularly in the details that so often determine side effects.

But actual situations must differ even more than the rooms they (sometimes) occur in. As a result, stereotypes for situations (or for changes in situations) cannot possibly have the same kind of broad, reliable specificity as can stereotypes for horses, fountain pens, etc. Either they must disregard middle-level detail (mention the furniture and windows, but say nothing about what they're like or where) or else they must leave lots of open slots or "variables" to be filled in with specifics on each occasion. In the former case, the frame problem is not addressed because side effects always depend on situation-specific details: Is Baby resting on Papa (this time) or on the table next to him? On the other hand, if the crucial details are left as variables to be assigned, then there must be some mechanism for making and updating these assignments: When Papa moves, how are the slot-holders for the living room stereotype to be readjusted? But that's just the frame problem all over again, in the guise of applying stereotypes concretely, in real time.

In its quarter century, Artificial Intelligence has grown enormously, both in scope and in sophistication. Problems that could not even be posed in the late fifties, let alone tackled, are now the topics of elaborate and vigorous research. By disciplining theory, the computational model also liberates it: issues can be formulated and accounts developed that were hitherto essentially inconceivable. Certainly these early explorations have encountered unanticipated complexities and difficulties, but even they constitute a wealth of unprecedented empirical knowledge. In the meantime, AI is not standing still, but getting better. Each year there are systems with capabilities that none had before, and no end is in sight. Can we, then, extrapolate from present trends to ultimate success? To approach this question, we need a clearer idea of the goal.

6 Real People

Pragmatic Sense

Artificial intelligence has always been modeled on people. Our story began with the (philosophical) invention of the modern mind—especially the idea, inspired by the new science, of thought as *symbol manipulation*. Since then, however, we have focused more on the project of mechanizing that theory. Starting with notions of formality, automation, and interpretation, we developed a conception of *computation* as fundamentally symbol manipulation. From there we fleshed out the abstractions with five distinct computational architectures and then addressed Artificial Intelligence more specifically with a brief sampling of premier research and accomplishments. As it happens, AI is hard: among its discoveries, new problems loom as large as lasting solutions. Perhaps it is fitting, then, fo finish back at the beginning, with one clear specimen of intelligence known to science—ourselves.

Our aim is still to understand AI, but now, so to speak, from the other end. Instead of looking forward from its background and achievements, we will try to look backward from the goal, taking real people as its measure. The plan, in other words, is to scout around for omissions: phenomena that may be important to intelligence but have not been (perhaps cannot be) assimilated within the GOFAI tradition. Our explorations are tentative; in particular, no "disproofs" of AI are proposed, but at most some issues to ponder.

Let's begin by returning to the unsolved problem of *making sense*. In chapter 3 we saw that interpretation (hence computation) depends on it, but it's hard to define. For symbol systems, telling the truth is an exemplary way of making sense, though not the only one. Nonsymbolic systems, however, can also make sense, for instance, by *acting* in ways that exhibit intelligence.

Consider mice: they sport a modest worldly savvy but utter precious few symbolic expressions, true or otherwise. Whether they manipulate symbols inside their brains is beside the point; we credit them wits on quite different grounds—namely, their crafty little deeds. Wee Juan, for example, catches the aroma of cornbread on the sideboard, mingled, alas, with a scent of Felix below. After a moment's hesitation, he retreats warily into the wall and scampers up the back route, to emerge unseen behind the dishrack. What's intelligent about that? Well, we assume that Juan has various beliefs (about cats, cornbread, and the kitchen situation), various preferences (about eating versus being eaten), and that, on the basis of these, he acts *rationally*; that is, he thinks over his options, puts two and two together, and makes a canny move.

Ascribing mental states on the basis of behavior is much like interpreting a body of alien symbols; above all, the system must end up making sense—*pragmatic sense*, we could call it. For instance, it would be absurd to ascribe to Juan:

1. the *belief* (as he glances, trembling, toward Felix) that he beholds a stately sycamore;
2. the *intent* (as he scurries up the studs) of lying still and drifting off to sleep; or
3. the considered *decision* (based on sniffs and evinced in scrambling) to run for Governor of Utah.

These are absurd because there is no sensible relation between the ascribed states and the perceivable situation and/or the actions performed. Note that *truth* enters here as a "sensible relation" between perception and perceived; and that it is joined by a counterpart relation, *success*, between intent and accomplishment. We can summarize these points in the pithy principle:

ASCRIPTION SCHEMA: Ascribe beliefs, goals, and faculties so as to maximize a system's overall manifest competence.

Competence is the ability to achieve goals by making rational decisions in the light of knowledge and perception. The point, in other words is to "rationalize" the system's behavior, relative to its circumstances, by interpolating just the right mental structure to do the job.[1]

People, of course, both talk and act; hence interpretation and ascription must be coordinated. For instance, if Blanche, after saying "Watch out! That chair is hot," proceeds to sit on it herself, then something is amiss. We may have misinterpreted her; perhaps (unlike most of us) she likes to heat her seat; or maybe she was just lying to save her place. One way or another, however, word and deed must jibe, as the work of a single mind; in effect, symbolic and pragmatic sense together define a more general condition on meaningful coherence.

The complete robot is likewise both speaker and agent. In principle, however, it might seem that AI could concentrate on language alone and simply ignore the sense in actions. After all, Turing's test (with which we have not quarreled) essentially makes English fluency a sufficient condition for intelligence, so why bother with pragmatics? The answer is a fact about language so fundamental that it's easy to overlook: talking is itself a kind of action. *Speech acts* are at once symbolic expressions and things we *do* to further our ends. Accordingly, pragmatic sense is built into the notion of linguistic competence already and cannot be ignored by AI.

For instance: if you would like help at the library, the sensible move is to ask for it; if you want your neighbor to know his dog is loose, tell him; but if you need your plans to stay secret, keep them to yourself. In each case, the focus is not so much on what is said as on the practical effect of saying it. Similarly, if I agree to a trade (e.g., by saying "I accept your offer"), then I both express my consent and pursue my goals. In this case, however, I also participate in the institution of property exchange, which adds further pragmatic constraints: if I (knowingly) promise what I can't deliver, then my agreement is as defective as my morals. No system negligent of such matters could truly speak the language.

Box 1
Semantic Intrigue

The "ascription schema" constrains mental ascriptions once a system is specified; but it puts no limit on which systems should have mental states ascribed to them, as we can see by shifting from mouse psychology to:

MOUSETRAP PSYCHOLOGY: The trap *wants* to kill mice and *believes* it can whenever one nibbles the bait. Further, whenever it *feels* its trigger move, it comes to believe a mouse is nibbling. It now so feels, and straightaway it *acts*.

Painstaking observation confirms that the trap has mostly true beliefs and reliable perceptions; moreover, it acts on them consistently and rationally, achieving its goals with enviable success. But surely this is all silly and gratuitous. Satisfying the ascription schema is not sufficient to justify a set of mental ascriptions.

What else is required? Consider *Supertrap*, a system with a more versatile repertoire. When a mouse is soaked with gasoline, Supertrap strikes a match; when a mouse is under the shelf, he topples a dictionary; when a mouse is in a blender, he trips the switch; and of course, when a mouse nibbles the bait, he snaps shut. These habits betray a common malevolent thread, which is generalizable by (and only by) ascribing a persistent goal: dead mice. Without malice aforethought, it would be just a grisly (and incredible) coincidence that each gesture happened to be potentially lethal, not to mention exquisitely timed so as to realize that potential.

Mental ascriptions are like revolutionary warriors: either they hang together or they hang separately. Optimally, each ascription will figure in many rationalizations, in various combinations with other ascriptions. Thus, just as murderous intent helps explain several proclivities, in conjunction with sundry beliefs about gasoline, blenders, and the like, so also those beliefs should work together with other goals in still other accounts: how Supertrap starts a bonfire or makes a

milkshake, say. Subtler combinations reveal why he declines
to harm cats and barn owls, even when they nibble the bait
or reek of gas. Such tangled "conspiracy" of rationalizations
(through their common constituents) I call *semantic intrigue*; it
is how mental ascriptions "hang together" (cohere), and it is
what they need (over and above the ascription schema) to be
nongratuitous.

Ascription, like interpretation, is a way of discerning order
(nonrandomness) that would otherwise go unnoticed or be indescribable. The discovered pattern, of course, need not be
perfect; but flaws are identifiable as such only against the
backdrop of a pattern that is largely clear and reliable. (There
are no flaws in chaos.) Accordingly, semantic intrigue—the
pattern behind intelligently nonrandom behavior—makes possible the ascription of (scattered) *errors*. Suppose I jiggle a
mousetrap's trigger with a feather, and it snaps shut. Shall
we say it tried to kill "that mouse," believed the unlikely dic-
tum "Crush a feather, kill a mouse," or merely took the op-
portunity for some target practice? None of these makes any
more sense than the rest of mousetrap psychology. But if we
switch to Supertrap, and if we have independent evidence
that he expects some sneaky mice to try disguises, knows
where they might get feathers, etc., then there could be
enough intricacy to justify attributing some (particular) error.[2]

Much more interesting, though, is the way pragmatic sense can
"piggyback" on symbolic content and contribute something extra
to the communication. Consider the following "implications":

1. Mary asks Peter: "Where's Paul?" Peter replies: "He's in one
   of the Dakotas." Mary surmises that Peter doesn't know
   which Dakota.
2. A gourmet friend, leaving the restaurant as we enter, says:
   "Don't order the quiche tonight; it's dreadful." We assume
   she has tasted it.
3. Son: "I wish I had money for a movie." Father: "The lawn
   needs to be mowed." The son infers there's money in lawn
   mowing.

4. Marsha: "John is my mother's sister's husband's son." Presumably John is not Marsha's mother's sister's son, that is, not Marsha's cousin.

In no case is the conclusion logically entailed by the preceding remarks, even in conjunction with common knowledge. Rather, each inference involves suppositions about the other person's reasons: Why did he say *that*? Why did she put it that way?

Philosopher Paul Grice accounts for such inferences by treating talk as rational (inter)action. Thus we can draw conclusions not only from the views people actually express, but also from the way they conduct themselves as participants in this joint communicative venture. More specifically, Grice proposes four "maxims" of *conversational cooperation*, by which we can expect one another to abide:

1. Provide as much information as will be useful and appropriate.
2. Take care not to say false things.
3. Be relevant (stick to the topic, etc.).
4. Be perspicuous (clear, orderly, brief, and so on).

These are meant as general guidelines for the practice of conversation. They are, of course, neither complete not inviolable; but they do provide a rough standard, which, other things being equal, we can all take for granted.[3]

This has remarkable consequences. Since Mary assumes that Peter is being cooperative (there's no reason to doubt it), she assumes, in particular, that he is abiding by the first maxim to the best of his ability; so he must not know which Dakota Paul is in, or he would have said. Likewise, our gourmet friend, being careful not to say false things, wouldn't damn a quiche she hadn't tried. The father's remark about the unmowed lawn would violate the third maxim (relevance), unless it bore on the son's money problem; so the son figures it does. Finally, why would Marsha use the long, complicated description of John's relationship if she could use the more perspicuous "cousin"? So, apparently, she can't. By counting on pragmatic sense, more information is actually conveyed than given by the total content of the symbols as such (including entailments). Yet nothing other than words, no facial expressions, telltale intonations, or whatever, need be used: it could all be done by teletype.

Grice calls implications generated in this way (via presumption of conversational cooperation) *conversational implicatures*. Though examples like the foregoing are perhaps the most common, the most striking are transgressions deliberately contrived by speakers to *exploit* the maxims. Suppose a prospective employer wants my assessment of a former student and asks for a letter. I write: "I have known Mr. Frump for six years. He is always quietly pleasant and has no nasty habits. Yours truly,. . . ." Here I have flagrantly violated the expectation of providing as much pertinent information as I possess. The reader will not only notice this, but also realize that I anticipate his noticing. So I must be up to something that I expect him to "get": namely, the hidden message that Frump, though nice, is not particularly bright.

Unfortunately, conjoining pragmatic to symbolic sense does not render the underlying notion of "making sense" any clearer. In fact, the overview seems even messier, with less hope of any single unifying theme, such as truth, rationality, or competence. What's worse, these complications are only the beginning. A coherent, intelligible conversation, for instance, is far from just a random sequence of true utterances and/or successful speech acts: truth salad and success salad make as little sense as word salad. Yet in what do the continuity, development, legitimate digression, etc., of ordinary discourse (not to mention ordinary life) consist? These matters, of course, are much studied; but precise criteria are not forthcoming. I am myself unable to formulate a sharper general characterization than this:

NONASININITY CANON: An enduring system makes sense to the extent that, as understood, it isn't making an ass of itself.

Box 2
Metacognition

Most of our cognitive states concern things and events in the "outside world"; but some are instead about other cognitive states, either our own or somebody else's. Thus we can have beliefs, hopes, fears, etc., not only about external facts, but also about other beliefs, hopes, or fears. I call such thinking *metacognition*, to signal its special status as cognition about cognitions.

Drawing specific conclusions about other people's knowledge, motives, etc. on the basis of what they do is an example of metacognition; and understanding conversational implicatures is a special case of that. But we can also infer what people have in mind from their other actions, from what they tell us explicitly, from observing their situations (she must wish that bear would leave her alone), and from our general knowledge of what "everybody thinks."

Inasmuch as people are the most important, the most common, and the most complicated fixtures in our daily lives, it is essential that we be able to anticipate their actions and reactions in various possible circumstances. (Note that this generates a special version of the frame problem.) But such anticipation is impossible without considerable appreciation of their individual points of view, values, and goals. (This is, indirectly, the lesson of "semantic intrigue.") Hence metacognition is crucial to intelligent action, including, of course, intelligent speech.

Not only do we think about other people's thoughts; we also *reflect* on our own. Indeed, many philosophers have deemed reflection the essence of consciousness, or at least of (distinctively human) *self-consciousness*. Whether or not that's the case (and I'm not persuaded that it is), reflective self-awareness is certainly a criticial element in much that we regard as particularly mature, sophisticated, profound, insightful, and the like. Needless to say, no system incapable of metacognition could reflect.[4]

Mental Images

A three-inch cube is painted blue on two opposite sides and red on one side ("bridging" the blue sides). If this cube were sliced up into twenty-seven one-inch cubes, how many of the smaller cubes would have exactly one red and one blue side?

Think of the house you know best (perhaps the one you grew up in or where you live now) and ask: How many windows are there on the back wall of that house?

Imagine yourself riding on a giraffe; more specifically, imagine you are being chased across the African savanna, and your trusty giraffe is speeding you away at a full gallop. In this fantasy, where are your arms?[5]

Most people say they answer these questions not by reasoning in words, but by forming and inspecting *mental images*. Thus, to solve the cube puzzle, subjects "picture" the cube as sliced and then count the smaller cubes along the two edges where red and blue touch. The windows example is more memory than problem solving, but it's interesting because respondents fall into two camps. One group imagines looking at the house from the backyard and counting the visible windows; whereas the other imagines walking from room to room, looking at the back walls, and counting windows from the inside.[6]

The giraffe fantasy is different again: it's not a puzzle to solve (e.g., with a right answer), nor, for most of us, is it a recollection of anything we've ever seen or done. Yet nearly everybody says their arms are around the giraffe's neck. This can't be by extrapolation from more familiar horse- or camel-back riding, since riders don't normally embrace horses or camels by the neck. I suspect that, instead of just visualizing a scene, people somehow imagine themselves "into" the situation—whereupon they confront the problem of not falling off, and there, right in front of them, is a tall neck to grab.

Of course not all questions are (or even seem to be) answered using imagery. If I ask "How many dimes make up a dollar?" or "Is arsenic good for hamsters?" no images would be particularly helpful or relevant. Other questions are intermediate: they could be answered with images, but needn't be. For instance, most adults can tell how many ears a tiger has without forming an image and counting (though they could do the latter, if they wanted). On the other hand, if you ask them what shape a tiger's ears are, they'll most likely have to check the image. (Going still further, however, if you ask how many stripes the tiger has, probably even the image won't help.)

Apparently, then, there are (at least) two different kinds of mental representation:

QUASI-LINGUISTIC representations are complex symbols, with meanings jointly determined by syntactic structure and the interpretations of their simple constituents (e.g., English sentences, AI "stereotypes," computer programs).

QUASI-PICTORIAL representations "depict" their objects by resembling or mimicking them in some way that's hard to characterize; but pictures, scale models, and (perhaps) mental images are prime examples.

This is a bit ironic. Recall that Hobbes and Descartes, in developing the symbol-manipulation view, strove mightily to overcome Aristotle's "resemblance" theory of representation; yet, in the end, we may need both. Rehabilitating mental images, however, faces significant difficulties quite apart from historical irony.

The main problem is understanding what they might be. They can't be literal *pictures* in the brain, because there's no third eye inside the skull to look at them (and, besides, it's dark in there, and surgeons have never seen any, even with flashlights, and so on). But so what? There's also no inner eye (or homunculus) to read quasi-linguistic symbols "written" in the brain; and we now know that none is needed. The computer model proves in principle that it suffices to have internal structures (whether neural or electronic) that preserve certain *essential features* of language (digital syntax, mode/content distinction, semantic compositionality, etc.) together with *operations* that can take proper account of these features. Might an analogous reply work for inner images?

What are the essential features of pictorial representations, and what operations take account of them? Consider a floor plan of a house:

Box 3
Imagination and Perception

When we have a mental image, the experience is subjectively similar to the experience of perceiving the imagined object, only fainter and less definite. Thus visualizing the back of the house is rather like looking at it (with "the mind's eye"), imagining the sound of trumpets is like hearing them, and so on. A natural assumption, then, is that some of the same equipment that subserves perception is also used in imagery.

Moreover, there is independent support for this assumption. For one thing, it is notorious that imagination (dreaming, hallucination, etc.) can be mistaken for perception; and it has been shown experimentally that subjects can be fooled the other way as well (mistake perception for imagination). Further, it has been found that perceiving and imagining in the same modality at the same time is much harder than perceiving and imagining simultaneously in different modalities (seeing and hearing, say). This suggests that, at some level specific to the modality in question, perception and imagination compete for the same resources. Lastly, certain stroke victims who suffer peculiar visual impairments suffer exactly analogous impairments in their ability to form and use visual images. The implication is that the stroke-damaged tissue was involved in both processes.

Doesn't that settle it? If vision isn't "pictorial," what is? (Quick answer: pictures.) Unfortunately, it's not that simple. Grant that the experience of looking at a house is similar to the experience of looking at a picture of the house; that could show, at most, that the house and picture are similar to each other, not that the experience (or mental representation) is similar to either. In particular, it doesn't show that perception is anything like picturing. Again, grant that imagining a house is similar to seeing one; that still doesn't show that either representation is at all similar to a house (or to a picture of one).

In sum: perception and imagination seem to be in the same boat with regard to quasi-pictorial representation; but that alone doesn't show which boat they're in.

1. its *parts correspond* to relevant parts of the house (lines to walls, rectangles to rooms, etc.); and
2. the *structure of relations* among the corresponding parts is the same (since the hall is to the kitchen as the bath is to the bedroom, so the hall rectangle is to the kitchen rectangle as the bath rectangle is to the bedroom rectangle).

The second clause is essential; otherwise anything can "correspond" to anything. We could say the stairwell corresponds to the skin of a pomegranate, the parlor to three seeds scattered within it, and so on; but then the "structure of relations" is not preserved.[7]

The relations in a blueprint match those in a house almost trivially: all the relevant features are essentially the same, except for scale. Other cases, however, are trickier. For instance, some maps represent altitude not with scaled-down height but with gradations of color. The cartographer must then ensure that relational structures are maintained: for example, whenever A is shown higher than B, and B than C, then A must be higher than C. How are imagined distances, shapes, etc., represented in the brain? Nobody knows, but probably neither by scale model nor by color gradations; on the face of it, brains are more like pomegranates than sheets of paper.[8]

Typical *operations* involving images (think of the floor plan again) would include:

—moving the focus of one's attention from one part to another (scanning and/or panning);
—changing the orientation of the image (rotating);
—changing its scale (zooming);
—adding, deleting, or repositioning salient pieces ("cut and paste");
—recognizing (and counting) salient pieces or features;
—superimposing two images to compare them.

Such operations are easy to understand for images printed on paper, manipulated by hand, and inspected by eye; but what could they mean for mental images? How, for instance, can a mental image be rotated or zoomed without twisting or stretching some chunk of brain tissue? How can the "mind's eye" scan when it has no socket to roll in?

Astonishingly, however, all these operations and more seem to be possible with mental images, subject to certain interesting limitations. Let's begin with the *imaginal field* upon which images are viewed (and which is remarkably similar to the ordinary visual field):

—it has a measurable (though fuzzy-edged) shape and size, about the same as the visual field; and
—it has limited acuity (resolving power for fine details), sharper at the center, but not as sharp as vision.

Images and this field are distinct, since the images can be rotated, zoomed, and moved around relative to the field, which itself remains fixed. For instance, if you form an image of your TV set, the screen is quite prominent, with the control knobs roughly visible off to the side. But if you "zoom in" on those knobs, they get much bigger and clearer, with the rest of the set now enlarged out of view. Thus resolution and field of view stay the same, while visible detail and area vary with magnification.

How do psychologists know these things? Partly, no doubt, by examining their own experience and by compiling the introspective reports of others. But, in addition, there are a number of experimental techniques that provide impressive (though indirect) confirmation, while also making the results more precise and definite. The usual trick (widely used in psychological research) is to arrange an experimental setup so that *time* becomes the critical dependent variable—basically because it's involved in everything and easy to measure. Then other factors can be systematically altered to see how they affect the timing, either singly or in combination.

A famous and striking example is Shepard and Metzler's (1971) mental rotation experiment. They showed subjects pairs of line drawings (see figure 1) and asked them whether the two drawings depicted the same object. Sometimes the objects were the same but oriented at different angles; at other times, they were different

Figure 1   Mental Rotation

Shepard and Metzler showed subjects 1600 different pairs of perspective drawings and asked whether the two drawings depicted the same object. Three of the pairs are shown above: the first pair shows the same object, rotated in the plane of the paper; the second two drawings also depict the same object, but this time rotated in a horizontal plane perpendicular to the paper; the drawings in the third pair do not depict the same object (no rotation could make them coincide).

objects. Participants claimed that they answered by *rotating* one object *in their minds* until it lined up with the other, permitting them to see whether it matched. To check this claim, the experimenters measured how fast the subjects answered and then plotted these times against the angles of rotation required to line up the respective pairs. The reaction time (minus a small constant) is *directly proportional* to the amount of rotation needed.[9] It's hard to see how this could happen if subjects weren't really rotating images; so the natural conclusion is that they are—and, moreover, at a constant angular velocity. (The rate varies from person to person, but averages about 60 degrees per second or 10 rpm.)

Subsequent experiments supported that interpretation by confirming that images pass through intermediate angles as they rotate, just as if they were glued to a rigid turntable. Nothing, however, is easy: it turns out that larger and/or more complex images rotate more slowly. Further, if subjects are asked to rotate an image of something heavy (perhaps an object that they've just been handling), then the rate of rotation is not constant. It takes a while to get the image up to speed and also to slow it down at the other end—much as if the image itself were heavy. So rotating mental images can't be very like rotating photographs.

But I have saved the best for last. The original Shepard and Metzler experiment actually involved two different kinds of rotation: rotation in a plane perpendicular to the line of sight (like a wheel seen broadside) and rotation in a plane parallel to the line of sight (like a wheel viewed edge on). The latter is far more complicated because it involves all three dimensions. Different parts of the object pass into and out of view as they are rotated toward or away from the viewer or as one part passes temporarily behind another. Yet, astonishingly, subjects performed both rotations at virtually the same rate. This suggests that in both cases subjects are rotating not an inner copy of the experimenter's drawing, but a full three-dimensional image (inner "scale model"?) of the object depicted. To rationalize this discovery, one could solemnly point out that imagery evolved in a 3-D world, and so on; but I find it amazing, all the same.[10]

Though hundreds, if not thousands, of imagery experiments have been reported, there is much to learn. We know next to nothing about how these feats are performed in the brain, and there is no artificial analog nearly as compelling as the computer is for quasi-linguistic representations. Indeed, it remains controversial just what (if anything) ultimately distinguishes quasi-linguistic and quasi-pictorial representation[11]; nor, on the other hand, is there any strong reason to assume these two are our only modes of mental representation. In the meantime, we know distressingly little about how the two kinds of representation might interact; "pattern recognition" is perhaps a special case of this problem. Last but not least, it's far from clear what limits there are on the power of imagination (see box 4 for a speculation).

Why does imagery matter to Artificial Intelligence? On the one hand, computers can certainly form and manipulate images, as "computer graphics" graphically demonstrates. And, on the other hand, it wouldn't matter if they couldn't, since cognitive processes needn't explain everything about the mind. The reply to the first point is familiar but fundamental: not every computer simulation is GOFAI. Artificial Intelligence processes (in our strict sense) are essentially cognitive: that is, more or less rational manipulations of complex quasi-linguistic symbols.[12] Computer graphics techniques do not have anything like this character and are therefore quite irrelevant.

So the second issue is important. How much would GOFAI lose if it omitted imagination? To this the answer is much less clear. If it turns out that image manipulation is always fairly stupid and low-level, then cognitive science could safely adopt the following:

SEGREGATION STRATEGY: Assume that cognition and "phenomenon-X" (e.g., imagery) are realized in entirely different mental faculties and that they interact only via a well-defined cognitive input/output interface.

Thus intelligence is one thing, imagery another—and GOFAI concerns only the former. That's not to say that imagery is unreal or unimportant, but just that it's somebody else's problem. As with perception, cognitive science would get involved only at the "inside" of the symbolic interface. That all presupposes, however,

Box 4
Dynamic Imagery and the Frame Problem

The beauty of images is that (spatial) side effects take care of themselves. If I imagine myself astride a giraffe, my feet "automatically" end up near its belly and my head near the middle of its neck. If I have a scale model of my living room, and I put the model couch in the front alcove, it "automatically" ends up by the bay window and opposite the door. I don't have to arrange for these results deliberately or figure them out; they just happen, due to the shapes of the images themselves.

How far can such mimicry go? If I leave the tiny lamp on the model table while I move the table over by the couch, will the lamp come along for the ride? Probably. If I leave the model windows unlocked, will tiny thieves steal in at night and rip off the tiny stereo? Probably not. What about in imagination? Of course, we can well imagine robbers taking the stereo; but that isn't quite the question. The issue is what happens *automatically*, given the structure of the image and the operation performed. A robbery won't follow automatically in imagination any more than in a scale model. On the other hand, putting the couch into the alcove will *ipso facto* get it next to the window, even in imagination. The interesting question is the intermediate case: will the lamp "automatically" ride along with the table in a mental image, just as it does in a scale model?

I don't know; but two points seem worth stressing. First, the relevant relation between lamp and table is not purely spatial; it is crucial that the lamp is physically resting on and supported by the table. In scale models, spatial relations are modeled by (scaled down) spatial relations, and dynamic (physical) relations are modeled by (scaled down) dynamic relations; that's why the model works. We don't know what models what in the brain physiology of imagination; but it seems quite unlikely that spatial relations map straightforwardly onto (scaled down) spatial relations. Some more elaborate system must be at work; and if that's so, then I see no obvious reason why that more elaborate system couldn't model dynamic relations as well. My second point is then easy: automatic modeling of dynamic side effects may be just what is needed to solve the frame problem.

that image manipulation is basically peripheral to intelligence. Were imagination to be more intimately involved in sophisticated problem solving and daily competence, then it would become a serious alien intruder in the home territory of GOFAI, and thus a challenge to the fundamental adequacy of cognitivism. It could be that intelligence is *not* essentially symbol manipulation.[13]

Feelings

By common prejudice, robots have no feelings. Rational they may be, but coldly so: logical, efficient, insensitive. Fiction and its culture are curiously uncertain whether this is a blessing or a curse—whether thinking engines are spared the aggravating disruptions of mood and emotion, or, instead, forfeit all that makes life worth living. Either way, however, the view presupposes that thought and feeling are separate things, that understanding and affect are fundamentally distinct and disparate. And insofar as it addresses only cognition, Artificial Intelligence seems to rely on the same assumption. But that just underscores the essential questions: *Could* AI accommodate feelings? Does it *need* to?

Like all general presumptions about the mind, the thought/feeling separation has roots deep in the history of philosophy; it goes at least as far back as Plato and is well articulated in Hobbes and Descartes. To examine it, we would like a better idea of what feelings are; yet even today the psychology of affect is relatively underdeveloped. Experiments are difficult to design and assess (because variables are hard to measure and control); and theories tend to be offshoots or adaptations of ideas that originated elsewhere. Thus a philosopher might try a *conceptual analysis* of an emotional state (regret-P = know-P plus wish-not-P), while a behaviorist would prefer an *S-R construct* (fear = agitation plus disposition to flee). Psychoanalysts see passions as clues to the *subconscious* (revulsion = repressed Oedipal aggression), whereas psychobiologists emphasize *autonomic arousal* (lust = fired-up midbrain plus sweaty palms). And, predictably, cognitive psychologists look for *symbol structures* that can interact sensibly with knowledge and decision making (jealousy = "own" stereotype with inflated "threat" and "defend" values). This is not to suggest that nothing about affect is known, but only that a settled overview remains elusive.[14]

The aims of the present section are therefore modest: I offer merely a rough sorting of feelings into seven intuitive categories— in order, first, to keep the *variety* of phenomena conspicuous (lest simple answers appeal), and, second, to provide a framework for some tentative remarks about affect and Artificial Intelligence. The classification itself is neither complete nor sharp, and no systematic support or consequences are claimed (see tables 1 and 2).[15]

SENSATIONS (as of color or pain) are "raw inputs" from sense organs or other parts of the body. They always have definite input locations and modalities and are associated with particular stimulus conditions (on which their persistence depends); hence they can be induced easily and accurately in the laboratory. Sensations are closely tied to specific physiological functions and are remarkably independent both of cognition and of one another. Thus a person can be insensate in one respect (color-blind, nonticklish, numb gummed), but otherwise perfectly normal. By the same token, it's easy to imagine dumb animals experiencing a full range of sensations, even ones that we lack (sonar, for example).

REACTIONS (PASSIONS) are, like sensations, "automatic" responses to the current input. But, unlike sensations, they are not associated with particular input organs or modalities; indeed, the input can be news of distant events or even a sudden realization. Still, passionate reactions are immediate and involuntary, often "visceral," usually short lived. Knowledge is involved, to the extent of recognizing relevant circumstances (you can't be horrified at the carnage without noticing the mangled bodies), but careful distinctions and inferences are quite beside the point. Reactions as such are never justified; they are at best appropriate, at worst out of proportion.

Table 1   Seven Kinds of Feelings

Sensations

seeing green	hunger/thirst	pain (stab, burn, hit)
hearing a tone	breathlessness	electric shock
taste of salt	full bladder/release	stomach cramps
felt warmth, pressure	tingling (foot asleep)	throbbing headache
felt acceleration	tickling	tired, aching muscles
nausea	being petted, nuzzled	too loud, too bright
dizziness	orgasm	itching

Reactions (Passions)

delight	revulsion	amazement
attraction	fright	exasperation
compassion	horror	being taken aback
lust	rage	being dumbfounded

Emotions

gratitude	regret	jealousy
being pleased	anger	envy
eagerness	grief	pity
exultation	fear	indignation
satisfaction	sorrow	worry

Interpersonal feelings

love	affection	devotion
friendship	goodwill	trust
hatred	enmity	being tired of

Sense of merit—other people

respect	esteem	admiration
contempt	spite	scorn
appreciation	disdain	reverence

Sense of merit—oneself

pride	embarassment	conceit
self-respect	shame	modesty
self-righteousness	feeling guilty	hurt feelings

Moods

joy, elation, walking on air	misery, depression, dejection
cheer, gaiety, bubbliness	melancholy, gloom, the blues
interest, having fun, entertainment	boredom, ennui, the blahs
feeling pleasant, agreeable, sweet	feeling grumpy, grouchy, sour
patience, tolerance, even temper	testiness, irritability, petulance
serenity, calm, peace	agitation, nervousness, the jitters
feeling loose, easy-going, casual	feeling tense, uptight, stiff
optimism, confidence, encouragement	pessimism, resignation, discouragement

Table 2   *Seven Kinds of Feelings: Comparison*

	"Object" to which feeling pertains	Subtle sense of object involved	Rational support is relevant	Dimension of variation	Durability	Animals (dogs) can feel them
Sensations	Stimulus quality	No	No	Intensity	Low	Yes
Reactions (passions)	Event or situation	Only a little	No	Fervor	Low	Only a little
Emotions	Event or situation	Some	Some	Fervor	Medium	Only a little
Interpersonal feelings	Familiar person	Yes	Only a little	Depth	High	Only a little
Sense of merit— other people	Person & deeds	Yes	Yes	Conviction	High	No
Sense of merit— oneself	Self & deeds	Yes	Yes	Conviction & depth	High	No
Moods	Everything (nothing)	???	No	Depth	Medium	Only a little

What I call EMOTIONS, on the other hand, are more measured, more discriminating. The point is not that they are less powerful—fear and anger are not fright and rage watered down—but rather they are more intelligent, more responsive to argument and evidence. Anger and fear can perfectly well be justified (or not), while still being notoriously hard to control. Emotions are more related to current beliefs than to current input; hence they can build up more slowly and last longer. Like reactions, emotions vary in fervor *with regard to* some event or situation; by contrast, sensations vary only in the intensity with which the stimulus seems to strike.

INTERPERSONAL FEELINGS focus not on events or situations, but on particular, familiar individuals. Devotion, friendship, hatred—these are only indirectly responsive to reason and evidence: one can love a rascal, quite irrationally. They are, however, richly sensitive to the scope and nuance of the other person, appreciating him or her profoundly, as a complete individual. Accordingly, though these feelings can certainly vary in ardor (especially in the short run), I think a more significant dimension is *depth*: the degree to which a full sense of the other person is integrated within the feeling and thereby within oneself. We know the flaws and foibles and love them too, on good days and bad. Such feelings make a difference to who we are; they can last a lifetime.

By comparison, our SENSE of someone's MERIT (as in respect, contempt, etc.) is more specific and more detached. I can both admire a man's eloquence and scorn his views, while having little personal involvement in either. Rational considerations are highly relevant and apt to be subtle and penetrating. Hence these feelings vary not so much in depth as in conviction: my esteem may be hesitant at first but later firm and durable. Indeed, the character of judgment is so apparent here that it threatens to eclipse the affective factor. Yet respect, reverence, and disdain are clearly and essentially felt; they are not mere cognitive estimates or apathetic evaluations (like ratings of socks or toasters), but powerful, sometimes moving responses to people and their deeds.

Our sense of our OWN MERIT is much like our sense of another's, except that it involves our selves. That difference, however, is crucial; we shall return to it in the next section.

MOODS are the odd ducks on this pond. Unlike the other categories, moods pertain to nothing in particular but somehow "color" the whole world at once. When one is melancholy, no sky is cheery: fluffy clouds are at best invisible, at worst a taunting mockery. Though events (and chemicals) can influence them, moods are not automatic responses to stimuli, nor are they ever rational or justified (though perhaps, like passions, they can be "out of proportion"). To describe the onset of moods, we resort to saying they "descend on" or "fill" or "come over" us. They're like vapors that seep into and infect everything we're about: what we think and what we notice, what's desirable and what seems likely, what's worth pursuing and how best to proceed. Moods are of intermediate duration (hours to weeks) and vary neither in fervor nor in conviction, but again in some kind of depth. Existentialists love them.

It is surprisingly difficult to gauge the bearing of these matters on Artificial Intelligence. Even sensation, which ought somehow to be the easiest case, is deeply perplexing. There's no denying that machines can "sense" their surroundings, if all that means is discrimination—giving different symbolic responses in different circumstances. Electric eyes, digital thermometers, touch sensors, etc. are all commonly used as input organs in everything from electronic toys to industrial robots. But it's hard to imagine that these systems actually feel anything when they react to impinging stimuli. Though the problem is general, the intuition is clearest in the case of pain: many fancy systems can detect internal damage or malfunction and even take corrective steps; but do they ever hurt? It seems incredible; yet what exactly is missing? The more I think about this question, the less I'm persuaded I even know what it means (which is not to say I think it's meaningless).[16]

But, baffling or not, perhaps it doesn't matter. If robots can "sense" well enough to do their work and get around in the world, who cares whether they feel any subjective experiences (whatever those might be)? Or, to put it in terms of psychology, if the felt quality of sensation makes no difference to intelligent behavior, except as a cause of inputs, then it's no problem for cognitive science. The *segregation strategy* introduced earlier could work here as well: sensations, though real and important, are noncognitive and hence can be safely relegated to some other faculty. Of course, they would still affect our thoughts and goals, but only by generating special quasi-linguistic inputs to the cognitive computer: "red here now" or "fierce, stabbing pain in left shin this instant." Thinking would take over from there.

Passions are not so easily dispatched. On the face of it, robotic rage and delight, not to mention lust or revulsion, are even harder to swallow than electronic pains and visions; yet they seem more intimately cognitive than mere input modes. Nevertheless, a subtler segregation might handle the case: it could be that passions are fundamentally compound, with one component rooted in mammalian physiology, another allocated to the faculty of sensation proposed above, and a third being genuinely cognitive. That neatly accommodates the obvious arousal aspect, the powerful affective quality, and the element of recognition, while also, via the physiological factor, accounting for the absurdity of computer lust.[17] Moreover, it supplies the needed segregation without rendering the states completely noncognitive; rather, the cognitive and noncognitive *components* are segregated and interact (bidirectionally) only through suitable input/output channels. Incidentally, it is often supposed that the cognitive component provides much of the differentiation among passionate reactions, with the arousal and affective components being comparatively nonspecific; but that's not essential to the segregation.

Now, if this "divide and conquer" tactic works for passions, maybe it could apply also to emotion and sense of merit. Not only would the parallel itself be gratifying, but there might be a basis for explaining the similarities and contrasts among the different categories. Arousal, for instance, is less conspicuous in reverence and scorn than in fright or horror, whereas thoughtful estimation is less notable in the latter. Meanwhile, gratitude and grief fall somewhere in between on both scales, suggesting, perhaps, that varying proportions within the compound are what differentiates these classes of affect. Of interest to us, however, is that intellect could then do without them all, apart from their cognitive components. To be sure, ability to feel compassion, fear, admiration, and the like would make a powerful difference to AI systems; but need it make a difference to their intelligence? The above common prejudice assumes otherwise, and a suitable segregation just might support that view.

What about interpersonal feelings? Why is a machine being "in love" such an alien idea? Not, I think, because it lacks the hormones and midbrain—for blushing and tingling are at most incidental. Nor could it be that beliefs and goals are not involved in these states. Indeed, from one perspective, friendship, enmity, and devotion seem just like cognitive structures: complex combinations of adjusted values and assessments, hopes and plans, assumptions and commitments. What's distinctive is the way these relationships flesh out and give meaning to our own lives. An existence without friendship or love, or at least hatred or enmity, would be hopelessly barren and hollow, as if there weren't really anybody there—just a contentless, pointless cognitive skeleton. Apparently, then, interpersonal feelings presuppose personality; to love or trust or hate, you have to be somebody, with a "life" of your own to fill and devote. Whether intelligence and ego can be segregated is the topic of the next section.

Moods, it seems to me, are the toughest of all, if only because they are so peculiar. Since they're not generally localized to any particular stimulus or condition, they can hardly be conceived as inputs ("melancholy here now" or some such). But since they're also not localized in topic or content, it's equally difficult to attribute their cognitive relevance to any determinate cognitive component within them. Yet moods do profoundly affect what and how we think, in their own nonvoluntary, nonrational, and oddly pervasive way. Thus the segregation strategy doesn't have the same kind of plausible foothold it seems to have for other cases: there's no obvious "joint" at which to carve. I suspect that moods may turn out to be an important problem for cognitive science; it is, however, quite puzzling what that might imply for GOFAI.

This section has been modest. I neither endorse nor reject the suggestion that (some) affects may be composite or the associated thought/feeling segregations; nor dare I put much weight on any of the difficulties noted. I do believe the following: (1) affective phenomena are rich and varied; (2) their relation to intellect and cognition is far from clear; and therefore (3) they deserve a lot more study, even in AI.

Ego Involvement

CATLAP: Why did the computer move its queen over here?
DOGLEG: To attack my rook and pawn, I assume.
C: I see; but why is it attacking your rook and pawn?
D: Well, they're the key to my whole defense; if it could get past them, it would have a clear path to my king.
C: And what does it want that for?
D: To win. Capturing the opposing king is how you win.
C: Of course, of course; but why is the computer trying to win?
D: Oh, (mumble)
—it hopes to make a good impression on all its new friends.
—conscience (it donates prize money to Hackers Anonymous).
—it's a feisty little bastard with an inferiority complex.
—it can't help it, it's just built that way.

What is Dogleg to say? We have, I think, conflicting intuitions. In some sense, the computer *is* "trying" to win (so the first three replies seem okay); but at the same time it doesn't "give a damn" at all (so the final exchange seems bizarre). Apparently, there's a difference between something having a high goal-value and it really mattering. Could a GOFAI system ever truly care about anything?[18]

Most practical reasons and actions are *instrumental*: we undertake one thing in pursuit of another. Thus I go to the store in order to buy bread, in order to make a sandwich, and so on. Clearly, however, such rationales, such further goals, cannot go on forever—some goals must be "ultimate," in the sense that they are pursued for no (other) reason. How can that be? Biological wiring sets some goals: under certain conditions, my body will make me hungry, whether I like it or not (I'm just built that way). Also, occasionally, we act on whim: What the heck, let's take the scenic route. More often, we follow blind habit or social custom: How do *you* hold a fork, or pronounce the word 'either', and why? Wiring, whim, habit, and custom—those don't seem so hard to automate. Are they the extent of ultimate reasons?

Return to the chess example, but substitute for the computer a lanky lad from Brooklyn. Why is *he* trying to win? There are many possible answers, of course, but the following might be typical:

1. To earn public recognition and esteem and thereby validate or augment his own self-esteem. (Were he defeated, he might lose face and feel smaller or less worthy.)
2. For the pride and personal satisfaction that come from accomplishing something difficult (as opposed, perhaps, to frustration or disappointment in himself).
3. To show off, strut his stuff, or prove his prowess (the underside of vanity being humiliation and fear of inadequacy).

These have in common that the young man's *self-image* is at stake, his *ego* is involved. Thus his performance reflects on who he is, and how he may regard himself—an issue that matters to him not for any ulterior end (not instrumentally), but *for its own sake*. We are all familiar with "ego" as a potent motivator in matters large and small; yet machine and beast alike are utterly devoid of it.[19] Perhaps that's one reason why the computer can't really "care" about its chess game (or anything else).

But what has ego to do with cognition and intellect? Evidently nothing, sometimes. In showing that chess computers lack the personal involvement of their human opponents, we show also that they don't need it—for they play excellent chess. This point extends from simple pocket calculators through elaborate expert systems: each is competent within its domain, and quite selfless. Can AI rest assured, then, that understanding and ego are independent in principle, that intellect and self can be segregated? I suspect not.

A friend of mine tells a story about when she was in college and kept a white rat as a pet. It was tame enough to follow quietly at her heels, all around campus; but one day, startled by a dog, it took hasty refuge far up her pantleg. Unfortunately, it lodged itself so tightly that it couldn't back out; and, in the meantime, she didn't dare move, for fear of crushing it. So, after a moment's hesitation, she sheepishly let down her jeans, eased out a quivering rodent, and won a round of applause from delighted passersby.

Most people find this anecdote amusing. Why? Much of it, surely, is that we identify with the young heroine and share vicariously in her obvious embarrassment, while at the same time feeling relieved that it didn't happen to us. Embarrassment (and the corresponding relief), however, can be experienced only by a being that has some sense of *itself*—a sense that is important to it and that can be awkwardly compromised on occasion. If no personality or "self-consciousness" were at stake, there would be nothing to be embarrassed (or relieved) on behalf of. The point is not merely that my friend's ego was involved in her original embarrassment, but that *our* egos are engaged as we hear the story, share in that embarrassment, and smile.

I suggest that such ego involvement may be integral to the process of understanding. This isn't just a variation on empiricism—that you can't know what 'embarrassing' means until you've experienced it yourself (as: you can't imagine licorice unless you've tasted some). Rather, the idea is more radical: that actual, current feelings (such as embarrassed twinges, vicarious excitement, and the like) may be essential factors in real-time understanding. People do get involved in what they hear, and their own reactions affect the listening—what they notice, how they conceptualize, what it reminds them of, and so on. Storytellers count on these responses, much as they count on common sense, taking advantage of them for efficiency, for disambiguation, for effect.

For instance, in recounting the tale of the rat, I used the word 'sheepishly'. Did I equivocate? Obviously, I didn't mean that my friend acted like a sheep; common sense quickly eliminates that. But 'sheepish' can mean stupid or meek as well as bashfully embarrassed; and this is reflected in alternative translations, for example into German. It would take some fairly delicate intellection to rule out the misreadings rationally; yet any translating machine that got them wrong surely wouldn't have understood the story. *We* don't have that problem, because we put ourselves into the heroine's position and feel the embarrassment firsthand.

A different perspective is illustrated by what happened when Ralph asked his new friend Lucifer: "Why, when you're so brilliant, beautiful, and everything, did you ever get kicked out of Heaven?" Rather than answer right away, Lucifer suggested they play a little game. "I'll sit up here on this rock," he said, "and you just carry on with all that wonderful praise you were giving me." Well, Ralph went along, pouring out all the glory and adulation he could think of. But, as the hours passed, it began to get tiresome; so, finally, he said: "Look, why don't we add a little variety to this game—say, by taking turns?" "Ahh," sighed Lucifer, "that's all I said, that's all I said."[20]

Here we feel both with and for Ralph, as he and we are together manipulated by Lucifer's adroit dodge. First, we are sucked in by the irksome pointlessness of the adoration game and easily appreciate Ralph's eventual impatience. Then suddenly the trap set for Ralph springs on us, and we land in Lucifer's shoes, getting tired of Paradise. Helplessly, then, we also share his innocent indignation at "our" modest proposal getting blown into the crime of the ages by God's infinite vanity. But that reaction is taboo; in being driven to it, we relive not only Lucifer's impossible rationalization, but also the unbearable shame behind it—hence we laugh.

One final example will demonstrate the range of the phenomenon I'm getting at and also illustrate a different way in which the reader's personal involvement can be essential. It is a fable of Aesop's.

One day a farmer's son accidentally stepped on a snake and was fatally bitten. Enraged, the father chased the snake with an axe and managed to cut off its tail. In return, the snake nearly ruined the farm by biting all the animals. Well, the farmer thought it over and finally took the snake some sweetmeats, saying: "I can understand your anger, and surely you can understand mine. But now that we are even, let's forgive and forget, and be friends again." "No, no," said the snake, "take away your gifts. You can never forget your dead son, nor I my missing tail."

Obviously, this story has a moral, which a reader must get in order to understand.

Getting a moral, however, is more than just figuring it out and making it explicit; for otherwise Aesop could have conveyed his

Box 5
Wouldn't a Theory Suffice?

The examples are meant to show that listeners' personal involvements and reactions are an integral constituent in the
process of understanding. The implication is that a system
that lacked any ego or personality would be incapable of
such understanding. But does the conclusion follow?
Wouldn't it be enough to know about personality (and how it
affects people), without actually having any? Thus, imagine
Flo, a cognitive system with no ego of her own but supplied
with a rich and detailed theory of Curly, ego and all. Couldn't
Flo understand stories purely intellectually, by consulting her
theory, figuring out how Curly would react, and drawing appropriate inferences from that?

This suggestion is curiously self-defeating. Suppose for a
moment that a suitable theory could be formulated, and consider how it would be used. Note first that no theory could
predict Curly's responses without working through his salient
intervening thoughts (a person's input/output function has no
simpler description than its generating process). In other
words, the theory must take the form of a model—inevitably
named Moe—that yields its predictions by "simulating" Curly
in detail. In particular, the simulation must include Curly's
cognitive processes along with his ego, because cognitive
states crucially shape and guide ego involvement.

But now what have we got? Flo is selfless and hence cannot understand certain stories except by activating Moe. He,
in turn, cannot simulate Curly's involved reactions without
simulating his thoughts as well; so, basically, Flo has to give
Moe the whole story and then simply plagiarize his response.
In other words, the idea of Flo understanding the stories cog-
nitively, with occasional reference to her theory of selves, is
a total scam. Moe (in whom there is no such segregation) is
doing all the work, while Flo contributes nothing.

So what about Moe? Does he merely simulate Curly (the
way computer models simulate hurricanes), or does he actually understand the stories and feel the involvements? That

depends; we don't know what kind of theory Moe instantiates. One beauty of automatic formal systems is medium independence: to simulate one is to *be* one. Hence, if Moe is based on a GOFAI-type theory of Curly, then he actually has a mind of his own and literally understands. But, by the same token, he also has a self of his own—not just a theory of one.

point more directly by just saying what he meant, and skipping the allegory:

A child is like a part of oneself, such as a limb. The similarities include:
1. losing one is very bad;
2. if you lose one, you can never get it back;
3. they have no adequate substitutes; and thus
4. they are literally priceless.
Therefore, to regard trading losses as a "fair exchange" or "getting even" is to be a fool.

But this is just a list of platitudes. It's not that it misrepresents the moral, but that it lacks it altogether—it is utterly flat and lifeless. By comparison, Aesop's version lives: it has a moral because we as readers identify with the farmer. Hence we too are brought up short by the serpent's rebuke, and that makes us look at ourselves.

The terrifying thing about losing, say, one's legs is not the event itself, or the pain, but the thought of being a legless cripple for the rest of one's life. It's the same with losing a son, right? Wrong. Many a parent indeed would joyously give both legs to have back a little girl or boy who is gone. Children can well mean more to who one is than even one's own body. So who are you, and what is truly valuable in your life? The folly—what the fable is really about—is not knowing.

"But," someone will protest, "sense of humor, religious appreciation, and/or literary refinement should never be confused with *pure* intelligence." The vision of a pure intellect—the idea that reason has a character and validity of its own, independent of living situations—is as old as pure logic and pure mathematics. But how do we test it? Importantly, AI itself has already tarnished the dream by showing that knowledge representation is critical to commonsense understanding. Equally important, that fundamental discovery was not (and could not have been) made in the sterile context of toy puzzles and contrived domains. Only when the discourse itself is fully natural can the lurking richness of natural understanding truly show itself. In other words, any test systematically less demanding than Turing's test runs the risk of "purifying" the hardest problems right under the rug.

Though the examples in this section are not transcripts of unrehearsed dialogue, neither are they specimens of highbrow literature or obscure transcendental philosophy. Perfectly ordinary people can understand these passages without unusual effort; hence, any artificial system that could not understand them would not have attained the level of ordinary human understanding.

It is interesting to note that the tactic employed here might have wider application. Thus we have argued against the segregation of self and intellect on the grounds that real-time ego involvement can be an integral factor in the process of understanding ordinary discourse; those are essentially the same grounds that earlier torpedoed the segregation of intelligence and knowledge. But everyday conversation is fraught with life and all its perils; the listener's involvement goes far beyond common knowledge and self-image. A skillful raconteur can engage our emotions and our passions; we love the heroes and despise the villains as their adventures catapult us from optimism through tension to miserable gloom and back again. I see no reason to doubt that these standard and predictable responses can contribute effectively to the process of normal understanding. GOFAI will not have succeeded until its systems can be gripped and wrenched by the dramas of daytime television.

Box 6
Artificial Ego

Suppose it's true that no system without a self of its own—no system that wasn't somebody—could understand ordinary English. Does that undermine the project of GOFAI? Not necessarily. It only makes the problem larger by requiring that AI systems include artificial egos as well. What that might entail is hard to say.

Obviously, a system with a "self-image" must be capable of self-representation and reflection; in fact, it will need a full repertoire of metacognitive abilities (see box 2) if, for instance, its public standing will ever be relevant. Further, to account for the motivating power of ego involvement, the current status or condition of this self-image must be a matter of peculiar importance and value, yet also vulnerable to the vicissitudes of performance and perception. And that implies, in turn, that the system has some standard and scheme against which it measures personal worth—both its own and others'.

But self involves more than that; it presupposes a kind of continuity and ongoing ownership. A single event cannot be shameful, embarrassing, or foolish in isolation, but only as an act in the biography of a responsible, historical individual—an enduring person whose personality and character it reveals and can therefore threaten. With embarrassment, whether original or vicarious, it is essentially and necessarily the same me who then bumbled and now blushes. Only a being who cares about who it is as a continuing, selfsame individual can care about guilt or folly, self-respect or achievement, life or death.

I suspect there is more: I suspect that moral integrity, conscience, and the courage of one's convictions—or at least the possibility of these—are also integral to the structure of self. And who knows what else?

The Very Idea

> FORT LAUDERDALE -- Former plastic surgeon and real estate tycoon Phyllis Crock disclosed today ambitious plans for artificial wine production in the Everglades region. The new wine will be synthesized entirely from swamp water and coal tar, Dr. Crock explained. Its quality is expected to be outstanding, at a very competitive price. Federal development grants have already . . .

Naturally, Dr. Crock's announcement sparks considerable comment—most of it falling into four main categories:

ENTHUSIASM: "Hey, terrific! Isn't science wonderful? Put me in for a dozen cases of Crypto-Cabernet."

ABOMINATION: "This hideous outrage jeopardizes not only thousands of jobs in the wine industry but also millions of discriminating palates in future generations; and it surely causes cancer."

DEBUNKING: "It's all a sham. No matter what the stuff tasted like, even were it identical to a fine Bordeaux, it couldn't possibly be *wine*, because [it's not fermented, it's not made from grapes . . .]."

SKEPTICISM: "Time will tell, but I'll be amazed if it's much tastier than kerosene: coal tar and swamp water are awfully contaminated, and they totally lack the organic molecules needed for decent wine."

By coincidence, analogs of these same attitudes are also common in public reactions to Artificial Intelligence. Enthusiasm and abomination—ranging from pipe dreams of permanent leisure to nightmares of super-smart robots usurping the human race—are alike in taking "real" AI for granted.[21] Many difficult and important issues are raised by these points of view; but, alas, they are beyond the scope of our discussion. Debunking and skepticism, on the other hand, take nothing for granted but focus instead on the principal question: Is GOFAI really possible?

By *debunking* I mean purporting to prove *a priori* that AI is not possible. Arguments *a priori* rest on general principles and/or conceptual intuitions and hence are more or less independent of empirical results. Thus debunkers also claim that Turing's test is irrelevant. Basically, their thesis is: no matter how good AI systems get at imitating honest-to-goodness (human) intelligence, they'll still be mere imitations—counterfeits, fakes, not the genuine article. Typically, the argument goes like this:

1. nothing could be intelligent without X [for some X]; but
2. no GOFAI system could ever have X; therefore
3. no GOFAI system could ever be intelligent.

What's X? Popular suggestions include feelings, creativity, personality, learning, freedom, intuition, morality, and so on. Unfortunately, once X is specified, the necessary support for one or both of the premises usually turns out to be rather thin. It really isn't self-evident, for example, that nothing could be intelligent without feelings or that no GOFAI system could ever be creative; and being intuitively certain "down in your bones" just doesn't change that.[22]

Far and away the most attractive candidate for X, however, is *consciousness*—a topic conspicuous for its absence from both this book and the technical literature in cognitive science. Indeed, it is tempting to suppose that such deafening silence must conceal a nasty little secret; and perhaps it does. But, before gloating too much, we might well remember that no other psychological theory sheds much light on consciousness either: it's pretty mysterious, no matter how you look at it. The point is not merely that all accounts are equally bad off (though that's true), but rather that we have so little grip on the phenomena that, again, premises 1 and 2 are very hard to defend. This doesn't meant that the issue can be dismissed, only that it's extraordinarily elusive. (Could consciousness be a theoretical time bomb, ticking away in the belly of AI? Who can say?)

Still, we dare not scorn intuition altogether: much of philosophy and even science is based on a refined and articulated sense of what "makes sense." How do we refine our intuitions? A strategy

Box 7
Cognition and Consciousness

Philosopher Daniel Dennett is rare among cognitivist sympathizers in trying to accommodate consciousness in an AI-like model.[23] He begins with the observation that consciousness is a kind of *access*: we can *tell* what's on our minds. This means two closely related things. First, we can *introspect* on our own minds (we know what we think); second, we can *speak* our minds (we say what we think). These are related in that introspection is like "telling oneself," though not necessarily in any public languge and perhaps more thoroughly and candidly.

Of course, we are neither aware of nor able to articulate everything that goes on in our heads; in fact, according to most theories, only a small fraction of our total mental contents and processing is accessible to telling (ourselves or others)—namely, the fraction of which we are conscious. So Dennett proposes a special memory component, called M, that happens to contain this particular fragment of our thoughts. M serves mainly as an intermediary or buffer zone between perception, verbal expression, and (via the inner referee) the rest of the mind: problem solving, long-term memory, commonsense inference, etc.

The next move is then the crucial one: it's a mistake, says Dennett, to suppose that we can tell what's on our minds *because* we have some "inner light" (awareness, consciousness, whatever), that makes the contents of M accessible. Rather, our verbal and other faculties have access to those contents simply because of the way we are built; and that access precisely *is* consciousness. In other words, all consciousness amounts to is a built-in ability to "tell" what's contained in a certain memory buffer—an ability that poets and philosophers then describe in terms of inner lights, etc., as if to provide an explanation.

This is a powerful idea; but still, I think, not really satisfactory. For one thing, it's too pat: consciousness has contents, so we make it a container. Presto, a theory! but what does that explain? Why for instance, should perceptions, feelings, reflections, and verbalizations be funneled through the same buffer? Why is careful, rigorous thinking always conscious? What does M have to do with self-control, "self-consciousness" (diffidence), intent, alertness, insight, presence, and so on? Closer to the core, why does M seem so different from all my other memory buffers—or rather, why is M the only one that "seems" any way at all?

that sometimes works is devising *thought experiments* that test the limits of a concept. Here's an example. Suppose someone designed a GOFAI system that would (allegedly) be conscious, have emotions, and all the rest. Then we know that, at some level of description, this system consists of inner players manipulating and exchanging formal tokens according to formal rules; and we also know that all such systems are essentially medium independent. So, imagine rewiring the city of Los Angeles to facilitate the required interactions and then recruiting millions of Angelenos to manipulate tokens according to those rules. By definition, this sprawling monstrosity—let's call it Gabriel—would be an actual instance of that GOFAI system, with all its relevant properties.[24]

Now ask yourself: could Gabriel—not the people in it, but the whole thing as a single unit—be conscious? One gasps at the thought; it seems preposterous on the face of it, which makes us suspicious of the original claim. That's how thought experiments work: they magnify our intuitions and sometimes clarify them. But they can also be treacherous. In this case, for instance, I am as appalled as anyone by the thought of a conscious Los Angeles; but I cannot say quite why—and that leaves me uncomfortable. Perhaps the example shows not so much the limits of possibility as the limits of my imagination.

Debunkers want to shoot AI down before it takes off, regardless of any actual research, as if the very idea were somehow crazy or incoherent. But the prospects for cheap victories strike me as slender. As I see it, cognitive science rests on a profound and distinctive *empirical* hypothesis: that all intelligence, human or otherwise, is realized in rational, quasi-linguistic symbol manipulation. This hypothesis might be true, and it might not (or maybe it's partly true and partly not).

Skeptics concede that the hypothesis is empirical, that it won't be settled by "armchair philosophizing," but are still doubtful about the outcome. Thus, the problems and open questions spelled out in this chapter might give one pause; and, of course, the same intuitive perplexities that inspire debunkers can equally support more moderate hesitations. (Even if I keep an open mind about Gabriel in principle, I can remain dubious in fact.) The important point, however, is that we look ultimately to the laboratory for answers.

Most people who know much about AI are very impressed—and rightly so, for it epitomizes the most powerful and successful approach to psychology ever known. Metaphysical paradoxes are dispatched with apparent ease; concrete theories are formulated with unprecedented scope and detail; technical discoveries are many and deep. Moreover, there is a "wave of the future" air about it: the AI bandwagon carries farsighted progressives, bold and unfettered. Yet, in some sense, Artificial Intelligence has not kept its "promise." There are today no arguably intelligent machines (discounting "micro-experts"); no plausible fraction of common sense has ever been programmed; no current system has the linguistic competence of a three-year-old child—and none is in sight.

But what would you expect? Well, back in 1957, just eighteen months after the Logic Theorist was announced (and six weeks after the first Sputnik), Herbert Simon said what he and Allen Newell expected:

1. That within ten years [i.e., by 1967] a digital computer will be the world's chess champion, unless the rules bar it from competition.
2. That within ten years a digital computer will discover and prove an important new mathematical theorem.
3. That within ten years a digital computer will write music that will be accepted by critics as possessing considerable aesthetic value.

4. That within ten years most theories in psychology will take the form of computer programs, or of qualitative statements about the characteristics of computer programs.

It is not my aim to surprise or shock you—if indeed that were possible in an age of nuclear fission and prospective interplanetary travel. But the simplest way I can summarize is to say that there are now in the world machines that think, that learn and that create. Moreover, their ability to do these things is going to increase rapidly until—in a visible future—the range of problems they can handle will be coextensive with the range to which the human mind has been applied.[25]

Shocking or not, the predictions were certainly overeager. Even today the best chess machines are barely master rated; no computer has ever come close to an important mathematical discovery; and machine composition seems mainly to have faded away. It must be acknowledged, however, that computational concepts have indeed become very prominent in psychological theories (though, interestingly, one could construe that as more a sociological success than a technical one).

But these are not the sort of failed predictions that falsify theories. If Kepler predicts the position of Mars and it comes out wrong, that's bad for his theory because the prediction is a consequence of it. But Simon and Newell's predictions were not so much consequences of their approach as enthusiasm on its behalf. They mistook not the world, but the research.[26] The lesson for us is therefore oblique: in the development of science, it's hard to know what to expect. By the same token, it's hard to tell when a field is not living up to expectations. Difficult problems take time and fortitude: "If at first you don't succeed . . . etc." Presumably, that's also why it's so hard to recognize crippling defects for what they are, until there's some better approach to compare them to.

Fulton's Folly is our heritage. Despite the scoffing, courageous Fulton persevered—and prevailed. We are all reluctant to mutter "it can't be done," for fear of being the blindered naysayers, the reactionary fogies of folklore, who end up eating crow. The heros are the ones who believe—and win. Perhaps it is well to cherish such images; but skeptics don't *always* lose. Nobody ever did

---

Box 8
Imposter Paradigm?

Living science is hard to criticize; but history lends perspective. Until the rise of cognitivism, behaviorism reigned almost unchallenged in American psychology departments. It could boast established experimental methods, tons of well-confirmed results, specialty journals carrying detailed technical reports, texts and curricula for teaching people to read and write those reports, and a coherent "philosophy" within which it all seemed inevitably right. In short, it had the institutional earmarks of an advanced and thriving science. In retrospect, however, behaviorism contributed little to our understanding of human behavior—let alone the mind—and seems hopelessly inadequate to the task.

In historian Thomas Kuhn's terms (1962/70), a *paradigm* is a major scientific triumph, so impressive in breaking new ground and yet so pregnant with unfulfilled possibilities, that a technical research tradition coalesces around it as a model. The pioneering achievements of Thorndike and Pavlov, for instance, inspired a vigorous and sophisticated investigation of the conditioning of birds, dogs, and rats—and also of people, to the extent that we are similar. Genuine intelligent behavior, however, turns out to involve processes qualitatively different from conditioned reflexes, etc. So, if the behaviorist paradigm is extended to psychology in general, it becomes a kind of *imposter*: an outlook and methodology adequate to one domain parading as adequate in quite another, where it has no credentials whatever.

Cognitivism is behaviorism's natural child. It retains the same deep commitment to objective experiments, mechanistic accounts, and the ideal of "scientific" psychology. But with the conceptual apparatus of symbol manipulation, knowledge representation, and heuristic control, it gains a vastly more powerful explanatory framework. Accordingly, it has now acquired the institutional earmarks of an advanced and thriving science—including enough fancy equipment, jargon, and data to intimidate almost anyone.

Might cognitive science also have an "imposter paradigm"? In Newell, Shaw, and Simon's classic implementations, symbolic "expert systems" have a model that is legitimately inspiring; and in that area progress appears to have been substantial.[27] The still unanswered question, however, is whether this limited but real success translates into an adequate approach to intelligence and psychology in general.

build a perpetual motion machine; moreover, the eventual explanation, energy conservation and the law of entropy, turned out to be important. Likewise, nobody ever managed to weigh phlogiston or measure the Earth's absolute velocity; and these "failures" were significant steps in the acceptance of oxygen and of relativity theory. Discovery overcomes misconception as often as ignorance.

Like their predecessors, cognitive scientists have made undeniable contributions to our knowledge of ourselves. But, also as before, these contributions are notably narrow, even small, compared to the depth and scope of psychology's pretheoretic purview. Lest the brilliance of what has been achieved blind us to the darkness that surrounds, let us recall how many shadows have yet to be illuminated. How is it, for example, that we recognize familiar faces, let alone the lives engraved in them, or the power of Rembrandt's portrayals? How do we understand conversational English, let alone metaphors, jokes, Aristotle, or Albee? What is common sense, let alone genius, wit, or good taste? What is character, let alone schizophrenia, neurosis, or moral integrity? We turn to psychology if we think these questions have scientific answers; and if we shouldn't, why shouldn't we?

Cognitivists are as vague and impressionistic on such matters as psychologists have always been. Of course, they too can buy time with the old refrain: "be patient, we're only just beginning (though so-and-so's preliminary results are already encouraging)." Promissory notes are legitimate currency in vigorous sciences, but too much deficit spending only fuels inflation. Perhaps the idea of automatic symbol manipulation is at last the key to unlocking the mind; or perhaps the programmable computer is as shallow an analogy as the trainable pigeon—the conditional branch as psychologically sterile as the conditioned reflex.

We hate to withhold judgment: skepticism is intellectual anemia. How much more fun, more vigorous, more apparently forthright to take sides! Yet, sometimes, the results are just not in. I am not really convinced that GOFAI is impossible; on the other hand, I'm certainly far from persuaded that it's inevitable. I am dubious: near as I can see, after thirty years, the hard questions remain open.

Notes

Introduction

1. Perhaps Artificial Intelligence should be called "Synthetic Intelligence" to accord better with commercial parlance. Thus artificial diamonds are fake imitations, whereas synthetic diamonds are genuine diamonds, only manufactured instead of dug up (compare also artificial maple flavoring versus, say, synthetic insulin). Despite the name, AI clearly aims at genuine intelligence, not a fake imitation.

2. Turing doesn't mention whether the interrogator is told that a computer has been substituted for the man; and that would surely make a difference to the questioning. But, as the next paragraph shows, the essence of the test is much simpler, and the ambiguity doesn't really matter.

3. One might reject this comparison on the grounds that *our* thoughts take place in *immaterial* (perhaps immortal) souls and have at most incidental relations to our brains. Such a position, however, would rule out Artificial Intelligence from the start. Hence, for purposes of discussion, this book must and will assume that human intelligence is (or at least could be) realized in matter—such as brains.

4. Philosopher Dan Dennett has been particularly assiduous in making this point in a variety of contexts (see, for instance, his 1978 and 1984).

5. Essentially this point was made a quarter of a century ago by McCarthy (1959): "We base ourselves on the idea that in order for a program to be capable of learning something it must first be capable of being told it" (Minsky 1968, p. 405). Time has borne McCarthy out; but see Schank (1983) for a plea that learning should now be reactivated as a central research topic.

Chapter 1

1. This view of the heavens was developed into a sophisticated mathematical theory mainly by the Greek astronomer Ptolemy in the second century A.D.; hence it is generally known as the Ptolemaic theory.

2. Quoted by Kuhn (1962/70), p. 69, and in a slightly different form by Koestler (1967). My colleague B.R. Goldstein informs me, however, that the story is

most likely a political slander, circulated by opponents of Alfonso's throne, who took advantage both of an old prophesy that blasphemy would bring Alfonso to a bad end and of his own known penchant for astrology. The earliest extant version is apparently that found recently by Jerry Craddock in a chronicle written in 1344. Whether the story is true or not, the fact that it was told (and believed) suffices for the point in the text.

3. Galileo (1623) *Il Saggiatore* (*The Assayer*), section 6; see Barbera (1968), volume VI, p. 232 (Translations of Galileo are my own.)

4. Galileo (1638) *Dialogs on Two New Sciences*, part II of the Third Day; see Barbera (1968), volume VIII, pp. 208f. This is Galileo's mature work on motion, published just four years before he died. Note: don't confuse Galileo's use of the term "momentum" with the modern, Newtonian sense (vector product of velocity and mass).

5. Mathematically minded readers will notice in this idea of "aggregating" lines an anticipation of the integral calculus, developed fifty years later by Newton and Leibnitz.

6. In free fall from rest, the distance covered is proportional to the square of the time elapsed. (This is essentially Theorem II, which immediately follows Theorem I, given in box 1.)

7. Galileo (1623) *Il Saggiatore* (*The Assayer*), section 48; see Barbera (1968), volume VI, p. 350.

8. Locke probably adopted these terms from the chemist Robert Boyle.

9. Hobbes (1656), chapter 1, p. 3. I suppose, by the way, that if Hobbes was the "grandfather" of AI, then Turing was the father, who planted the seed, and McCarthy the godfather, who gave it a name and a place in society; but Newell, Shaw, and Simon actually brought it into the world (see "Heuristic Search" in chapter 5).

10. Hobbes (1651), part I, chapter 5, pp. 29–30.

11. Hobbes (1651), part I, chapter 1, p. 2.

12. Hobbes (1656), chapter 2, p. 17.

13. Descartes (1637), p. 369. (Translations of Descartes are my own.)

14. Descartes (1637), near the end of part II of the *Discourse*, pp. 19–20.

15. Descartes (1637), near the end of part V of the *Discourse*, pp. 56–57. Incidentally, Descartes included animals in the category of unreasoning machines; so this passage is also what gets him out of attributing souls (minds) to beasts.

16. Only in the strictest contexts, of course, would the "rules of reasoning" be the same as the exact rules of logic or mathematics; for more ordinary thought and discourse, "reasonableness" is much more flexible, though perhaps still guided by rules.

17. Hume (1739–40).

18. Hume (1749), section 1.

19. Hume (1739–40), pp. 12–13.

20. By this Newton meant that he could do a lot of physics just knowing *that* the law of gravity holds, without knowing *why* it holds. But, since he didn't believe in action at a distance, he did think the "why" question had an answer, and he would have liked to know it. Hume himself saw clearly that in any science some principles must be accepted simply on the basis of experience and without further explanation; see, for instance, the concluding paragraphs of his introduction to the *Treatise*.

Chapter 2

1. Card games and many board games (such as backgammon, Scrabble, and Monopoly), which involve a random element (shuffling, drawing, rolling dice) are probably best conceived as formal games with an extra "input"; but, for present purposes, that's a distracting complication, which we can ignore.

2. A chess problem (of the white-to-mate-in-two variety) may be regarded as a formal game, mostly just like chess, except that it is played by only one person and there are many different starting positions.

3. The rules for legal moves implicitly determine what the positions are; that is, if the legality of any move ever depends on feature X, then feature X must count as part of the formal position. (This does not render self-containedness trivial because formal systems must also be digital and finitely playable.) Note that self-contained systems are *ahistorical*; that is, the earlier history of moves cannot affect what's legal now, except via effects on the current position (so fully formal chess needs a few tokens off to the side, marking whether the king and rook have ever moved, and the like).

4. The tolerances for the write techniques are effectively set by the precision of the read techniques, and vice versa; it's the write/read cycle that must be positive and reliable.

5. This is still a fairly strong notion of equivalence; mathematicians would often regard systems as equivalent even though they don't quite meet these conditions. The various possible qualifications are tricky and technical, however, and don't add much to the basic idea.

6. Many of these would be more difficult to understand or "play" than others, due to confusing complications in rules or lack of visible structure in the posi-

tions. Our chip game, for instance, is probably harder than the equivalent peg game because it's so hard to keep track of which chips can be legally exchanged (unless you lay them out to mimic the pattern of the peg board). Hence, from the point of view of game playing, formally equivalent systems can still be significantly different.

7. It's not clear, however, that all algorithms require inputs; thus one might deem the geometric procedure for constructing a regular pentagon with compass and straightedge an algorithm—but it doesn't seem to take any inputs.

8. This is not to deny that an oracle-like device (such as dice) could provide an input to a perfectly finite game.

9. This is a good place to reflect again on the significance of digitalness: if the ground-level operations were not positive and very reliable, then there's no telling what would happen to the enormous and intricate structures resting on them. (Recall the discussion of poker chips and sand.)

10. There are other kinds of analysis, such as explaining how an algorithm achieves its result, via a specified sequence of steps; explaining the properties of a chemical compound in terms of its molecular structure; or explaining the meaning of a sentence in terms of the word meanings. Also, of course, there are other kinds of explanation besides analysis. (For some comparisons, see Haugeland (1978) and the references cited there.)

Chapter 3

1. Though the general analogy between thought and discourse has been familiar for ages, the specific formulation in this paragraph and the two following is adapted (with modifications) from Searle (1983), chapter 1.

2. Not all correspondences are quite so straightforward. For instance, making a promise does more than just express the speaker's intentions: it also undertakes a (publicly binding) obligation, sometimes with legal force. Other speech acts, like pronouncing a couple husband and wife, making a bid in bridge, or calling signals in a football game, introduce other complications.

3. Sometimes the term 'syntax' is used more narrowly to mean only the "grammar" of a system's complex expressions (i.e., WFFs; see box 6).

4. Indeed, there was no rigorously formal system for geometry (i.e., interpretable as geometric) until David Hilbert (1867–1943), the great German pioneer of formal axiomatics, produced one in 1899.

5. This characterization quietly ignores various necessary technicalities such as axiom schemata, proofs by contradiction, and the like; but these only complicate the basic idea and don't matter for our purposes.

6. The term 'computer' is actually used in a number of different ways. Often it is generalized to include all automatic formal systems, regardless of whether or

how they are interpreted; sometimes it is restricted to programmable systems (see chapter 4), so as to rule out "mere" calculators; and sometimes it even includes interpreted automatic systems that aren't formal systems (for example, so-called "analog" computers). We stick to interpreted formal systems because they are the original inspiration for Artificial Intelligence. The basic idea is close to what Newell and Simon (1976) mean by "physical symbol systems"; my formulation is influenced by Smith (1982), chapter 1.

7. To the best of my knowledge, this basic distinction was first drawn (though in different terms) by Dreyfus (1965), pp. 59–60.

8. This powerful and important conception seems to have originated with Fodor (1968). Related ideas are also developed in Simon (1969/81), Dennett (1975), Haugeland (1978), and Lycan (1981), among others.

9. Cummins (1983), p. 92, makes a closely related point (but it isn't quite the same because he sorts out semantics, interpretation, and cognition a little differently).

Chapter 4

1. Schickard's plans and partially completed machine were destroyed in a fire, and never presented publicly. They only became known when some letters describing them were found among the papers of his fellow astronomer Johannes Kepler. Schickard not only automated addition and subtraction, but also incorporated a version of Napier's "bones," a device for simplifying multiplication and division. Leibnitz, however, was the first to automate multiplication and division fully; his basic mechanism was still used until fairly recently. (These stories, and several to follow, are taken from Goldstine, 1972, and Augarten, 1984.)

2. For an excellent account of the mechanical design and workings of the Analytical Engine, see Bromley (1982); most of the specifics reported here are drawn from that article.

3. Augusta's translation of Menabrae's summary (complete with notes) is reprinted in Morrison and Morrison (1961). This volume also has selections from Babbage's autobiography, including a brief chapter on the Analytical Engine.

4. Unfortunately, significant parts of that work were released only much later (or never) because of government security restrictions; indeed, it has been charged that overcautious regulations cost Britain an early lead in computational technology.

5. At about the same time, 1936, an American mathematician, Emil Post (1897–1954), had a number of very similar ideas but not as complete or well worked out as Turing's.

6. Turing's thesis is equivalent to Church's thesis (after Alonzo Church, who made an equivalent proposal, in different terms); some authors now refer to them together as the *Church–Turing thesis*.

7. Technically, Babbage programs can include subroutines, using purely relative access; but they are much more cumbersome to implement. Von Neumann is typically credited with the "stored program" concept—that is, putting the program code in the main memory, right along with the data—as his basic contribution to computer architecture. But besides overlooking the same fact about Turing machines, this misses the essential point: because the program is in main memory, the addresses in the control directives (e.g., return from subroutine) can be modified during execution.

8. "The Dartmouth Summer Research Project on Artificial Intelligence" (Dartmouth, 1956). Attendees included John McCarthy, Marvin Minsky, Trenchard More, Allen Newell, Nathaniel Rochester, Arthur Samuel, Oliver Selfridge, Claude Shannon, Herbert Simon, and Ray Solomonoff. (See McCorduck, 1979, pp. 93f.)

9. "LISP" is an acronym for "LISt Processing," which is a feature that-McCarthy adopted from a series of earlier systems called "IPLs" (for "Information Processing Languages"), designed by Allen Newell, Cliff Shaw, and Herbert Simon. In fact, LISP was inspired by the IPLs in several ways, including the use of recursive definitions and a common form for code and data. But LISP represents a deep rethinking of the basic ideas, resulting in a substantially cleaner and more elgant system, including an algebra-like "timeless" notation (function application), a theoretically motivated notion of function definition (the lambda operator), and efficient memory management (garbage collection). Incidentally, the LOGO system, developed by Seymour Papert at MIT and now widely available for home computers, is an offshoot of LISP and similar to it in many respects.

10. Babbage memory (the "store") can be accessed *only* by label; so unlike the others, its cups would not be arranged in a row at all, but scattered about in no particular order.

11. This presupposes an important technical restriction: you're not allowed to connect your Y-connectors in a circle or have any kind of closed loop in the tree branches.

12. "General recursive functions," which are intuitively computable, were defined by Kurt Gödel (1934); "lambda definable functions," which are also intuitively computable, were delineated by Alonzo Church and Stephen Kleene at about the same time. Church (1936) proved that these two approaches identify exactly the same class of functions and proposed that all intuitively computable functions are in this class. The following year, Turing proved that this class coincides with the class of functions computable by his machines; so "Church's thesis" and "Turing's thesis" turn out to be equivalent.

13. The school Newell left, though, was Princeton—host also (between 1935 and 1950) to Gödel, Church, Turing, von Neumann, McCarthy, and Minsky (but, alas, not Babbage). On the other hand, Rand did upstage Princeton by getting the first von Neumann machine (named "Johnniac") actually up and running.

14. Symbol manipulation was integral to their "Information Processing Languages," ancestors of LISP (see note 9); their "Logic Theorist" program is described further in the next chapter. Of course, other people were pursuing ideas in the same vicinity; but none so successfully. For further historical details, see McCorduck (1979), chapter 6.

15. Even more than von Neumann and LISP machines, production systems are the fruit of many minds. In the 1920s, Emil Post (who also nearly coinvented Turing machines; see Post, 1936) devised a kind of formal system based on "productions" (see Post, 1943); Chomsky's (1957) "rewrite rules" are basically Post productions. Markov (1954) added a deterministic control scheme, thereby making production systems algorithmic. And a few early string-manipulation languages (COMIT, SNOBOL) actually use productions as programming devices; but it is preeminently Newell who has developed and championed production systems as a general computer architecture (especially as relevant to AI programming).

16. Conflict-resolution schemes can be much more complicated than these; indeed, sophisticated systems can allow several productions to act simultaneously or one production to act on several patterns at once. The main requirement for such elaborations is a fancier and busier (more expensive) referee.

17. The Turing architecture supports no form of modularity (though, of course, since it's universal, it can *mimic* anything). Von Neumann machines support modularity through subroutines and loop constructs, *provided that* the entrance and exit conditions are well-defined and interactions are carefully channelled, which is the point of so-called "structured programming."

Chapter 5

1. The British Colossus machine, about a tenth the size of ENIAC, was actually operational almost two years earlier; but it had a special purpose architecture, dedicated exclusively to code cracking, and (more important), it remained so shrouded in military secrecy that it was out of date before anyone ever heard of it. By contrast, the Moore School's Electronic Numerical Integrator and Computer was proudly unveiled in February 1946, just a few months after it was completed, and immediately sparked a flurry of further developments.

2. For a sampling of all this hoopla, see *Newsweek*, November 12, 1945, p. 93; *Business Week*, February 16, 1946, p. 50; *Science Newsletter*, February 23, 1946, cover and p. 118; *New Republic*, June 23, 1947, pp. 14–18; and *Time*, January 23, 1950, cover and pp. 54–60.

3. ENIAC had twenty "words" (ten decimal digits each) of data storage, plus separate storage for three hundred instructions (equal to about two digits each); it cost just under half a million dollars. A Cray 1 or Cyber 205 can do twenty to one hundred million multiplications per second (64-bit floating point; hence more work than ENIAC's divisions); fully equipped, they have four million words (64 bits each, equivalent to about twenty decimal digits) and cost about fifteen million dollars (= three million 1946 dollars). For an overview of these machines, see Levine (1982).

4. According to the Introduction to Locke and Booth (1955), p. 5.

5. See Bar-Hillel (1960), especially Appendix III.

6. An engaging portrait of this period is drawn in McCorduck (1979), chapters 5 and 6. The early research is best represented in Feigenbaum and Feldman (1963), and most thoroughly criticized in Dreyfus (1972/79), chapter 1.

7. In fact, it was only retrospectively, from reflecting on a number of early programs and how they worked, that NS&S came to regard *search* as a common characteristic; but the reliance on heuristics was explicitly emphasized from the start.

8. There are a few techniques for reducing search, without danger of overlooking anything. For instance, certain redundancies can be ignored, as can the consequences of options that have already been eliminated. Seldom, however, are these reductions sufficient to avoid the explosion.

9. Semantics, as we saw in chapter 3, concerns the meanings of symbols, including the relationship to whatever is symbolized. Thus, in the fullest sense, NS&S's programs (interpreted as problem solvers) are as "semantic" as any other. But they had relatively few structures (interpreted as) conveying detailed factual information about specific aspects of the world; programs depending on more such information are "semantic" in a stronger sense.

10. Work representative of this period is reported in Minsky (1968); some of it is also summarized in Minsky (1966) and criticized in Dreyfus (1972/79), chapter 2.

11. Work representative of this period is reported in Minsky and Papert (1972), Bobrow and Collins (1975), and Winston (1975); there are good summaries in Boden (1977), chapters 6, 8, and 10; Dreyfus (1972/79), Introduction to the Revised Edition; and Waltz (1982).

12. The "action" routines are slightly more complicated, since they won't allow two blocks in the same place or anything to rest on top of a pyramid. (If you ask SHRDLU to stack something on a pyramid, he will "try" it and report that he can't, as if he had actually been thwarted by gravity.) Other programs from the same era did attempt "real" perception and action within the blocks world; they had some success, but suffer, in the end, from the same intrinsic flaws of idiosyncrasy and nongeneralizability that we will see presently in SHRDLU.

13. Also, needless to say, SHRDLU would have a lot more trouble with that dialogue than just the new words.

14. Micro-worlds researchers, however, were not the first to make this point. It was well known (though, of course, not established empirically) by such philosophers as Husserl, Heidegger, Dewey, the later Wittgenstein, and their students.

15. Yorick Wilks (1974) uses a similar example to test a translation system. In translating to French, for example, resolving the ambiguity is essential, since 'they' must be feminine if it refers to apples, but masculine if it refers to boys.

16. To be sure, in bizarre circumstances such commonsense arguments can be unreliable; but we shall find plenty of difficulties to entertain us in the normal case.

17. There is no established terminology. Roughly what I call "stereotypes" have also been called "noemata" (Husserl, 1913), "schemata" (Bartlett, 1932), "frames" (Minsky, 1974), "preference structures" (Wilks, 1974), "scripts" (Schank, 1975), and various other things.

18. Charniak (1974) (quoted in Minsky, 1974) gives a different example that illustrates much the same point:

A goat wandered into the yard where Jack was painting. The goat got paint all over himself. When Mother saw the goat, she asked, "Jack, did you do that?"

While the final pronoun is not exactly ambiguous, it's not easy to say just what it refers to. The antecedent is certainly no single word or phrase in the story, but rather something more abstract like "get all that paint on the goat." How will *that* be extracted from a commonsense encyclopedia?

19. The problem was first described (and named) by McCarthy and Hayes (1969); for recent discussions, see the essays in Pylyshyn (forthcoming; the present section is based on my contribution to that volume).

20. I believe that these are the basic factors that make the frame problem hard; but bear in mind that they are vastly compounded in real situations by continuous and/or irregular changes (the rat and mongoose kept darting about the dollhouse), simultaneous events with interacting side effects (Ajax spilled the turpentine just as Comet hit the lantern), cumulative effects (one last straw on old Dutch's back), and so on.

21. Thus basic facts are not independent in the sense that all combinations are allowed but only in the sense that if any allowed change is made, no other basic facts are thereby altered. (E.g., neither putting two chess pieces on one square nor moving the king into check are allowed; but when any piece moves, the others stay put.)

22. The point of the last two paragraphs is made by Dennett (1978), p. 118.

Chapter 6

1. The ascription schema amounts to a streamlined version of a condition Dennett (1971) formulates as follows:

Their [the creatures'] behavior will "manifest" their beliefs by being seen as the actions which, given the creatures' desires, would be appropriate to such beliefs as would be appropriate to the environmental stimulation. Desires, in turn, will be "manifested" in behavior as those appropriate desires (given the needs of the creature) to which the actions of the creature would be appropriate, given the creature's beliefs.

In my review (1982) of Dennett (1978), I called this condition "rational format." (Several other points in the present section are also drawn from that review.)

2. Philosophers will recognize the possibility of correctly attributing errors as a sign of the "referential opacity" of ascription; we see here that it rests fundamentally on semantic intrigue.

3. This is based on Grice (1967), an unpublished but widely circulated manuscript of his William James Lectures. (Grice (1975) is a condensed version of that manuscript.) I have taken liberties with Grice's exact formulation, mostly in accord with maxim 4.

4. Sometimes what I call "metacognitions" are called "second-order (or higher-order)" beliefs and desires. They have been discussed in many contexts; see, for example, Frankfurt (1971), Dennett (1976, 1983), and Smith (1982).

5. The first example is from Simon (1972), who attributes it to George Baylor; the second is from a lecture by H.L. Dreyfus (many years ago).

6. Block (1983) contains a nice summary of the philosophical issues surrounding mental imagery; Block (1981) is a collection of important papers on that topic by various philosophers and psychologists; Cooper and Shepard (1984) and Kosslyn (1983) are readable surveys of recent experimental results (the latter also sketches a psychological theory to account for those results).

7. Indeed, the respective relations in the model and the modeled must be independently definable (not ad hoc) or else the pomegranate "image" is still not ruled out.

8. The foregoing is but a sketch of ideas explored more fully in Shepard (1975), Palmer (1978), and Kosslyn (1983). The term "quasi-pictorial" is Kosslyn's.

9. The small constant subtracted from each reaction time is just the time required to detect a straight match (no rotation at all); the response times to detect a mismatch were generally longer.

10. Other results (e.g., Pinker 1980, Pinker and Finke, 1980) support the claim that full 3-D images are formed and manipulated as if in three dimensions. In-

terestingly, even in imagination our *access* to these models seems restricted to two-dimensional projections, from a particular point of view—just like visual perception of the 3-D world.

11. Pylyshyn (1973, 1978, 1981, 1984) argues forcefully that *all* mental representation (including any involved in imagination) is fundamentally quasi-linguistic. Anderson (1978) argues that there's no way to tell them apart.

12. Note: an image isn't automatically quasi-linguistic just because it's "digitized" or implemented as a data structure in a quasi-lingistic programming system. A quasi-linguistic representation must be a legal symbol in a symbolic system: a complex interpreted token, whose meaning *about the world* is a function of its syntax and the separate meanings of its parts. An image composed of "pixels" is not such a compound, regardless of how the pixels are instantiated.

13. Block (1983) develops this line of reasoning in an interesting way.

14. See Clarke and Fiske (1982) for a collection of current review papers on affect in relation to cognition.

15. I have not drawn these lists from any source, though I assume they must be typical of many, and cruder than some.

16. For further relevant discussion of sensation, see, for example, Shoemaker (1972), Dennett (1978a), and Block (1980).

17. Devices like this are popular among psychologists. It should be noted, however, that merely *saying* that states are composite is a far cry from a theory of *how* they are composed—what the parts have to do with one another, what holds them together, and so on.

18. Most of this section is adapted from the last few pages of Haugeland (1979).

19. Do you think cats are embarrassed when they fall flat or dogs contrite when caught stealing? I am dubious, but nothing hangs on it.

20. This is a no doubt garbled version of a story I heard years ago, attributed to the movie *Bedazzled*.

21. Actually, Joseph Weizenbaum (1976) argues eloquently that AI might be dangerously dehumanizing even if people merely believe in it. (That is, he finds it abominable, even without taking it for granted.)

22. John Searle (1980) vigorously debunks AI, taking original meaning (which he calls "intrinsic intentionality") as the value of X. He assumes premise 1 without argument and constructs many ingenious examples in a careful defense of 2. Our section "Paradox and Mystery Dispelled" in chapter 3 is in part a reply to Searle.

23. See especially Dennett (1978b); it goes without saying that this brief sketch oversimplifies Dennett's actual position.

24. This image has been around for a while. Dennett (1978) attributes it to Davis (1974); it appears also in Block (1978); and the central example in Searle (1980) is a variation on the theme.

25. From an address to the Operations Research Society of America, November 14, 1957. Though Simon delivered the speech, it was coauthored with Newell, and the text was published with both names (Simon and Newell, 1958).

26. In later interviews (apparently around 1977 or 1978; see McCorduck, 1979, pp. 187–91), Simon (and also Minsky) attributed the failures to an underestimate of how much work would actually be invested. Simon also acknowledged underestimating the knowledge representation required.

27. I say "appears to have been" because appearances can be deceiving. In an eye-opening new book, Dreyfus and Dreyfus (forthcoming) argue forcefully that even the apparent "expertise" of narrow specialist systems is often illusory and never comparable to human expertise.

Bibliography

Adam, Charles, and Paul Tannery, eds. (1897–1910). *Oeuvre de Descartes*, Paris: Léopold Cerf (republished, 1973, Paris: Librairie Philosophique J. Vrin).

Alt, F.L., ed. (1960). *Advances in Computers*, Volume 1, New York: Academic Press.

Anderson, Alan Ross, ed. (1964). *Minds and Machines*, Englewood Cliffs, NJ: Prentice-Hall.

Anderson, John R. (1978). "Argument Concerning Representations for Mental Imagery," *Psychological Review*, 85, 249–277.

Augarten, Stan (1984). *Bit by Bit*, New York: Ticknor & Fields.

Augusta, Ada (see Menabrea, 1842).

Babbage, Henry Prevost, ed. (1889). *Babbage's Calculating Engines*, London: E. and F. N. Spon. (This is a collection of Charles Babbage's papers, published posthumously by his son; a facsimile edition, with a new introduction by Allan G. Bromley, was published in 1982, Los Angeles: Tomash Publishers.)

Barbera, G., ed. (1968). *Le Opere de Galileo Galilei*, Nuova Ristampa della Edizione Nazionale, Rome: Ministero della Pubblica Istruzione.

Bar-Hillel, Yehoshua (1960). "The Present Status of Automatic Translation of Languages" (in Alt, 1960).

Bartlett, F.C. (1932/61). *Remembering: A Case Study in Experimental and Social Psychology*, Cambridge, England: The University Press.

Bauer-Mengelberg, Stefan (1966). Review of Davis, 1965, *Journal of Symbolic Logic*, 31, 484–494.

Blake, D.V., and A.M. Uttley, eds. (1959). *Proceedings of the Symposium on Mechanization of Thought Processes*, National Physical Laboratory, Teddington, England. London: H.M. Stationery Office.

Block, Ned (1983). "Mental Pictures and Cognitive Science," *The Philosophical Review*, XCII, 499–541.

———— ed. (1981). *Imagery*, Cambridge, MA: Bradford Books/The MIT Press.

———— (1980). "Are Absent Qualia Possible?" *Philosophical Review*, 89, 257–274.

———— (1978). "Troubles with Functionalism" (in Savage, 1978).

Bobrow, Daniel, and A.M. Collins, eds. (1975). *Representation and Understanding*, New York: Academic Press.

Boden, Margaret (1977). *Artificial Intelligence and Natural Man*, New York: Basic Books.

Bromley, Allan G. (1982). "Charles Babbage's Analytical Engine, 1838," *Annals of the History of Computing*, 4, 196–217.

Chomsky, Noam (1957). *Syntactic Structures*, The Hague: Uitgverij Mouton.

Church, Alonzo (1936). "An Unsolvable Problem of Elementary Number Theory," *American Journal of Mathematics*, 58, 345–363 (reprinted in Davis, 1965).

Clark, Margaret Syndor and Susan T. Fiske, eds. (1982). *Affect and Cognition: The Seventeenth Annual Carnegie Symposium on Cognition*, Hillsdale, NJ: Lawrence Erlbaum Associates.

Cooper, Lynn A., and Roger N. Shepard (1984). "Turning Something Over in the Mind," *Scientific American*, 251:6, 106–114 (December 1984).

Cummins, Robert (1983). *The Nature of Psychological Explanation*, Cambridge, MA: Bradford Books/The MIT Press.

Davidson, Donald, and Gilbert Harman, eds. (1975). *The Logic of Grammar*, Encino, CA: Dickenson Publishing.

Davis, Martin, ed. (1965). *The Undecidable. Basic Papers on Undecidable Propositions, Unsolvable Problems, and Computable Functions*, Hewlitt, NY: Ravens Press. (See Bauer-Mengelberg, 1966, for corrections.)

Dennett, Daniel C. (1984). *Elbow Room*, Cambridge, MA: Bradford Books/The MIT Press.

———— (1983). "Intentional Systems in Cognitive Ethology: the 'Panglossian Paradigm' Defended," *Behavioral and Brain Sciences*, 6, 343–390.

————— (1978). *Brainstorms*, Cambridge, MA: Bradford Books/The MIT Press.

————— (1978a). "Why You Can't Make a Computer that Feels Pain," *Synthese*, 38, 415–456 (reprinted in Dennett, 1978).

————— (1978b). "Toward a Cognitive Theory of Consciousness" (in Savage, 1978; and reprinted in Dennett, 1978).

————— (1976). "Conditions of Personhood" (in Rorty, 1976; and reprinted in Dennett, 1978).

————— (1975). "Why the Law of Effect Won't Go Away," *Journal of the Theory of Social Behavior*, V, 169–187 (reprinted in Dennett, 1978).

————— (1971). "Intentional Systems," *Journal of Philosophy*, LXVIII, 87–106 (reprinted in Dennett, 1978, and in Haugeland, 1981).

Dertouzos, Michael L. and Joel Moses, eds. (1979). *The Computer Age: A Twenty-Year View*, Cambridge, MA: The MIT Press.

Descartes, René (1637). *Essaies Philosophiques*, Leyden: L'Imprimerie de Ian Maire; page citations to the edition of Adam and Tannery, 1897–1910, volume VI (1902).

Dreyfus, Hubert L. (1972/79). *What Computers Can't Do*, New York: Harper & Row.

————— (1965). "Alchemy and Artificial Intelligence," RAND Corporation Technical Report P-3244 (December 1965).

Dreyfus, Hubert, and Stuart Dreyfus (1985). *Mind Over Machine*, New York: Macmillan/The Free Press.

Edwards, Paul, ed. (1967). *The Encyclopedia of Philosophy*, New York: Macmillan.

Feigenbaum, Edward, and Julian Feldman, eds. (1963). *Computers and Thought*, New York: McGraw-Hill.

Fodor, Jerry A. (1981). *RePresentations*, Cambridge, MA: Bradford Books/The MIT Press.

————— (1968). "The Appeal to Tacit Knowledge in Psychological Explanation," *Journal of Philosophy*, LXV, 627–640 (reprinted in Fodor, 1981).

Frankfurt, Harry (1971). "Freedom of the Will and the Concept of a Person," *Journal of Philosophy*, LXVIII, 5–20.

Galilei, Galileo (1638). *Intorno a due Nuove Scienze (Dialogs on Two New Sciences)*; page citations to the edition of Barbera, 1968, volume VIII.

————— (1623). *Il Saggiatore (The Assayer)*; page citations to the edition of Barbera, 1968, volume VI.

Gödel, Kurt (1934). "On Undecidable Propositions of Formal Mathematical Systems." Mimeographed notes, taken by Stephen Kleene and Barkley Rosser, from Gödel's 1934 lectures at the Institute for Advanced Study, Princeton (reprinted in Davis, 1965).

Goldstine, Herman H. (1972). *The Computer from Pascal to von Neumann*, Princeton, NJ: Princeton University Press.

Gregg, L.W., ed. (1972). *Cognition in Learning and Memory*, New York: John Wiley.

Grice, Paul (unpublished). "Logic and Conversation," The William James Lectures, Harvard, 1967.

————— (1975). "Logic and Conversation" (in Davidson and Harman, 1975, 64–75; this is a portion of the above).

Haugeland, John (forthcoming). "An Overview of the Frame Problem" (in Pylyshyn, forthcoming).

————— (1982). "The Mother of Intention," *Nous*, XVI, 613–619.

————— ed. (1981). *Mind Design*, Cambridge, MA: Bradford Books/The MIT Press.

————— (1979). "Understanding Natural Language," *Journal of Philosophy*, LXXVI, 619–632.

————— (1978). "The Nature and Plausibility of Cognitivism," *The Behavioral and Brain Sciences*, 1, 215–226 (reprinted in Haugeland, 1981).

Hobbes, Thomas (1656). *Elements of Philosophy*; page citations to the edition of Molesworth, 1839–45, volume 1.

————— (1651). *Leviathan*; page citations to the edition of Molesworth, 1839–45, volume 3.

Hume, David (1749). *An Enquiry Concerning Human Understanding*; page citations to the edition of Selby-Bigge, 1902.

————— (1739–40). *A Treatise of Human Nature*; page citations to the edition of Selby-Bigge, 1888.

Husserl, Edmund (1913). *Ideen zu einer reinen Phänomenologie und phänomenologischen Philosophie, I. Buch: Allgemeine Einführung in die reine Phänomenologie,* Halle: Max Niemeyer Verlag. (Translation by W.R. Boyce Gibson, 1931, *Ideas: General Introduction to Pure Phenomenology,* London: George Allen & Unwin.)

Koestler, Arthur (1967). "Kepler, Johannes" (in Edwards, 1967).

Kosslyn, Stephen M. (1983). *Ghosts in the Mind's Machine,* New York: W.W. Norton.

Kuhn, Thomas S. (1962/70). *The Structure of Scientific Revolutions,* Chicago: University of Chicago Press.

Levine, Ronald D. (1982). "Supercomputers," *Scientific American,* 246:1, 118–135 (January 1982).

Locke, William and Donald Booth, eds. (1955). *Machine Translation of Languages,* Cambridge, MA: The MIT Press.

Lycan, William G. (1981). "Form, Function, and Feel," *Journal of Philosophy,* LXXVIII, 24–50.

Markov, A.A (1954). Translation: "The Theory of Algorithms," *American Mathematical Society Translations* (Series 2) 15, 1–14 (1960).

McCarthy, John (1959). "Programs with Common Sense" (in Blake and Uttley, 1959, 75–84; reprinted and enlarged in Minsky, 1968, 403–418).

McCarthy, John, and Pat Hayes (1969). "Some Philosophical Problems from the Standpoint of Artificial Intelligence" (in Meltzer and Michie, 1969).

McCorduck, Pamela (1979). *Machines Who Think,* San Francisco: W.H. Freeman.

Meltzer, B., and D. Michie, eds. (1969). *Machine Intelligence,* Vol. 4, Edinburgh: Edinburgh University Press.

Menabrea, L.F. (1842). "Sketch of the Analytical Engine Invented by Charles Babbage" (in French), *Bibliothèque Universelle de Genève,* 82 (October 1842). (Translation, with extensive notes, by Ada Augusta, Countess of Lovelace, reprinted in Morrison and Morrison, 1960, 225–297.)

Minsky, Marvin (1979). "Computer Science and the Representation of Knowledge" (in Dertouzos and Moses, 1979, 392–421).

———— (1974). "A Framework for Representing Knowledge," MIT AI Lab Memo #306 (different abridged versions reprinted in Winston, 1975, TINLAP-75, and Haugeland, 1981).

———— (1968). *Semantic Information Processing*, Cambridge, MA: The MIT Press.

———— (1967). *Computation: Finite and Infinite Machines*, Englewood Cliffs, NJ: Prentice-Hall.

———— (1966). "Artificial Intelligence," *Scientific American*, 215, 247–260 (September 1966).

Minsky, Marvin, and Seymour Papert (1972). "Progress Report on Artificial Intelligence," MIT AI Lab Memo #252.

Molesworth, Sir William, ed. (1839–1945). *The English Works of Thomas Hobbes of Malmesbury*, London: John Bohn.

Morrison, Philip, and Emily Morrison, eds. (1961). *Charles Babbage and His Calculating Engines*, New York: Dover Publications.

Newell, Allen, and Herbert A. Simon (1976). "Computer Science as Empirical Inquiry: Symbols and Search," *Communications of the Association for Computing Machinery*, 19, 113–126 (March 1976; reprinted in Haugeland, 1981).

———— (1961). "GPS, A Program that Simulates Human Thought," *Proceedings of a Conference on Learning Automata* (Lehrenden Automaten), Munich: Oldembourg KG (reprinted in Feigenbaum and Feldman, 1963).

Palmer, Stephen E. (1978). "Fundamental Aspects of Cognitive Representation" (in Rosch and Lloyd, 1978).

Pinker, Steven (1980). "Mental Imagery and the Third Dimension," *Journal of Experimental Psychology: General*, 109, 354–371.

Pinker, Steven, and Ronald A. Finke (1980). "Emergent Two-Dimensional Patterns in Images Rotated in Depth," *Journal of Experimental Psychology: Human Perception and Performance*, 6, 244–264.

Post, Emil (1943). "Formal Reductions of the General Combinatorial Decision Problem," *American Journal of Mathematics*, 65, 197–215.

———— (1936). "Finite Combinatory Processes—Formulation 1," *Journal of Symbolic Logic*, 1, 103–105 (reprinted in Davis, 1965).

Pylyshyn, Zenon (forthcoming). *The Frame Problem and Other Problems of Holism in Artificial Intelligence*, Norwood, NJ: Ablex Publishing.

———— (1984). *Computation and Cognition*, Cambridge, MA: Bradford Books/ The MIT Press.

————— (1981). "The Imagery Debate: Analogue Media versus Tacit Knowledge," *Psychological Review*, 88, 16–45 (reprinted in Block, 1981).

————— (1978). "Imagery and Artifical Intelligence" (in Savage, 1978).

————— Pylyshyn, Zenon (1973). "What the Mind's Eye Tells the Mind's Brain: A Critique of Mental Imagery," *Psychological Bulletin*, 80, 1–24.

Rorty, Amelie O., ed. (1976). *Identities of Persons*, Berkeley: University of California Press.

Rosch, Eleanor, and Barbara B. Lloyd, eds. (1978). *Cognition and Categorization*, Hillsdale, NJ: Lawrence Erlbaum Associates.

Savage, C. Wade (1978). *Perception and Cognition: Issues in the Foundations of Psychology* (Minnesota Studies in the Philosophy of Science, Vol. IX), Minneapolis: University of Minnesota Press.

Schank, Roger (1983). "The Current State of AI: One Man's Opinion," *AI Magazine*, 4:1, 3–17 (Winter–Spring 1983).

Schank, Roger, and the Yale AI group (1975). "SAM—A Story Understander," Yale Computer Science Research Report No. 55.

Searle, John R. (1983). *Intentionality, an Essay in the Philosophy of Mind*, Cambridge, England: Cambridge University Press.

————— (1980). "Minds, Brains, and Programs," *Behavioral and Brain Sciences*, 3, 417–424 (reprinted in Haugeland, 1981).

Selby-Bigge, L.A., ed. (1902). *Enquiries Concerning the Human Understanding and Concerning the Principles of Morals* (by David Hume), Oxford: Clarendon Press.

————— ed. (1888). *A Treatise of Human Nature* (by David Hume), Oxford: Clarendon Press.

Shepard, Roger N. (1975). "Form, Formation, and Transformation of Internal Representations" (in Solso, 1975).

Shepard, R.N., and J. Metzler (1971). "Mental Rotation of Three-dimensional Objects," *Science*, 171, 701–703.

Shoemaker, Sydney (1972). "Functionalism and Qualia," *Philosophical Review*, 81, 159–181.

Simon, Herbert A. (1969/81). *The Sciences of the Artificial,* Cambridge, MA: The MIT Press.

———— (1972). "What Is Visual Imagery? An Information Processing Interpretation" (in Gregg, 1972).

Simon, Herbert A., and Allen Newell (1958). "Heuristic Problem Solving: The Next Advance in Operations Research," *Operations Research,* 6, 1–10.

Smith, Brian Cantwell (1982). *Reflection and Semantics in a Procedural Language,* MIT Laboratory for Computer Science, Technical Report #272 (doctoral dissertation).

Solso, R.L., ed. (1975). *Information Processing in Cognition: The Loyala Symposium,* Hillsdale, NJ: Lawrence Erlbaum Associates.

TINLAP-75 (1975). *Theoretical Issues in Natural Language Processing,* proceedings of a conference held in Cambridge, MA, June 10–13, 1975.

Turing, Alan (1950). "Computing Machinery and Intelligence," *Mind,* 59, 434–460 (reprinted in Feigenbaum and Feldman, 1963, and in Anderson, 1964).

———— (1936–37). "On Computable Numbers, with an Application to the *Entscheidungsproblem,*" *Proceedings of the London Mathematical Society,* Series 2, 42, 230–265 (reprinted in Davis, 1965).

Waltz, David (1982). "Artificial Intelligence," *Scientific American,* 247:4, 118–133 (October 1982).

Weaver, Warren (1949). "Translation" (circulated privately to about 200 people in 1949; first printed in Locke and Booth, 1955).

Weizenbaum, Joseph (1979). "Once More: The Computer Revolution" (in Dertouzos and Moses, 1979, 439–458).

———— (1976). *Computer Power and Human Reason,* San Francisco: W.H. Freeman.

Wiener, Norbert (1948a). *Cybernetics,* New York: John Wiley and Sons.

———— (1948b). "Cybernetics," *Scientific American,* 179:5, 14–19 (November 1948).

Wilks, Yorick (1974). "Natural Language Understanding Systems within the AI Paradigm," Stanford AI Memo #237.

Winograd, Terry (1971). *Procedures as a Representation for Data in a Computer Program for Understanding Natural Language,* Project MAC (MIT) Technical Report #84 (doctoral dissertation); revised version later published as "Understanding Natural Language," *Cognitive Psychology*, 3 (1972) 1–191, and as *Understanding Natural Language*, New York: Academic Press (1972).

Winston, Patrick, ed. (1975). *The Psychology of Computer Vision*, New York: McGraw-Hill.

Index

Illustration Credits

ARTIFICIAL INTELLIGENCE
The Very Idea
by John Haugeland

"Machines who think—how utterly preposterous," huff beleaguered humanists,
defending their dwindling turf. "Artificial
Intelligence—it's here and about to surpass
our own," crow techno-visionaries, pro-
claiming dominion. It's so simple and
obvious, each side maintains, only a fanatic
could disagree.

Deciding where the truth lies between these
extremes is the main purpose of John
Haugeland's marvelously lucid and witty
book on what artificial intelligence is all
about. Although presented entirely in non-
technical terms, it neither oversimplifies the
science nor evades the fundamental philosophical issues. Far from ducking the really
hard questions, it takes them on, one by
one.

Artificial intelligence, Haugeland notes, is
based on a very good idea, which might
well be right and just as well might not.
The idea that human thinking and
machine computing are radically the same
provides the central theme for his illumi-
nating and provocative book about this
exciting new field. After a brief but revealing digression in intellectual history,
Haugeland systematically tackles such basic
questions as, What is a computer really?
How can a physical object "mean" anything? What are the options for computational organization? What structures have
been proposed and tried as actual scientific
models for intelligence?

In a concluding chapter he takes up several
outstanding problems and puzzles—including intelligence in action, imagery, feelings,
and personality—and their enigmatic prospects for solution.